A Student Guide to Object-Oriented Development

A Student Guide to Object-Oriented Development

Carol Britton and Jill Doake

ELSEVIER
BUTTERWORTH
HEINEMANN

AMSTERDAM • BOSTON • HEIDELBERG • LONDON • NEW YORK • OXFORD
PARIS • SAN DIEGO • SAN FRANCISO • SINGAPORE SYDNEY • TOKYO

ELSEVIER BUTTERWORTH-HEINEMANN
Linacre House, Jordan Hill, Oxford OX2 8DP
30 Corporate Drive, Burlington MA 01803

First published 2005

British Library Cataloguing in Publication Data
A catalogue record for this book is available from the British Library

Library of Congress Cataloguing in Publication Data
A catalogue record for this book is available from the Library of Congress

ISBN 0 7506 61232

For information on all Elsevier Butterworth-Heinemann publications
visit our website at http://books.elsevier.com

Working together to grow
libraries in developing countries

www.elsevier.com | www.bookaid.org | www.sabre.org

ELSEVIER   BOOK AID International   Sabre Foundation

Typeset at Neuadd Bwll, Llanwrtyd Wells
Printed and bound in Great Britain

Preface and acknowledgements

This is a book for beginners to the object-oriented way of developing software systems. We hope that it will also be useful for students who already have some idea of what object-orientation is all about, but we do not assume any prior knowledge, and we try to explain everything in the simplest way possible.

The book is based on our own experience of teaching object-oriented development, and we have concentrated on those aspects that students find most difficult to grasp, in particular how the different models are related to each other, and how each model progresses through the system development process. One of the most important aspects of the book is the exercises at the ends of the chapters, since it is only by working through these that students will really learn to master the techniques.

The book is based around the development of a small bike hire system, from the initial identification of customer requirements, through the construction of models for the system, to the final code. We have included source documentation, analysis and design models, and also a partial implementation in the final chapter. Our aim is to provide an understanding of the object-oriented system development process, and to give students the opportunity to become competent in some of the techniques involved in it.

Many thanks are due to Matthew Britton, who provided technical advice on programming issues and helpful comments on the final chapters of the book. Once again, we are very grateful to David Howe for providing useful and constructive comments on the text, and to Dave Hatter and Alfred Waller for continuing support during the writing process. At Anglia Polytechnic University we are indebted to Alan Curtis for technical advice and some code for the final chapters, and Jacqui McCary for trialling the material. At the University of Hertfordshire, thanks go to Sarah Beecham for working through all the exercises and asking useful questions (even if they were sometimes hard to answer). Finally, thank you to Christopher and Oliver for putting up, once again, with temporarily distracted wives – we were going to dedicate the book to them, but we don't really think it's their sort of thing.

Carol Britton and Jill Doake

Contents

1 Introduction

Learning outcomes

The material and exercises in this chapter will enable you to:

- Describe the concept of a system life cycle and the main features of traditional and object-oriented approaches

- Describe the principal characteristics of the Rational Unified Process

- Explain how models are used in system development

- Recognize features of the Unified Modelling Language

- Get to know the Wheels case study, which is the source of examples and exercises in the book.

Key words that you will find in the glossary:

- analysis
- component
- deliverable
- design
- development method
- framework
- implementation
- incremental development
- iteration
- milestone
- object
- Object Management Group (OMG)
- prototyping
- Rational Unified Process (RUP)
- requirements
- reuse
- system life cycle
- traceability
- Unified Modelling Language (UML)

How to get the best from this book

The aim of this book is to describe what happens when a computer system is developed for a small business, in this case the Wheels bike hire company. The approach used is object-orientation, which means that the whole development process is based round the object – a thing or concept that initially represents something in the real world and eventually ends up as a component of the system code. An object-oriented system is made up of objects that collaborate to achieve the required functionality, what the system has to do.

What sort of person did we have in mind when we wrote this book? Well, ideally, you are highly motivated, interested in how software systems are developed, keen to learn about the object-oriented approach, and prepared to work hard at practising the exercises. In reality, you are probably not sure why you've got the book, except that it appeared on the reading list for one of your modules, you don't know much about software systems, you haven't the first idea what the object-oriented approach is, and if you are a typical student, working hard at exercises may be pretty low on your list of priorities. So it all comes down to a compromise – we'll do our best to make sure that the book is as interesting as possible, and we'll try to write in a style that you'll find easy to understand; we'll also grade the exercises, so that they are not a huge hurdle to be overcome, and provide answers, so that you can see how you are getting on. In return, you will have to read the chapters, think about the material, grit your teeth and do the exercises.

The book describes how a software system is developed using an object-oriented approach, with examples and exercises based on Wheels, the bike hire system used as a case study. Table 1.1 lists the chapters with a very brief summary of how they fit into the structure of the book.

All the chapters in the main body of the book follow a similar structure, introducing the topic of the chapter with examples drawn mainly from the Wheels case study. In a number of the chapters there is a section on technical points – this covers more advanced issues that you can leave out on a first reading, but gives a more complete picture. Many of the chapters also have a section on common problems; this deals with the questions that are most frequently asked by students, and the main difficulties that they have with the topic. At the end of each chapter you will find quick check questions that will help you to recall the material covered and check your understanding. Where appropriate, there are also practical exercises that provide essential practice in the various techniques. You will find the answers to the quick check questions in the relevant chapter, and the answers to the exercises are in a separate section at the end of the book.

Table 1.1 explains the material that is covered in the rest of this book. However, simply reading the chapters will not teach you to

Table 1.1: The chapters in the book with a brief summary of each

Chapter	Contents
1	Introduction to the system life cycle, object-oriented development and the bike hire case study.
2	Requirements for the new Wheels system, using standard requirements techniques, such as interview, questionnaire and scenario. This chapter ends with a list of requirements for the system that is developed in the rest of the book.
3	The technique of use cases and how the system will interact with its users.
4	Objects, classes and the central ideas in object-oriented development.
5	How to construct a class diagram.
6	Class responsibilities and CRC cards. Sequence and collaboration (interaction) diagrams, showing how all the objects involved behave during a single use case.
7	State diagrams, showing how the different objects of a single class behave through all the use cases in which the class is involved.
8	Activity diagrams, providing details of the activities that take place during a system process.
9	Design at the overall system level, including designing the overall architecture of the system, selecting a strategy for coping with persistent data and designing the user interface.
10	Design at the detailed system level, showing how early models of the system are refined and enhanced as development moves towards program code.
11	The code for the Wheels bike hire system, illustrating the relationship between it and some of the models that have been produced during development.

develop a software system. Building systems is a skill – like playing a musical instrument or swimming – that can only be learnt by practice. It's no good knowing all about swimming if you can't actually swim, and it's no good knowing all about how to develop systems if you can't actually do it. If you simply want to be able to talk about development of software systems in theory, then all you need to do is read the book, but if you want to be able to make a useful contribution to a system development project, there is no alternative but to get stuck in and do the exercises.

There are a number of extra sections at the end of the book. Appendix A collects together all the material relating to the Wheels bike hire case study, and Appendix B contains introductory information about a second case study, which can be used as a vehicle for practising all the techniques covered in the book. There is also a bibliography for readers who want to find out about some of the topics in more detail, and a glossary of terms, giving definitions of all the key words used in the book. Finally answers are provided to all the practical exercises.

There are two websites for the book, one for students which can be found at http://books.elsevier.com/companions/0750661232 and one for lecturers at http://books.elsevier.com/manualsprotected/ 0750661232. These sites contain further models for the second case study, a complete set of lecture slides, electronic copy of the code and multiple choice questions for topics covered in the book. There is also a revision notes section that will be helpful as an aide-mémoire for students who are studying for exams.

The system life cycle

When undertaking any large project, it is important to have some kind of framework in order to help identify milestones, structure activities and monitor deliverables. The development of a software system is no different from any other kind of project in needing some kind of framework within which the developers can work together.

An agreed framework for development brings many advantages, and the larger and more complex the project, the more evident these advantages become. First, a framework provides an overall picture of the development process; this picture is not cluttered by detail of what goes on at any stage in the process, but is useful as a high-level view of the major areas of activity, milestones and project deliverables. A framework provides a basis for development and ensures a certain level of consistency in how the work is approached. Consistency of approach is important when a large number of developers are involved, and is helpful for new staff joining the project after it has started. A framework plays a significant role in ensuring quality, both of the development process and of the final system, by providing a structure for project management – planning, monitoring and controlling the development project.

In software system development, a framework has traditionally been known as a system life cycle model. Although life cycle models have been around for a long time, there is still no general agreement about the precise stages in the development process, the activities that take place at any particular stage, or what is produced at the end of it. This is hardly surprising, since factors such as the type of system being built, the software being used, the timescales and the development environment will all influence decisions about the detailed stages of a project.

However, at a higher level, there is agreement that there are certain life cycle stages that all projects must go through in order to reach a successful completion. Historically these stages have been referred to as requirements, analysis, design, implementation and installation. Each stage is concerned with particular issues and produces a set of outputs or deliverables, as shown in Table 1.2.

Traditional life cycle models

Over the years there have been a number of life cycle models based on the development stages outlined in Table 1.2. In this section we briefly introduce some of the most widely used models. You can find more information about traditional system life cycles in some of the books in the bibliography, for example Pfleeger (1998) and Sommerville (2000).

Waterfall. This early life cycle model represents the stages of development as a straightforward sequence, where one stage must be completed before the next begins. It was the first model to identify the different stages that make up the system development process, and its simplicity has made it a useful model for many years. However, the waterfall model is not really a true reflection of what actually happens in system development, since it does not emphasize the need to iterate over the stages.

V-model. This is a variation of the waterfall, where the stages are visualized in the form of the letter 'V'. It emphasizes how later stages of development are related to earlier stages; for example, how testing should be derived from the activities that are carried out during requirements and analysis.

Spiral. This model is also derived from the waterfall. It incorporates iteration of life cycle stages and focuses on identifying and addressing the risks involved in development.

Prototyping. In the prototyping life cycle, implementation takes place early in the development process. The working model produced is subsequently refined and enhanced during a series of iterations until it is acceptable to the client.

Table 1.2: A traditional high-level system life cycle

Stage of life cycle	Issues addressed	Deliverables
Requirements	What are the problems, needs and wishes of clients and users? What are the objectives and scope of the proposed system? What are the major risks involved?	List of requirements that can be used as a starting point for development. List of problem areas that fall within the scope of the proposed system. Assessment of risk factors.
Analysis	What does the system look like from the perspective of the clients and users?	A set of models, each taking a different view of the system, which together give a complete picture. The models may be text, diagrams or early prototypes.
Design	How can the system be constructed, so as to satisfy the requirements?	Models from the analysis stage, refined to illustrate the underlying architecture of the system. These models take account of technological considerations and constraints arising from the implementation environment.
Implementation	How can the models produced be translated into code?	A fully tested suite of programs.
Installation	What is needed to support clients and users so that they can use the new system effectively?	User manual, technical documentation, user training. Conversion from current system to new system.

Iterative development. This approach is closely related to the spiral model and to prototyping. A skeleton version covering the complete functionality of the system is produced and then refined as development progresses.

Incremental development. In this life cycle model the system is partitioned according to areas of functionality. Each major functional area is developed and delivered independently to the client. For example, in the bike hire system, tasks relating to issuing a bike might be developed and delivered, followed by returning a bike and then maintaining customer records.

The object-oriented approach

One of the differences that is immediately obvious between traditional life cycle models and the object-oriented approach is the way that the various stages are named. In traditional models the names, such as 'analysis' or 'implementation', reflect the activities that are intended to be carried out in that stage. In object-orientation, however, a clear distinction is made between the activities and the stages (generally referred to as phases) of development. The phases in object-oriented development are known as inception, elaboration, construction and transition, indicating the state of the system, rather than what happens at that point in development.

Inception covers the initial work required to set up and agree terms for the project. It includes establishing the business case for the project, incorporating basic risk assessment and the scope of the system that is to be developed. Inception is similar to a standard feasibility study, but frequently includes a small part of the requirements for the system that have been implemented in a working program.

Elaboration deals with putting the basic architecture of the system in place and agreeing a plan for construction. During this phase a design is produced that shows that the system can be developed within the agreed constraints of time and cost.

Construction involves a series of iterations covering the bulk of the work on building the system; it ends with the beta release of the system, which means that it still has to undergo rigorous testing.

Transition covers the processes involved in transferring the system to the clients and users. This includes sorting out errors and problems that have arisen during the development process.

In object-orientation, activities such as analysis or design are referred to as workflows. Figure 1.1 shows the different workflows that typically take place during a system development project.

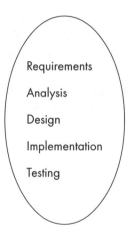

Figure 1.1   *Workflows that take place during development of a system*

It is recognized that a workflow may be carried out at more than one development phase and that developers may well engage in the whole range of workflows during every phase of building a system. For example, in inception, requirements engineering and analysis will obviously take place, but there may well also be some design activity and even some implementation if all or part of the system is to be prototyped. During the construction phase the main activities will be implementation and testing, but if bugs are found there will have to be some requirements and analysis as well.

Instead of the ordered table in Table 1.2, the object-oriented approach to development views the relationships between workflows and phases of development rather like the spider's web in Figure 1.2, where any phase may involve all workflows, and a workflow may be carried out during any phase.

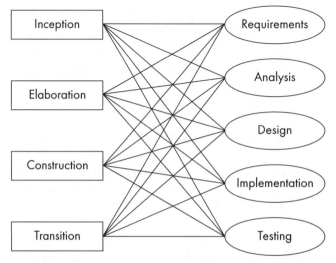

Figure 1.2   *An object-oriented view of development phases and workflows*

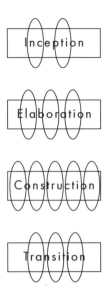

Figure 1.3   *Phases of object-oriented development with iterations of workflows*

The object-oriented approach also recognizes fully the reality of iterative development. Activities at any phase do not take place in a neatly ordered fashion. A developer may have to revisit a range of workflows several times during one phase of development, before it is possible to move on to the next phase. Figure 1.3 illustrates the phases of the object-oriented life cycle with iteration of workflows at each phase. You can see from the diagram that iterations are most likely during construction, but can occur during any phase of development. In the diagram each ellipse represents a range of workflows that may take place as shown in Figure 1.1.

In addition to the emphasis on iterative development, the object-oriented approach also differs from traditional life cycle models in that it stresses the importance of a seamless development process. This means that the separate phases are less distinct from each other than in a traditional system life cycle; it is not considered essential, nor is it often easy, to be able to say precisely when one phase is completed and another begins.

The seamless process is supported by the fact that object-oriented development is driven by a single unifying idea – that of the object. Objects initially represent things or concepts in the problem domain; they underpin the whole development process, and eventually become components of the code for the final system. Because the object is the foundation of all development work, object-orientation does not introduce new models to describe the system at different phases, but develops and refines early models from the inception phase right through the development process. This helps to preserve important information, and avoids the risk of inconsistency between multiple representations. It also brings the added advantage of traceability, allowing the developer to track an early requirement via the different phases of development right through to the code.

Although the traditional system life cycle was concerned about issues such as quality, ease of modification and potential reuse, it tended to regard them as add-ons to the core development process. In the object-oriented approach such issues are regarded as central, and developers are encouraged to bear them in mind throughout the time they are working on the system.

The Rational Unified Process (RUP)

A life cycle provides a high-level representation of the stages that a development project must go through to produce a successful system, but it does not attempt to dictate how this should be achieved, nor does it describe the activities that should be carried out at each stage. A development method,[1] on the other hand, is much more prescriptive, often setting down in detail the tasks, responsibilities, processes, prerequisites, deliverables and milestones for each stage of the project.

Over the past decade, there have been a number of object-oriented development methods, such as Responsibility-Driven Design (Wirfs-Brock et al., 1990), Object Modelling Technique (Rumbaugh et al., 1991) and Open (Graham et al., 1998). It is beyond the scope of this book to describe these in detail, but you can find references to all of them at the end of the chapter and in the bibliography.

Nowadays, almost all object-oriented projects use the Unified Modelling Language (see following section) as the principal tool in their development process. Use of the UML has been approved by the Object Management Group (OMG), which controls issues of standardization in this area. This has resulted in conformity between projects in terms of notation and techniques. However, UML is simply a notation or language for development; it is not in itself a development method and does not include detailed instructions on how it should be used in a project. The creators of the UML, Ivar Jacobson, Grady Booch and James Rumbaugh, have proposed a generic object-oriented development method in their book *The Unified Software Development Process* (Jacobson et al., 1999) and this generic method has been adopted and marketed by the Rational Corporation under the name of the Rational Unified Process (RUP).

RUP incorporates not only modelling techniques from the UML, but also guidelines, templates and tools to ensure effective and

---

1. *Development methods used to be referred to as 'methodologies', and sometimes still are. As the true meaning of methodology is 'study of methods', we prefer to use the simpler term 'method' in this book.*

successful development of software systems. The tools offered by RUP allow a large part of the development process to be automated, including modelling, programming, testing, managing the project and managing change.

RUP is based on the following six 'Best Practices' which have been formulated from experience on many industrial software projects:

1 Develop software iteratively

2 Manage requirements

3 Use component-based architectures

4 Visually model software

5 Verify software quality

6 Control changes to software.

1 *Develop software iteratively*

RUP follows the phases of the generic object-oriented life cycle (inception, elaboration, construction and transition) described earlier in this chapter. It is built on the central concept of iterative development (as shown in Figure 1.3) and each of its phases defines a series of activities that may be performed once or a number of times. Each iteration is defined as a complete development loop resulting in the release of an executable product that is a subset of the final system. In this way RUP supports incremental development – the frequent release of small packages of software that gradually build up to become the final system. Iteration and incremental development encourage involvement and feedback from clients and users; they make it easier to cope with changes, and reduce the risk factors associated with any development project.

2 *Manage requirements*

RUP offers sound support for eliciting, organizing and recording requirements. Precise documentation of requirements facilitates traceability through the development process, which enhances the quality of the final system. The emphasis on the activities that take place early on in the life cycle provides a sound foundation for the later stages and results in systems that are robust, reliable and meet the needs of their users.

3 *Use component-based architectures*

RUP prescribes the early identification and development of a system structure that is at the same time robust enough to ensure system reliability, and flexible enough to accommodate changes. This is achieved through the use of components – subsystems that each have a single, well-defined function. RUP describes how to construct an architecture combining both new and previously existing components, thus encouraging the reuse of software as part of the development process.

4 *Visually model software*

RUP is based around the Unified Modelling Language (UML) as a vehicle for development. UML has become an industry standard, and incorporates a wide range of techniques and tools to support developers. The techniques offered by UML bring with them all the advantages of visual modelling. For example, UML diagrams facilitate communication between developers and users and between members of the development team, they offer a number of different views of the system which combine to give a complete picture, they help developers to decompose the problem into smaller, more manageable chunks, and they provide a means of abstraction, concentrating on important information while hiding details that are currently irrelevant.

5 *Verify software quality*

RUP provides the techniques to support quality assessment of functionality, reliability and performance throughout the development process. The RUP approach to quality is based on objective measures and criteria for success; it involves all members of the development team and applies to all the activities that are carried out as part of the system development.

6 *Control changes to software*

Changes are the norm in a software development project, so an effective development process must be able to monitor and control them. RUP provides tools to do this, and also supports the work of developers by offering protection in one area of development from changes that occur in another.

RUP is an increasingly popular approach to developing software systems, and is already laying claim to be the industry standard. However, it would be overkill to work through all the details of RUP in this book, since the book is based around the development of a small, simple information system. We therefore describe the development of the Wheels bike hire system within a simplified object-oriented framework.

The Unified Modelling Language (UML)

The Unified Modelling Language, or UML, is a set of diagrammatic techniques, which are specifically tailored for object-oriented development, and which have become an industry standard for modelling object-oriented systems. The UML grew out of the work of James Rumbaugh, Grady Booch and Ivor Jacobson, and has been approved as a development standard by the Object Management Group. Before discussing the UML in detail, we should explain briefly what we mean by 'modelling' in this context, and why it is an important part of software system development.

Modelling

Architects and engineers have always used special types of drawing to help them to describe what they are designing and building. In the same way, software developers use specialized diagrams to model the system that they are working on throughout the development process. Each model produced represents part of the system or some aspect of it, such as the structure of the stored data, or the way that operations are carried out. Each model provides a view of the system, but not the whole picture.

As an example, let us consider a small girl, Jane, and imagine that we have a photograph of her. The photograph is one possible model of the real-life Jane; it tells us what she looks like, and may give some idea of her character. Figure 1.4 shows two more possible models of the real-life Jane.

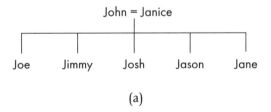

John = Janice

Joe   Jimmy   Josh   Jason   Jane

(a)

Jane Jones

Date of birth: 4th April 1997
Address: 21 Parsons Drive, Letterbury
School: Letterbury Junior School
Class: 3B

(b)

Figure 1.4   *Different models showing different information about one real-life person*

Unlike a photograph, the family tree in Figure 1.4(a) tells us nothing about Jane's appearance, but it does provide information about her family. We can see that she has four brothers and is the youngest child; we also discover the first names of Jane's parents and siblings. The family tree is a graphical, diagrammatic model. Figure 1.4(b), on the other hand, is a textual model; it tells us some details about Jane, her birth date, address, school and which class she is in. Each model (the photograph, the family tree and the piece of text) tells us something about Jane, but we can only get all the information by looking at all the models (in fact we would need many more detailed models to get a complete picture of her).

The characteristic of a model to provide some but not all the information about the person or thing being modelled is known as *abstraction*. We can say that each of the models in Figure 1.4 is an abstraction of the real-life Jane, focusing on certain aspects of her and ignoring other details. In the same way, each of the modelling techniques in the Unified Modelling Language provides a particular view of the system as it develops; each UML model is an abstraction of the complete system.

Abstraction is a very important tool in modelling any sort of software system because typically the problems developers have to deal with are much too complex for one developer to hold all the details in his head at once. Abstraction provides a means of concentrating on only those aspects of the system that are currently of interest, and putting other details to the side for the time being.

Another, equally important tool for modelling software systems is *decomposition*. This is the breaking down of a large, complex problem or system into successively smaller parts, until each part is a 'brain-size' chunk and can be worked on as an independent unit. Traditionally software systems used to be decomposed according to their functions – the tasks that the system had to carry out. As we shall see later, however, object-oriented systems are decomposed according to the data that they have to store, access and manipulate.

Initially, the models that are constructed using the techniques provided by the UML help the developer to impose a coherent structure on the information gathered from clients and users. One of the principal uses of the models is as a basis for discussions, since talking about the system as represented helps to identify gaps and inconsistencies in the information. As the project progresses, the original models are enhanced with details relating to design and implementation issues, so that eventually they become a blueprint for the development of the system.

Table 1.3: The principal UML diagrams with brief descriptions

Model	View of the system
Use case	How the system interacts with its users.
Class	The data elements in the system and the relationships between them.
Interaction (sequence and collaboration)	How the objects interact to achieve the functionality of a use case.
State	How the different objects of a single class behave through all the use cases in which the class is involved.
Activity	The sequence of activities that make up a process.
Component	The different software components of the system and the dependencies between them.
Deployment	The software and hardware elements of the system and the physical relationships between them.

UML models

As we mentioned in the previous section, the UML is not a development method since it does not prescribe what developers should do; it is a diagrammatic language or notation, providing a set of diagramming techniques that model the system from different points of view. Table 1.3 shows the principal UML models with a brief description of what each can tell us about the developing system.

The 4 + 1 view. The authors of UML, Booch *et al.*, (1999), suggest we look at the architecture of a system from five different perspectives or views:

- The use case view

- The design view

- The process view

- The implementation view

- The deployment view.

This is known as the 4 + 1 view (rather than the 5 views) because of the special role played by the use case view. *The use case view* of the system is the users' view: it specifies what the user wants the system to do; the other 4 views describe how to achieve this. The use case view describes the external behaviour of the system and is captured in the use case model, discussed in Chapter 3. In the early stages of development, the software architecture is driven by the use cases; we model the system's software in terms of collaborations of the classes[2] required by each use case. *The design view* (sometimes called the logical view) describes the logical structures required to provide the functionality specified in the use case view. The design view describes the classes (including attributes and operations) of the system and their interactions. This view is captured in the class diagram, discussed in Chapter 5 and the interaction diagrams, discussed in Chapters 6 and 10. *The process view* is concerned with describing concurrency in the system; concurrency is beyond the scope of this book, but we briefly discuss how sequence diagrams can be used to achieve it. *The implementation view* describes the physical software components of the system, such as executable files, class libraries and databases. This view of the system can be modelled using component diagrams (see Chapter 9). *The deployment view* of the system describes the hardware components of the system such as PCs, mainframes, printers and the way they are connected. This view can also be used to show where software components are physically installed on the hardware elements. Deployment diagrams describe this view of the system. Not all of these views will be required for every system. For instance, if your system does not use concurrency, you will not need a process view. If your system runs on a single machine, you will not need the deployment view or the component view, as all of the software components will be installed on one machine.

The 4 + 1 view gives us five different ways of viewing a system and is supported in UML by modelling techniques to capture each view. Just as a photograph, family tree and description give us different views of a person, the UML views show us a system from different points of view. Each one offers a different perspective, no one gives us the whole picture. To gain complete understanding of the system all of the views must be considered.

UML and CASE tools. One of the advantages of a standardized language for producing diagrams during system development is that a number of CASE tools have been developed to provide automated support for developers.

---

2. *A collaboration of classes is the set of classes required to provide the functionality of a specific use case (see Chapter 3).*

CASE (Computer Aided Software Engineering) refers to any piece of software that has been designed to help people develop systems. In theory, a CASE tool can be a simple drawing program or basic debugger, but today almost all CASE tools cover the whole of the system life cycle, and provide automated support for all development activities, both technical and managerial. For object-oriented systems, tools such as Rational Rose™ and Together™ allow developers to produce UML models of the system which are syntactically correct, consistent with each other and which can be refined and developed to produce executable code. The diagrams in this book were originally produced using both Rational Rose™ and Together™, but the code has been written from scratch in order to show how the system develops from diagrams to code, and to emphasize certain points that we think are important when you are learning about object-oriented development. However, it would have been perfectly possible to generate the skeleton of a running program from the diagrams shown here. Even though we did not use this facility, we still benefited from the 'nanny' characteristics of the CASE tools, which remembered details of previous diagrams, allowed us to navigate between diagrams that were related, and pointed out when we made stupid mistakes.

Introduction to the case study

The case study which is used as the basis for examples and exercises in this book is a typical bicycle hire shop. If you have ever hired a bicycle, you will already be familiar with some of the details; in fact, if you have ever hired anything, such as a car or even a video, you will see that the basic processes are very similar.

The bike hire shop is called Wheels, and was started by Mike Watson, the current owner, about ten years ago. Mike has always been a keen cyclist, and still competes regularly in local races and rides for charity. He has an encyclopaedic knowledge of all types of bike, and is very proud of the range and quality of his stock. The business has done well, and now occupies large premises near the centre of town with a big storage and workshop area in the basement. Wheels attracts a lot of passing custom because of the position of the shop, and also gets many returning customers who know that they will be given a good quality bike that will suit their needs.

As well as Mike, who is very much involved in the day-to-day running of the business, there is a full-time shop manager, Annie Price, the head mechanic, Naresh Patel, and three other mechanics who work part-time. There is a computer in the reception area, and all the Wheels bikes are recorded on file, with details such as the bike number, type, size, make, model, daily charge rate and deposit. Unfortunately, however, that's all there is on the computer, and the actual hire and return procedures are carried out in much the same, slightly disorganized way that they always have been.

Mike has recently come to realize that, although he has a successful business, he will not be able to expand as he would like to unless he gets his business processes up to date, and that to do this he will have to make much more effective use of the computer. He decides to hire a small local firm to investigate the way things are done at the moment, suggest possible improvements, and develop a computer system that will bring the Wheels business into the twenty-first century.

Chapter summary

This chapter provides advice on how to get the best from the book as a whole, explaining that developing software systems is a skill that can only be learnt by practice. The chapter fills in some of the background relating to system life cycles and the main features of traditional and object-oriented approaches to development. It also describes briefly the Rational Unified Process (RUP) and the Unified Modelling Language (UML), which is used for the diagrams in the book. Finally, the chapter introduces the Wheels bike hire case study that is the source of examples and exercises in the book.

Bibliography

Booch, G., Rumbaugh, J. and Jacobson, I. (1999) *The Unified Modeling Language User Guide,* Addison-Wesley, Reading, MA.

Britton, C. and Doake, J. (2000) *Object-oriented Systems Development: A Gentle Introduction,* McGraw-Hill, London.

Britton, C. and Doake, J. (2002) *Software System Development: A Gentle Introduction* (3rd edition), McGraw-Hill, London.

Graham, I., Henderson-Sellers, B. and Younessi, H. (1998) *The OPEN Process Specification,* Addison-Wesley, Harlow, UK.

Jacobson, I., Booch, G. and Rumbaugh, J. (1999) *The Unified Software Development Process,* Addison-Wesley, Reading, MA.

Pfleeger, S.L. (1998) *Software Engineering, Theory and Practice,* Prentice Hall, Upper Saddle River, NJ.

Quatrani, T. (1998) *Visual Modeling with Rational Rose and UML,* Addison-Wesley, Reading, MA.

Rumbaugh, J., Blaha, M., Premerlani, W., Eddy, F. and Lorensen, W. (1991) *Object-oriented Modeling and Design,* Prentice-Hall, Englewood Cliffs, NJ.

Sommerville, I. (2000) *Software Engineering.* (6th edition, Addison-Wesley, Wokingham.

Wirfs-Brock, R., Wilkerson, B. and Wiener, L. (1990) *Designing Object-oriented Software,* Prentice Hall, Englewood Cliffs, NJ.

Quick check questions

You can find the answers to these in the chapter.

a   Why is it not enough just to read the book if you want to make a useful contribution to a software development team?

b   What is a system life cycle?

c   What are the main stages of a traditional system life cycle?

d   List four life cycle models that are based on the traditional approach to developing software systems

e   What are the main phases of object-oriented system development?

f   In object-oriented development, what is the relationship between phases and workflows?

g   List three ways in which object-oriented development differs from the traditional structured approach.

h   What is the difference between a life cycle and a development method?

i   What are (a) RUP and (b) UML?

j   What do we mean by (a) abstraction and (b) decomposition in the context of modelling software systems?

k   What is a CASE tool?

2 Requirements for the Wheels case study system

Learning outcomes

The material and exercises in this chapter will enable you to:

- Familiarize yourself with the details of the Wheels case study

- Explain the role of requirements engineering in the system development process

- Describe the principal stages of requirements engineering

- Recognize and use some of the most popular techniques in requirements elicitation.

Key words that you will find in the glossary:

- elicitation
- Fagan inspection
- problem definition
- problems and requirements list
- scenario
- specification
- validation

Introduction

One of the main aims of this chapter is to fill in some of the details of the Wheels case study which was introduced in Chapter 1 and which is used in examples throughout the rest of the book. We describe Wheels through techniques that are typically used early in the development process to establish how things are done at present and identify what the client wants and needs from the new system. The activities that capture and record client requirements are known collectively as requirements engineering. Requirements engineering is a crucial and complex part of any system development, not just object-oriented projects. It is not possible to do justice to the whole of requirements engineering within the scope of this book, but if you are interested in the topic and want to read more about it, you will find a list of useful texts at the end of the chapter and in the bibliography. In this chapter we simply give a brief description of the main stages of requirements engineering, and show how some of the most useful techniques can be applied to the Wheels case study.

Towards the end of the chapter you will find a list of requirements that must be satisfied by the new Wheels system. These requirements form the starting point for the object-oriented development of the Wheels system that is described in the rest of the book.

Requirements engineering

Interest in requirements engineering as a topic in its own right is relatively recent compared to system design or programming, but it is now universally agreed that getting the requirements right is a crucial part of any system development project. We can see this most clearly by imagining what happens if we get the requirements wrong: it will not matter how well the system is designed or how elegant the code, if the system does not do what the clients and users want, it is useless. It is therefore essential that users, designers and programmers have a clear, comprehensive and agreed specification of requirements to use as a basis for developing the system; the goal and purpose of requirements engineering is to produce such a specification.

Requirements engineering is traditionally divided into three main stages:

- Elicitation, when information is gathered relating to the existing system, current problems and requirements for the future

- Specification, when the information that has been collected is ordered and documented

- Validation, when the recorded requirements are checked to ensure that they are consistent with what the clients and users actually want and need.

Requirements elicitation

During requirements elicitation, the focus is on collecting as much information as possible about what the clients and users want and need from the new system. This usually involves a large amount of work examining the way in which the system operates at present, whether it is manual, automated, or a mixture of both. Techniques for requirements elicitation include interviews, questionnaires, study of documents, observation of people carrying out day-to-day tasks, and assessment of the current computer system if there is one. Each of these techniques is appropriate in particular situations, but to gather all the information needed, a range of elicitation techniques should be used. In the following section of this chapter we provide illustrations of how the techniques of interviewing and questionnaires might be applied in eliciting requirements for the Wheels case study system.

Interviews. Successful elicitation of requirements depends on good communication with clients and users, and one of the most effective ways of achieving good communication is through one-to-one interviews. Ideally, a developer should interview everyone in the client organization, from secretaries and office juniors to bosses and managers. However, in a large business this is clearly not practicable, so it is important that those members of staff who are interviewed are a representative cross-section of the people who will be involved in the new system. In the case of the Wheels system development project, the developer should interview at least the owner of the business, the shop manager and one of the mechanics. The opinions of Wheels' customers should also be canvassed, but it is more appropriate to do this using a questionnaire; this is discussed later in this chapter.

The main purpose of an interview at this stage of the system development process is to elicit the interviewee's views on how the business functions at present, any problems that arise from this and ways in which the interviewee thinks that things could be improved. In order to gather as much relevant information as possible, the interview must be well prepared. It is useful to produce a plan that is given to the interviewee in advance, stating the time and place of the interview, the kind of topics that will be covered and any documents that the interviewee should bring along. Figure 2.1 shows the plan for an interview with Annie Price, the shop manager at Wheels. The interviewer is Simon Davis, a system developer on the Wheels project.

A plan, such as the one in Figure 2.1, helps to put the interviewee at their ease and provides a basic structure for the interview. However, it is important that such a plan should not dominate the process of the interview, as valuable information may be lost if the interviewer sticks rigidly to pre-prepared questions. A good interviewer will direct an interview, but not dominate it and, most importantly, will always be prepared to listen to what the

Interview Plan			
System: **Wheels**		Project reference: **Wheels/04**	
Participants:	**Annie Price (Shop manager for Wheels)** **Simon Davis (Developer)**		
Date **10 February 2004**	Time **14.30**	Duration **45 minutes**	Place **Manager's office**
Purpose of interview **Preliminary meeting to discuss procedures and problems with the current system**			
Agenda • **current procedures for hiring bikes** • **problems with the current system** • **initial ideas on how these could be addressed** • **follow-up actions**			
Documents to be brought to interview • **bike card** • **any other documents relating to current procedures**			

Figure 2.1   Interview plan for interview with Annie Price, shop manager at Wheels

interviewee has to say. Below you can see an extract from the interview between Simon Davis, the system developer and Annie Price, the shop manager at Wheels.

SD: …so could you tell me what happens typically when someone wants to hire a bike? Just talk me through it bit by bit.

Annie: OK, well say someone comes in and says they want to hire a bike for that afternoon, so I ask them if they know what sort they want – it's always easier in that case. Then, when I've got an idea of what they're looking for, I get Naresh or one of the other mechanics to come and suggest a couple of bikes that might suit.

SD: And is the customer always happy with that?

Annie: Yes, usually they go with whatever Naresh says. He's the head mechanic and he's pretty clued up about bikes. We hardly ever get any of them coming back and complaining after the ride.

SD: So what's next?

Annie: I get the bike's number – that's stencilled onto the bike – and then I use that to look up the bike card. There's a card for each bike and we keep them under the counter in this box.

SD: Ok, and what order do you keep them in?

Annie: We keep them in the order of the bike numbers – it's the only way really – though it does cause problems with queries. For example, the other day I had a man on the phone wanting to know if we had two bikes, a Raleigh Pioneer for him and a Dawes Galaxy for his partner, and how much it would cost for three day's hire. First of all I had to look on the shop floor to see if we'd got the right bikes, then I had to search through all the cards and then I had to work out how much it was going to cost him. He was very patient, but that sort of thing takes ages. Anyway, I'll show you one of the cards.[1]

Bike Number: 1591 Clour: Black	Make: Scott Daily rate: £8	Model: Atlantic Trail Deposit: £50	Type: mountain Size: womans	
Customer	**Start date**	**Return date**	**Paid**	**Extras**
Mrs V. Patel 16 St Johns Road	31/08/03	2/9/03	£74	
Ms C. Wilson 112 Regent Street	9/9/03	12/9/03	£82	£8
Dr F. Green 67 Grange Road	4/10/03	4/10/03	$58	
Ms C. Wilson 112 Regent Street	19/1/04	19/1/04	£58	

Figure 2.2   *Example bike card from the current Wheels system*

SD: Thanks. Can you tell me – are the hire charge and the deposit the same for all the bikes?

Annie: No, they vary a lot. Well, you couldn't charge the same for a child's bike as for an 18-gear racer, could you? Anyway, then I fill in all the details on the bike card, the customer gives me the money to cover the hire and deposit and off they go.

SD: Don't they get a receipt?

Annie: Oh yes, sorry, I forgot. I write one out from the receipt book. It would be nice if we could use the computer system for that, but all we've actually got on it is a list of the bikes that

---

1. *The bike card is shown in Figure 2.2.*

we own and all their details like make, model, size, cost and all that. Even that can be a bit of a problem – for Naresh that is – he's the one who has to enter all the details about the bikes that the boss buys in and that can be really tedious.

SD: Well, I'm sure we can improve on that. So tell me, if a customer hires more than one bike, how do you record that?

Annie: Well, you can see this card only has details for this particular bike, so if a customer is hiring three bikes I have to put the details on three separate cards, including writing out their name and address three times. We have to do it like that because sometimes people hire more than one bike, but for different times. For example, we get families on holiday who hire bikes for the children for the whole week, but maybe just a couple of days for the parents. When people do want a number of bikes it's a bit of a pain looking out all the cards and filling in the same customer details on each one, not to mention working out what it all costs. We once had a customer who hired 20 bikes for his daughter's birthday party, which took me ages. That was a bit of a one-off though; we do get requests for parties and events, but it's generally the special stuff that they want.

SD: Special stuff?

Annie: Sorry, I should have told you about that. We have some novelty items that Mike (he's the boss) has picked up at auctions, like a couple of genuine working penny farthing cycles. Those are very popular for period style photos and charity events. People tend to notice them, so they're a really good advertisement for us as well. Last year we had a local couple who hired one of our old tandems for their wedding and we got loads of publicity from that.

SD: Presumably hiring those out is rather more complicated.

Annie: Oh yes, we have to write on the card extra details about our special bikes, such as their age, value and restrictions on what they can be hired for.

SD: OK, so just to get back to the actual hire procedures. You fill in the details on the card, the customer pays and you give them a receipt.

Annie: Yes that's it really.

SD: Thanks, that's very helpful. So what happens when the customer comes back with the bike?

Annie: Well they come in, usually all hot and sweaty, but never mind that. I get the bike number and I check that the bike they're returning is the one on the card. And I have to check the return date as well, because if they're late they have to pay extra.

SD: And you return the customer's deposit if they bring back the bike on time?

Annie: Usually, but not if the bike's been damaged of course. One of the mechanics gives every bike a quick check to make sure it's in reasonable condition. If there's a problem we keep some of the deposit and if it's really bad then we keep all of it. We once had one that was a write-off; goodness knows what the customer had been doing with it. The bikes are insured of course, but keeping deposits helps keep down the claims.

SD: Can you tell me about your customers in general, do you think they're happy with the hire system as it is, or do you get a lot of complaints?

Annie: I don't think it's too bad, though we do get complaints occasionally. I don't think the system's very efficient; for example, it can be really slow if I'm trying to work out the cost of hiring more than one bike. If it's my day off and one of the others is in charge it's even slower because they're not used to it. Sometimes I think the customers are just too nice to complain. They can see that I'm doing my best and they don't want to get me into trouble. I think if you asked them they might say that there are quite a few things that could be improved.

SD: Well I'm thinking of doing just that. Would it be all right to leave a short questionnaire on the counter for customers to fill in and return to you? I think it would give us a good idea of how your customers view the hire system and where they think the problems are.

Annie: That's a great idea. You can leave them on the counter and I'll make sure that every customer gets one...

We can see from this extract from the interview with Annie that, although the developer sticks fairly closely to the original plan, he allows Annie to expand on particular topics, such as the specialist bikes. The extract also contains an example of the sort of document that is used in the current system and should be studied by the system developer. The bike card is obviously causing some problems and slowing down the hire process; careful study of the card itself, together with input from Annie and other members of staff, will help the developer to produce a new and better computerized version.

The extract from the interview with Annie is fairly typical in that relevant information does not emerge in a structured, coherent order. From what Annie says, we can identify a number of areas that seem to be causing problems.

- It takes a long time to deal with queries such as 'Have you got 5 women's mountain bikes?' or 'How much would it cost to hire two adult racers for three days?'

- The only way Annie can tell if a bike is in the shop and available for hire is by looking on the shop floor.

- The bike cards are kept in number order, so Annie has to know the bike number before she can find its card.

- Wheels does not seem to keep any records of their customers' details or the bikes that they hired on previous occasions.

- When a customer hires more than one bike, Annie has to fill out a separate card for each one.

- Annie has to write out receipts for the customers by hand.

- Bike return is slow because it takes Annie a while to calculate whether the whole deposit can be returned.

- Important information about novelty bikes has to be written on the standard bike card.

Questionnaires. In order to build up a comprehensive list of requirements for the new system, it is important for the developer to find out as much as possible about what the bike shop's customers think about the current bike hire procedures. It is unlikely that the developer will be able to interview customers, and in any case, he is only looking for a small amount of information from each person, so the most effective method of elicitation is to use a questionnaire. Figure 2.3 shows a questionnaire that could be used to carry out a survey of customer opinions on the current system at Wheels. The purpose of the

Wheels customer survey

Our aim is always to give you the best service possible. We are investigating our current hiring procedures to identify any problems and improve the present system. It would be very helpful if you could give us your opinion on what you like or dislike about how we do things now and how we could improve.

Please spare a few minutes to answer the questions below and return the form to Annie in reception.

Please answer questions 1 and 2 by ticking one of the boxes:

1. Roughly how many times have you hired a bike from us in the past year?

   no hire ☐   once only ☐   2–5 times ☐   6–10 times ☐   more than 10 times ☐

2. Roughly how many times have you hired a specialist bike from us in the past year?

   no hire ☐   once only ☐   2–5 times ☐   6–10 times ☐   more than 10 times ☐

3. For each of the statements (a)–(e) below, circle the number that is closest to your own view. 1 means that you strongly agree with the statement, and 5 means that you strongly disagree.

		strongly agree				strongly disagree
a	The hire service is easy to understand	1	2	3	4	5
b	The hire service is fast and efficient	1	2	3	4	5
c	I always get a bike that suits me	1	2	3	4	5
d	It is easy to work out how much it's going to cost	1	2	3	4	5
e	The bike checking is quick and fair	1	2	3	4	5

4.

Overall are you happy with our curent bike hire system? YES/NO	Please give details of any concerns:
Do you have any suggestions for improving the bike hire system?	Any further comments or observations?

If you would like more information about our bikes please give your details:

Your name: _____

Your address: _____

_____

Thank you for completing this questionnaire.

Figure 2.3   Questionnaire for Wheels customer survey

- A customer, Steve Chen, arrives at the shop with a bike to return

- Annie contacts the mechanics to ask for someone to come and check the bike

- Annie gets the bike number, looks out the relevant bike card and checks Steve's name and address

- Annie makes sure that the bike being returned is the one on the card

- She confirms that the bike is being returned on time by checking the return date against the current date

- One of the mechanics checks the bike and confirms that it has been returned in good condition

- Annie returns Steve's deposit.

Figure 2.4   *Simple scenario for the return of a bike in the current Wheels system*

questionnaire and instructions on how to return it are stated clearly at the top, and there are different types of question. Most importantly, the questionnaire is relatively short and will only take customers a few minutes to fill in; it could easily be completed while customers are waiting for their bikes to be checked.

Scenarios. Scenarios have been popular as a method of requirements elicitation for many years and have now become closely associated with object-oriented development of systems. A scenario is a sequence of interactions between a user and the system carried out in order to satisfy a specified goal. Scenarios may be recorded in a variety of ways, including diagrams, storyboards or even videos, but they are generally documented in textual form as in the examples in this book. Figure 2.4 shows a scenario from the current Wheels system where the specified goal is to return a bike successfully.

As we can see from the example in Figure 2.4, a scenario is a sequence of particular events, not a general description. This example illustrates the straightforward return of a bike, without any problems. However, this is only one possible scenario for a bike return, and it is the developer's job to find out what happens in all possible cases. Figure 2.5 shows another scenario for bike return, which is slightly more complicated.

It is also important for the developer to find out about what happens when a goal is not achieved, for example a customer may come into Wheels to return a bike, but the bike card is missing. A scenario should be written for this sort of situation in the same way as for normal cases, so that the developer knows how the system should respond when things are not straightforward.

- Two customers, Paul and Debbie White, arrive at the shop with bikes to return

- Annie contacts the mechanics to ask for someone to come and check the bikes

- Annie gets the bike numbers, looks out the relevant bike cards and checks Paul and Debbie's names and addresses

- Annie makes sure that the bikes being returned are the ones on the cards

- She checks to see if the bikes are being returned on time by verifying the return date against the current date

- Annie finds that the bikes are one day overdue

- She tells the customers that there is a charge for the extra day's hire

- One of the mechanics checks the bikes and confirms that they have been returned in good condition

- Annie returns the customers' deposit, minus the extra day's hire charge

- Annie writes out a receipt for the extra charge.

Figure 2.5   *A more complicated scenario for the return of a bike in the current Wheels system*

Scenarios are a very effective technique in requirements elicitation because their narrative structure helps users to remember and describe what happens in different processes in the system. A detailed scenario can be built up by first constructing a simple version and then walking through it with the user to add more information. The scenario technique can be used both to uncover information about the current system and also to visualize requirements for the future; for example, the developer might ask Annie to think about what changes she would like to make to the bike return system and imagine a scenario of how these would work.

A further advantage of using scenarios in object-oriented development is that they can later be translated into interaction diagrams, which are part of the toolbox of object-oriented techniques. There are two types of interaction diagram, sequence and collaboration diagrams. These are discussed in Chapter 6. Finally, scenarios are a useful and effective way of testing the system, since they can be used as the basis of walkthroughs to check that the system behaves as the clients and users expect.

Requirements specification

The main purpose of requirements specification is to collate, order and record the mass of information gathered during the elicitation

Problem Definition

Client Wheels

Problems with current system

- It is difficult to answer queries
- The hire and return processes are slow
- Having one card for each bike means that Annie has to look out a number of cards and write the same name and address on each one if a customer hires more than one bike
- Producing one receipt for a hire of more than one bike is very complicated and can lead to miscalculations
- Staff have a feeling that customers are not particularly happy with the current hire system.

Objectives of new system

- To provide an efficient and speedy hire process
- To simplify the situation where a customer hires more than one bike
- To record details of customers and previous hires for marketing purposes, and to simplify dealing with requests for the same bike as hired previously
- To improve overall customer satisfaction.

Scope of new system

- The project will encompass the following areas of the business:
- Hire procedures
- Return procedures
- Recording bike details
- Some marketing to regular customers.
- The project will not cover payroll, personnel or general accounting.

Preliminary ideas

- Carry out a customer survey about current procedures
- Design a user-friendly, computerized bike card
- Provide facilities for the system to handle hiring of multiple bikes more efficiently.

Recommended action

- Design and agree questionnaire for customer survey
- Investigate information to be stored about customers
- Review design of the bike card using the computer.

Figure 2.6   Initial problem definition for Wheels

stage. The problems and requirements list that is produced from this stage is a crucial deliverable in the development process.

In this chapter we illustrate two ways of recording requirements in the early stages of development. One of these is the problems and requirements list, and the other is the problem definition, which is a brief initial summary of what has been discovered during the requirements elicitation process. An example of an initial problem definition for the Wheels system is shown in Figure 2.6.

The second, more detailed approach to recording requirements at this stage is the problems and requirements list. Requirements are recorded more formally and more comprehensively, so that the clients and users can check that the developer has a good understanding of what is wanted. Each requirement should be given a unique number or code, so that it can be clearly identified right through the development process. There should be a brief description of the requirement, including where it came from and the date it was identified. It is impossible for a developer to satisfy all the wishes of clients and users, so requirements should be prioritized by designating each one as essential, desirable or optional. It is also helpful to document any related requirements and any documents that are associated with this requirement. Finally, if there are changes to a requirement during development, these should also be documented, including the reason for the changes and the effect this may have on the system. Figure 2.7 shows two examples of early requirements specifications from the Wheels system.

No.	Source	Date	Description	Priority	Related Reqs.	Related Docs.	Change Details
5.1	Meeting with Annie Price at Wheels	10 Feb. 2004	Keep track of how many bikes a customer is hiring, so that he gets one unified receipt	Essential	1.3 2.3 6.1	Bike cards	

No.	Source	Date	Description	Priority	Related Reqs.	Related Docs.	Change Details
2.2	Customer survey	March 2004	Keep record of previous bikes hired by customers	Desirable	2.1 2.4	Bike cards	

Figure 2.7   *Two examples from the problems and requirements list for the Wheels system*

Requirements validation

The purpose of the validation stage of requirements engineering is to make sure that the developer has understood and recorded correctly the wishes and needs of the clients and users of the new system. Some validation can be carried out in parallel with elicitation, for example by summarizing during an interview what has been said, but there are also a number of more formal validation techniques that are used to ensure the accuracy of the requirements specification.

A written summary of each interview should be prepared by the developer and given to the interviewee shortly after the interview. This gives the interviewee an opportunity to check for any gaps or errors in the information that the developer has recorded from the interview. The summary should cover the main points raised during the discussion and any future action to be taken. A summary of the interview with Annie Price, the Wheels' shop manager, can be seen in Figure 2.8.

One of the most effective methods of validation is to cross-reference information obtained from different elicitation approaches. For example, scenarios produced in conversations with users may be compared with notes from observations of the same users carrying out day-to-day tasks. In the interview with Annie, she says that she gives the customers a receipt when they hire a bike, but observation may show that she often forgets to do this. Comparing information from different elicitation activities allows the developer to pick up any disparity between what people say they do when they carry out a task, and what they actually do. Comparisons can also be made between information obtained from questionnaires and information from interviews, observation or a study of documents.

Once requirements have been documented more formally, they may be subject to a Fagan inspection. This is a systematic and structured method of checking the documented output from any stage of the system development process in order to identify omissions and errors. A Fagan inspection is carried out by a small team of people, including the developer who produced the documentation that is being inspected and one or more people whose job it is to look through it in detail and identify any defects. Any omissions, inconsistencies or mistakes in the documentation are pointed out to the developer, so that these can be remedied if necessary through further consultation with clients and users of the system. In the development of the Wheels system, the problems and requirements list (see extract in Figure 2.7) would be the subject of a Fagan inspection to ensure that all requirements have been fully documented.

Interview Summary

System: Wheels   **Project reference:** Wheels/04

Participants: Annie Price (Shop manager for Wheels)
               Simon Davis (Developer)

Date	**Time**	**Duration**	**Place**
10 February 2004	14.30	45 minutes	Manager's office

Purpose of interview
Preliminary meeting to discuss procedures and problems with the current system

No.	Item	Action
1	Difficult to deal with queries.	Bike details and availability should be easily accessible.
2	No records of customer details or hires, so there is a problem when a customer wants the same bike as previously.	A record of previous bikes hired could be stored with customer details.
3	A customer hiring more than one bike is very complicated and makes a lot of extra work.	Investigate ways of simplifying hire procedures for more than one bike.
4	Receipts written out by hand.	New system must produce a computerized receipt.
5	Need to write extra details about specialist bikes on card.	Redesign card to cater for specialist as well as standard bikes.
6	Feeling that customers may not be happy with the current system.	Produce questionnaire about current procedures and ask customers to complete. Arrange interviews with Mike, Naresh and other staff.

Figure 2.8   Summary from interview with Annie Price

List of requirements for the Wheels system

The list below is a brief summary of the requirements for the Wheels system that have been gathered during the requirements elicitation process. Problems with the current system have already been covered in the interview with Annie and the section following the interview, but the implications for the new system have not yet been explicitly identified. This list will serve as a basis for the object-oriented development of Wheels that is the subject of the rest of the book.

The new Wheels system must:

R1   keep a complete list of all bikes and their details including bike number, type, size, make, model, daily charge rate, deposit (this is already on the Wheels system)

R2   keep a record of all customers and their past hire transactions

R3   work out automatically how much it will cost to hire a given bike for a given number of days

R4   record the details of a hire transaction including the start date, estimated duration, customer and bike, in such a way that it is easy to find the relevant transaction details when a bike is returned

R5   keep track of how many bikes a customer is hiring so that the customer gets one unified receipt not a separate one for each bike

R6   cope with a customer who hires more than one bike, each for different amounts of time

R7   work out automatically, on the return of a bike, how long it was hired for, how many days were originally paid for, how much extra is due

R8   record the total amount due and how much has been paid

R9   print a receipt for each customer

R10   keep track of the state of each bike, e.g. whether it is in stock, hired out or being repaired

R11   provide the means to record extra details about specialist bikes.

Chapter summary

This chapter provides more details about the Wheels bike hire system that is used as a source of examples in the rest of the book. The chapter also introduces the three stages of requirements engineering: elicitation, when requirements are gathered from clients and users of the system; specification, when the requirements are documented; and validation, when the requirements documentation is checked to ensure that the clients' and users' needs and wishes have been accurately recorded. The chapter illustrates some of the techniques from each of these stages by showing how they can be applied to the Wheels case study system. It also provides a summary of the requirements for Wheels which form a starting point for the object-oriented development described in the rest of the book.

Bibliography

Britton, C. and Doake, J. (2002) *Software System Development: A Gentle Introduction* (3rd edition), McGraw-Hill, London.

Kotonya, G. and Sommerville, I. (1997) *Requirements Engineering. Processes and Techniques*, John Wiley and Sons, Chichester.

Macaulay, L. (1996) *Requirements Engineering*, Springer-Verlag, London.

Pfleeger, S.L. (1998) *Software Engineering, Theory and Practice*, Prentice Hall, Upper Saddle River, NJ.

Sommerville, I. and Sawyer, P. (1997) *Requirements Engineering: A Good Practice Guide*, John Wiley and Sons, Chichester.

Quick check questions

You can find the answers to these in the chapter.

a   What are the main stages of requirements engineering?

b   What documents should be produced by the developer before and after an interview with a client or user of the system?

c   When are questionnaires useful?

d   What is a scenario?

e   What are the typical sections of a problem definition?

f   What features of a requirement should be recorded in the problems and requirements list?

g   What is the purpose of a Fagan inspection?

Exercises

2.1   Design an interview plan for an interview with Naresh, the chief mechanic at Wheels.

2.2   List five questions that it would be useful to ask Naresh during the interview.

2.3   This chapter includes a list of requirements that have been identified during the requirements elicitation process. Suggest two further requirements that it would be useful to have in the new Wheels system.

2.4   Mike, the owner of Wheels, is wondering whether to expand the hire business to include sports items such as skateboards, surfboards, golf clubs and tennis rackets. He wants to find out whether this would be attractive to his current customers.

Using the example in Figure 2.3 as a guide, design a questionnaire to find out whether there is a market for hire of sports items among Wheels' current customers.

2.5 Following the example scenarios in Figures 2.4 and 2.5, write a scenario to illustrate what happens when a customer, Sheena Patel, returns a bike on the due date, but there is some damage to the front wheel which is charged at £10.

2.6 Following the layout of the problems and requirements list in Figure 2.7, document the details of a requirement to keep records of customer details. You can assume that this requirement has come from Annie and that it is essential. It is related to the second requirement shown in Figure 2.7 to record details of previous bikes hired.

3 Use cases

Learning outcomes

The material and exercises in this chapter will enable you to:

- Explain the purpose of the use case model
- Recognize and describe the components of the use case model: use case diagram, actor descriptions, use case descriptions, scenarios
- Identify the use cases and actors in a system
- Draw a use case diagram
- Write use case descriptions and actor descriptions
- Explain what dictates the granularity of a use case
- Write scenarios and understand how they relate to use cases
- Explain the role of use cases in the creation of other UML models of the system
- Specify at what stages use cases are used in the development of object-oriented software.

Key words you will find in the glossary:

- «extend»
- «include»
- actor
- actor description
- collaboration
- communication association
- essential use case
- expanded use case description
- high-level use case description
- initiating actor
- participating actor
- real use case
- scenario
- stereotype
- use case
- use case beneficiary
- use case description
- use case realization

Introduction

Use cases model the user's view of the functionality of a system, i.e. what the system does as far as the user is concerned; what it does that is of value to the user. The use case model provides a means of organizing, structuring and documenting the mass of information discovered during requirements elicitation; it therefore forms an integral part of the requirements specification stage of the development process. Use cases are normally presented in a graphical form, the use case diagram, supported by textual descriptions, use case and actor descriptions, and scenarios. Both the diagrams and the supporting text are simple and intuitive which makes them an ideal vehicle for discussions with the user and for clarifying the developer's understanding of the user's requirements.

Once the use case model has been completed and checked with the user, it forms an essential pool of structured information on which the other models of the system will draw. The model is also useful for testing the system. Use case modelling is done at various stages during the object-oriented software development process. The amount of detail and the type of information shown at each stage depends on what the model will be used for. In the early stages where the main purpose is to communicate with the user, no information is included that relates to the detailed design or implementation of the system. Later on technical details relating, for example, to the design of the user interface, are added for the information of the programmer.

It is important to realize that although the use case model divides and structures the system, this structure is not used as a basis for the design of the new software system – that is provided by the class diagram (see Chapter 5). The use case model structures the system into the user's view of its main tasks, the class diagram structures the system into logical software units.

This chapter explains the main use case concepts and illustrates them with examples from the Wheels case study.

Use case diagram

The use case model consists of a use case diagram, a set of use case descriptions, a set of actor descriptions and a set of scenarios. The use case diagram models the problem domain graphically using four concepts: the use case, the actor, the relationship link and the boundary. The UML symbols used to model these concepts are shown in Figure 3.1.

Figure 3.2 shows a use case diagram of the Wheels case study. The functionality of the new system has been divided into five use

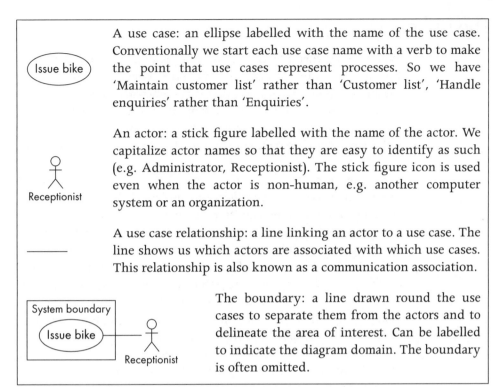

A use case: an ellipse labelled with the name of the use case. Conventionally we start each use case name with a verb to make the point that use cases represent processes. So we have 'Maintain customer list' rather than 'Customer list', 'Handle enquiries' rather than 'Enquiries'.

An actor: a stick figure labelled with the name of the actor. We capitalize actor names so that they are easy to identify as such (e.g. Administrator, Receptionist). The stick figure icon is used even when the actor is non-human, e.g. another computer system or an organization.

A use case relationship: a line linking an actor to a use case. The line shows us which actors are associated with which use cases. This relationship is also known as a communication association.

The boundary: a line drawn round the use cases to separate them from the actors and to delineate the area of interest. Can be labelled to indicate the diagram domain. The boundary is often omitted.

Figure 3.1   The UML symbols for use case diagrams

cases: 'Maintain bike list', 'Maintain customer list', 'Handle enquiries', 'Issue bike' and 'Handle bike return'. Conceptually a use case diagram is similar to a top-level menu which lists the five main things that the system does. Each use case is linked by a line to an actor. The actor, represented by a stick figure, is the person (sometimes a computer system or an organization) who uses the system in the way specified in the use case or who benefits from the use case.

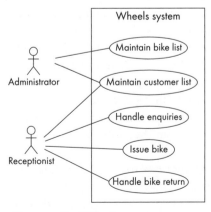

Figure 3.2   Use case diagram for Wheels

The use case

What we do when identifying use cases is to divide up the system's functionality into chunks, into the main system activities. What dictates the split is what the user sees as the separate jobs or processes – the tasks he will do using the system. We are not attempting in the use case model to achieve a division of the system into logical software units; we are just attempting to capture the user's view of the system.

Identifying use cases from the actors. There are several ways of approaching use case identification. One is to identify the actors, the users of the system, and for each one, to establish how they use the system, what they use it to achieve. If we look at the interview in Chapter 2 we can see that Annie and Simon start off by talking about issuing bikes, one of the main jobs that make up Annie's working day. Issuing bikes therefore will be one of the use cases. Issuing bikes involves finding a suitable bike, calculating the hire charge, collecting the money, issuing a receipt and recording details of the customer and the hire transaction.

The interview moves on to discuss dealing with the return of a bike. Annie sees this as a separate job from issuing the bike, it is separated in time and involves a different set of procedures – checking the date and the condition of the bike and returning the deposit.

Annie tells us in the interview that a list of bikes is already held on the computer, but they do not seem to be able to use it to help them in their work. The bike list needs to be stored so that it can be used to answer queries about what bikes Wheels have, whether they are available or on hire, what their deposit and hire charges are and so on. Maintaining this bike list is another use case. Handling queries is seen by Annie as a separate job from issuing bikes. She often gets people coming into the shop or phoning just to check on the range of bikes available and get an idea of costs. This sometimes leads to a hire, but more often it does not. We can therefore identify 'Handle enquiries' as a separate use case.

It also emerges from the interview that no record is kept of customer details or of what bikes they have hired on previous occasions. This sort of information would be useful for marketing purposes and to simplify dealing with requests for the same bike (see the Problem Definition (Figure 2.6), the Problems and Requirements List (Figure 2.7) and the Interview Summary (Figure 2.8)). 'Maintain customer list' can therefore be identified as a use case.

Identifying use cases from scenarios. Another approach to identifying use cases is to start with the scenarios. We have already mentioned scenarios in Chapter 2 – a scenario describes a series of interactions between the user and the system in order to achieve a specified goal. A scenario describes a specific sequence of events, for example what happened when Annie successfully issued a bike to a customer (see Figure 3.3). Depending on the stage they have reached, system developers can use scenarios to describe what did actually happen (or might typically have happened) on one occasion or how they want things to happen in the new system. A careful study of scenarios depicting both typical and exceptional uses of the system is a very good way to understand what the system does and how it is used. It's a bottom up approach to understanding a system. You start by looking at the details of how the system is used and from this work out what the overall aims and objectives are and from this what the use cases are.

Each use case represents a group of scenarios. Scenarios belonging to the same use case have a common goal – each scenario in the group describes a different sequence of events involved in achieving (or failing to achieve) the use case goal. Figures 3.3 and 3.4 describe scenarios belonging to the 'Issue bike' use case; in both cases Annie is trying to issue a bike to a customer.

- Stephanie arrives at the shop at 9.00am one Saturday and chooses a mountain bike
- Annie sees that its number is 468
- Annie enters this number into the system
- The system confirms that this is a woman's mountain bike and displays the daily rate (£2) and the deposit (£60)
- Stephanie says she wants to hire the bike for a week
- Annie enters this and the system displays the total cost £14 + £60 = £74
- Stephanie agrees this
- Annie enters Stephanie's name, address and telephone number into the system
- Stephanie pays the £74
- Annie records this on the system and the system prints out a receipt
- Stephanie agrees to bring the bike back by 9.00am on the following Saturday.

Figure 3.3   Successful scenario for the use case 'Issue bike'

- Michael arrives at the shop at 12.00 on Friday
- He selects a man's racer
- Annie see the number is 658
- She enters this number into the system
- The system confirms that it is a man's racer and displays the daily rate (£2) and the deposit (£55)
- Michael says this is too much and leaves the shop without hiring the bike.

Figure 3.4   Scenario for 'Issue bike' where the use case goal is not achieved

Coming to grips with the required functionality by studying typical user interactions with the system is a technique that has been used informally by software developers since long before the arrival of object-orientation. Use cases are not essentially object-oriented; they are a useful tool whatever method of developing software is being used. Use case modelling formalizes and documents a long-standing practice. Jacobson (1992) was responsible for raising the profile of the use case to the extent that it is now almost universally adopted by the object-oriented community, is formally included in the UML notation and is part of almost all object-oriented methods of developing software.

It would be an inefficient use of time for a developer to write scenarios for every possible sequence of events in a use case. A software tester writes test cases to test an intelligent selection of cases; he tests to agreed coverage criteria. In much the same way a developer should write a representative set of scenarios. The scenarios should document:

- A typical sequence of events leading to the achievement of the use case goal – e.g. a customer hires one bike

- Obvious variations on the norm – e.g. a customer hires several bikes for a fixed period; a customer hires several bikes for different periods; a customer hires a specialist bike etc.

- Sequences of events where the use case goal is not achieved – e.g. the customer cannot find a bike he likes; the customer thinks the cost is too great, etc.

The developer needs to be sure he understands and documents how the system should respond in every eventuality. He will probably write detailed scenarios to document large or complicated use cases, but small, simple use cases can be adequately described by use case descriptions (see below).

To summarize, the purpose of the use case model is to describe, from the user's perspective, what the system does. A use case describes a cohesive piece of the system's functionality as the user perceives it. The user may see it as a task that he uses the system to achieve, one of the jobs that make up his daily workload, or it may produce a list or a report that he gets from the computer. A use case is a complete end-to-end use of the computer, a complete path through the system. A use case must deliver some benefit to the actor associated with it – it must have a goal. Each use case will have several scenarios associated with it. Some will be successful, i.e. achieve the use case goal, some will not. The software developer needs to be aware of all possible scenarios because the system must be able to cope with them all and respond appropriately. However, it would be tedious and not particularly useful to document them all in detail. Instead, scenarios can be produced to illustrate what happens typically and interesting exceptions. A use case description is used to describe the use case in general terms and document the main variations from the norm.

Use case descriptions

The use case description is a narrative document that describes, in general terms, the required functionality of the use case. Typically it describes the use case goal and gives a general description of what usually happens, the normal course of events, adding a brief description of any minor variations. In other words the description is generic, it should be written in such a way that it encompasses every sequence of events, every scenario, relating to the use case.

The description is written in terms of what the system should do, not how it should do it. What happens behind the scenes in terms of coding, data storage structures and other implementation details is not relevant in a use case description, only what the user sees happening. In other words, the use case describes the system as the user sees it and does not aim to form the basis of a program specification or provide information about the internal processes of the system.

UML does not dictate any particular format for describing use cases. Different practitioners use different methods. The best advice is that we have a look at different techniques described by experts on the subject and choose something that works for us. The standard we will use in this book, which closely follows the style recommended by Larman (1998), is illustrated in Figures 3.5 and 3.6.

High-level description. It is useful to have two distinct types of use case description. In the early stages of software development, when no detailed decisions have been made about the design of the

---

Use case: Issue bike
Actors: Receptionist
Goal: To hire out a bike

Description:
When a customer comes into the shop they choose a bike to hire. The Receptionist looks up the bike on the system and tells the customer how much it will cost to hire the bike for a specified period. The customer pays, is issued with a receipt, then leaves with the bike.

Figure 3.5   High-level description of the 'Issue bike' use case

Use case: Issue bike
Actors: Receptionist
Goal: To hire out a bike

Overview:
When a customer comes into the shop they choose a bike to hire. The Receptionist looks up the bike on the system and tells the customer how much it will cost to hire the bike for a specified period. The customer pays, is issued with a receipt, then leaves with the bike.

Cross-reference:
R3, R4, R5, R6, R7, R8, R9, R10

Typical course of events:

Actor action	System response
1 The customer chooses a bike	
2 The Receptionist keys in the bike number	3 Displays the bike details including the daily hire rate and deposit
4 Customer specifies length of hire	
5 Receptionist keys this in	6 Displays total hire cost
7 Customer agrees the price	
8 Receptionist keys in the customer details	9 Displays customer details
10 Customer pays the total cost	
11 Receptionist records amount paid	12 Prints a receipt

Alternative courses:

Steps 8 and 9   The customer details are already in the system so the Receptionist needs only to key in an identifier and the system will display the customer details.

Steps 7–12   The customer may not be happy with the price and may terminate the transaction

Figure 3.6   Expanded description of the 'Issue bike' use case

system and particularly the design of the user interface, it is enough to have short unstructured descriptions, known as high-level descriptions (see Figure 3.5). These descriptions need only document the purpose of the use case, the actors involved and give a general overview of what happens. Subsequently it is useful to have more detailed structured descriptions known as expanded use case descriptions (see Figure 3.6).

Explanation of the expanded use case

Use case:	Name of the use case as it appears in the use case diagram
Actors:	List of actors associated with the use case
Goal:	The goal or purpose of the use case
Overview:	Copy of the high-level description
Cross-reference:	Relate this use case to the system requirement it covers

Typical course of events
Describes the most usual course of events in terms of the actor input and the system response

Alternative courses
This section describes the main alternative courses of action

---

Figure 3.7   *Template for an expanded use case*

Expanded use case description. This description is more detailed and structured than the high-level use case description. It should document:

- What happens to initiate the use case

- Which actors are involved

- What data has to be input

- The use case output

- What stored data is needed by the use case

- What happens to signal the completion of the use case

- Minor variations in the sequences of events (see Figure 3.7).

Preconditions. Some practitioners include a section for preconditions in the expanded use case descriptions. We might specify, for example, that the bike list needs to be up to date before the use case 'Issue bike' is performed, i.e. the use case 'Maintain bike list' must have been executed. The expanded use case description would then be presented as in Figure 3.8.

Use case: Issue bike
Preconditions: 'Maintain bike list' must have been executed
Actors: Receptionist
Goal: To hire out a bike

Overview:
When a customer comes into the shop they choose a bike to hire. The Receptionist looks up the bike on the system and tells the customer how much it will cost to hire the bike for a specified period. The customer pays, is issued with a receipt, then leaves with the bike.

Cross-reference:
R3, R4, R5, R6, R7, R8, R9, R10

Typical course of events:

Actor action	System response
1 The customer chooses a bike	
2 The Receptionist keys in the bike number	3 Displays the bike details including the daily hire rate and deposit
4 Customer specifies length of hire	
5 Receptionist keys this in	6 Displays total hire cost
7 Customer agrees the price	
8 Receptionist keys in the customer details	9 Displays customer details
10 Customer pays the total cost	
11 Receptionist records amount paid	12 Prints a receipt

Alternative courses:

Steps 8 and 9   The customer details are already in the system so the Receptionist needs only to key in an identifier and the system will display the customer details.

Steps 7–12   The customer may not be happy with the price and may terminate the transaction

Figure 3.8   Expanded description of the 'Issue bike' use case with preconditions

Actors and actor descriptions

Actors are external to the system – they represent people or things that interact with the system and receive some benefit from it. Normally an actor is a user, but sometimes it is another system such as a banking or accounting system; an actor can also represent a hardware device such as a printer. Typically an actor is someone who inputs information to the system or receives information from it (or both).

More precisely, an actor represents a particular way of using the system; a way of interacting with the system to achieve a use case goal. It is often referred to as the role someone plays in the use case. The actors in the use case diagram in Figure 3.2 are Administrator and Receptionist. The Receptionist issues the bike, the Administrator maintains the bike list and the customer list. Neither Administrator nor Receptionist are job titles within Wheels because we are not representing any particular person, rather we are representing anyone who is authorized to use the system to do a particular job. Each actor can represent several different people and several different job titles. For example, the Administrator can be Naresh, the head mechanic, or Annie, the shop manager, or even Mike the owner. Conversely, each person or job title can play several different roles. The Receptionist role will normally be played by Annie. However, on her day off, any of the mechanics or Mike can use the computer system as the Receptionist, i.e. they can play the role of Receptionist. Another way of thinking of it is that the users can be wearing different hats when they use the system; Naresh can use the system wearing the hat of an Administrator or a Receptionist.

Actors are identified during the requirements elicitation stage by asking such questions as:

- Who is involved in major system processes such as issuing bikes?

- Who will use the new system?

- Who supplies information to the system?

- Who will receive output from the system?

Actor descriptions. An actor description briefly describes the actor in terms of role and job title.

- *The Receptionist* uses the system to answer queries about bike availability and cost, to issue a bike for hire and to register a bike return. The Receptionist can be the shop manager (Annie), any of the mechanics or the owner (Mike).

- *The Administrator* uses the system to maintain lists of customers and bikes. The Administrator can be the head mechanic (Naresh), the shop manager (Annie) or the owner (Mike).

Use case relationships: communication association, include and extend

Communication association. In a use case diagram the line linking an actor to a use case is called a communication association (see

Figure 3.2). Communication associations tell us which actors are associated with which use cases. Each actor may be associated with many use cases and each use case may be associated with many actors.

Include. Two other types of relationship may be used on a use case diagram – «include» and «extend». Both «include» and «extend» are relationships between use cases. An «include» relationship is useful when you find you have a chunk of behaviour that is common to several use cases. Rather than repeat a description of that behaviour in several use case descriptions, the common behaviour can be split off into a separate use case which is then linked to all relevant use cases with an «include» relationship. This is a similar idea to the programming technique of using procedures or subroutines to code cohesive bits of functionality that may be used in more than one place in a program. It is important to identify functionality common to several use cases because it permits the developers to avoid wasting effort; a chunk of functionality can be identified, investigated and modelled once, then reused as required.

Figure 3.9 shows a refined version of the original Wheels use case diagram (see Figure 3.2). The use cases 'Maintain bike list', 'Handle enquiries', 'Issue bike' and 'Handle bike return' all need to find a particular bike from the list of bikes. We therefore create a new use case 'Find bike' and link it with an «include» relationship to the four use cases that need it. This tells us that each of these use cases will always use the 'Find bike' use case.

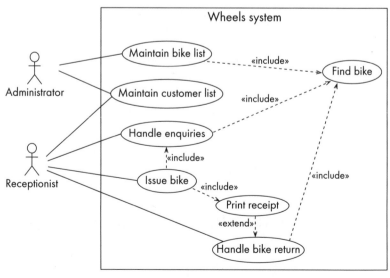

Figure 3.9   *Wheels system with includes and extends relationships*

In the same way, the first part of the use case description for 'Issue bike' repeats the behaviour of the use case 'Handle enquiries', Annie always tells customers the daily hire rate and deposit for a bike before going ahead with the issuing. Rather than repeat a description of this behaviour in both use cases, we can remove it from 'Issue bike' and have an «include» relationship between 'Issue bike' and 'Handle enquiries'. Notice that the dashed arrow points from the main use case to the one to be included, e.g. from 'Issue bike' to 'Handle enquiries'.

Extend. The «extend» relationship is used as a way of specifying significant alternative behaviour in a use case. It usually documents functionality that the user can opt to use over and above the norm. The practice of using an «extend» relationship in this way is only for documenting important variations from the normal course of events. Minor variations can be covered in the extended use case description. We would use an «extend» relationship if we want to describe:

- Extra functionality that is available if required, for example printing a list rather than just viewing it on the screen.

- Behaviour done only under certain conditions, for example printing an extra receipt if the whole deposit is not returned.

If, therefore, we want to specify a chunk of behaviour that is additional or exceptional to the normal sequence of events in a use case, we can create a new use case for that behaviour and specify an «extend» relationship between the new and the original use case. In Figure 3.9 we have created a new use case 'Print receipt' and an «extend» relationship between this use case and 'Handle bike return'. What this means is that sometimes returning a bike might involve printing a receipt, although this is not what normally happens. Printing a receipt will only be necessary if the customer has kept the bike for more days than they originally paid for, or if the bike is returned damaged. By contrast, printing a receipt is always part of the 'Issue bike' use case, so we have specified an «include» relationship between 'Issue bike' and 'Print receipt'. Notice that now the dashed arrow points from the new extending use case to the main use case, i.e. from 'Print receipt' to 'Handle bike return'. There seems to be no particular reason for this change of direction, it's just the rule.

If we decide that part of the use case 'Issue bike' will quite often involve adding a new customer, or updating our existing customer details, then it will be sensible to specify an «extend» relationship between 'Issue bike' and 'Maintain customer list' (see Figure 3.10). An «extend» relationship is more appropriate here than an

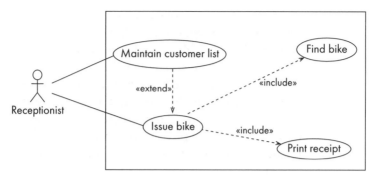

Figure 3.10   *Extract from the Wheels use case diagram showing the «extend» relationship between 'Issue bike' and 'Maintain customer list'*

«include» because we will not always add a new customer, or edit customer details as part of issuing a bike.

Notice that the minor use case is always modelled as an extension of the major one, i.e. the core functionality is specified in the base use case and the additional or exceptional behaviour in the extending use case.

The user sometimes has to select one of several options at a particular point in the use case; in such cases it may be useful to model each option as a separate extending use case. The 'alternative courses' section of the extended use case description (see Figure 3.7) is also used for specifying differences in use case behaviour. Which method you choose is a matter of judgement.

We have drawn a separate diagram (Figure 3.10) to illustrate the refined version of 'Issue bike' as our main diagram is getting a bit cluttered. This effectively makes the point that «include» and «extend» should be used sparingly. It is easy to get carried away with enthusiasm when identifying legitimate uses for these relationships, but the resulting model is not always an improvement.

Documenting «include» and «extend» in the use case description. If we have added «include» or «extend» relationships to a use case diagram, we must document them in the use case description. This is done using the keyword 'initiate'. For example, if the use case 'Issue bike' were to be modelled as specified in Figures 3.9 and 3.10, we would adjust its use case description to document the «include» and «extend» relationships, as in Figure 3.11.

Boundary

In general the concept of the system boundary is important as it delineates the domain of study. The system boundary may be included on a use case diagram (see Figures 3.2 and 3.9). It is shown

Use case: Issue bike
Preconditions: 'Maintain bike list' must have been executed
Actors: Receptionist
Goal: To hire out a bike

Overview:
When a customer comes into the shop they choose a bike to hire. The Receptionist looks up the bike on the system and tells the customer how much it will cost to hire the bike for a specified period. The customer pays, is issued with a receipt, then leaves with the bike.

Cross-reference:
R3, R4, R5, R6, R7, R8, R9, R10

Typical course of events:

Actor action	System response
1 The customer chooses a bike	
2 The Receptionist keys in the bike number	3 **Initiate** 'Find bike'
4 Customer specifies length of hire	
5 Receptionist keys this in	6 Displays total hire cost
7 Customer agrees the price	
8 Receptionist keys in the customer identification	9 **Initiate** 'Maintain customer list'
10 Customer pays the total cost	
11 Receptionist records amount paid	12 **Initiate** 'Print receipt'

Alternative courses:

Steps 7–12   The customer may not be happy with the price and may terminate the transaction

Figure 3.11   *Expanded description of the 'Issue bike' use case documenting «include» and «extend» relationships*

as a line round the use cases, separating them from the actors; normally it is labelled with the name of the system or subsystem. The drawing of a boundary on a use case diagram, however, adds very little to the meaning of the diagram as use cases are always inside the boundary and the actors outside it. The reason we have included the boundaries on our diagrams is simply that it comes as part of the CASE tool we used to draw the diagrams, i.e. Together[TM]. It is common practice, however, to omit the boundary and other CASE tools, for example Rational Rose[TM], do not draw a boundary on use case diagrams.

Using the use case model in system development

Each of the UML models concentrates on modelling its own particular aspects of the system while ignoring others: they provide complementary views of the system. The use case model gives the user coherent and detailed documentation of what the system does or will do. However, in addition to this, it also provides direct support for other parts of the software development process.

Checking the system using the use case model. The use case model provides an excellent basis for system testing. As each use case models a significant task, the use cases provide ready made testing units. The developer can take each use case in turn and check that the system does what it is meant to, i.e. provides the functionality specified. The scenarios provide instances of the normal sequence of events in the use case and the main alternatives; exactly what is required for testing purposes. The developer must check that the system can handle each scenario. Checking the design of the system can be done by walking through each use case to verify that it can be realized. When the system has been implemented, system tests can be derived from the use cases to check that the code produces the required functionality.

Estimating using use cases. Project managers find use cases useful for planning and estimating the development process. Once the system has been broken down into a set of use cases and the nature of each use case understood, the project manager will have a good idea of how long each will take to develop, how much risk is attached to each and how vital each is to the success of the project. This helps the project manager to produce an informed project plan; the system can be developed use case by use case. If the project manager knows that the system is not going to be produced as quickly as the customer would like, he can make sure that the most vital use cases are tackled first.

Basis for interaction diagrams. Use cases are closely related to interaction diagrams, i.e. sequence diagrams and collaboration diagrams (see Chapter 6). A use case provides a description of a particular task; the corresponding interaction diagram shows how that use case will work in terms of messaging between objects (see Chapter 6). Like the scenario, an interaction diagram shows what happens in a specific instance; loosely speaking the scenario gives a step-by-step account of what happens on the user's side of the computer screen and the interaction diagram gives a step-by-step account of what happens on the other side of the screen.

Starting point for the identification of classes. Use case descriptions and scenarios can provide the starting point for the identification of classes for the class diagram. One of the standard ways of finding classes is to examine the nouns in a clear and concise description of what the system does (see Chapter 5). One of the best places to find such a description is in the collection of use case descriptions provided by the use case model.

Technical points

The points discussed in this section may be ignored by readers who simply want a basic understanding of use case modelling. However, for those who want to probe a little deeper, this section will provide a more complete understanding of the topic.

Documenting extension points in a use case diagram. When a base use case has an «extend» link to another use case, it is sometimes useful to indicate on the use case diagram the point at which a jump to the extending use case is made. For example (see Figure 3.10), in the 'Issue bike' use case, we will want to use the extra functionality specified in the 'Maintain customer list' use case at the point where the Receptionist needs to add details about a new customer, or change the details of an existing one. Extension points can be documented on the use case diagram as in Figure 3.12. In the lower half of the use case ellipse we specify the names of the extension points – in this case 'Add customer' and 'Edit customer'.

We can also specify the circumstances under which the extending use case is executed by adding a comment on the relationship – in this case 'New customer or change customer details'.

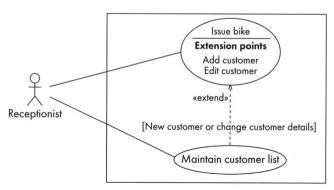

Figure 3.12   *Documenting extension points in a use case diagram*

Generalization. Both use cases and actors can be specialized, i.e. we can use an inheritance (otherwise known as a generalization/specialization) relationship between actors and between use cases. In object-oriented development inheritance is primarily associated with class diagrams (see section on inheritance in Chapter 4). If an inheritance relationship exists between two entities it means that one inherits the characteristics of the other. For example, in a classification of animals, a horse is a specialization of animal and a cart-horse is a specialization of horse. Each specialization both inherits characteristics from its parent in the hierarchy and adds features to reflect its own specialization. The parent has those features common to all of its descendants, those features they have in general – hence generalization.

Where use cases are concerned, the use of generalization is another way of specifying alternative courses of events. We could, for example, have modelled the situation shown in Figure 3.12 by using a generalization relationship as in Figure 3.13. This allows us to model what happens more precisely. If the Receptionist is issuing a bike to a completely new customer then she uses the specialized use case 'Issue bike to new customer'. This use case always executes the use case 'Maintain customer list'. However, if she is issuing a bike to an existing customer she uses the generalized use case 'Issue bike'. If she finds, in the course of executing this use case, that the customer has changed their address she can opt to execute the 'Maintain customer list' use case.

Actors can also be specialized if we wish to indicate that the specialized actor plays the same role as the generalized one but has some extra role.

Initiating actor and participating actor. It is worth understanding the differences between types of actors without getting too bogged down in the details. In any given use case, the initiating actor is the

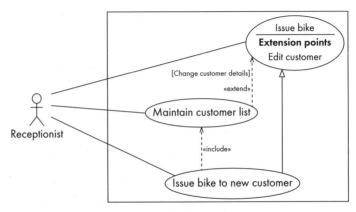

Figure 3.13   Generalization/specialization relationship

one who starts off the sequence of events, i.e. initiates the use case. The rest of the actors involved in the use case are the participating actors. The most important actor is the one known as the beneficiary, i.e. the one who gets benefit from the use case: the one using the computer, as specified in the use case, to do something useful for him.

There is some controversy about who should be modelled as the actors associated with a use case. Some practitioners like to show on a use case diagram everyone who is associated with a use case. Some show only the initiating actor, some show only the beneficiary.

In the Wheels case study we have not modelled Customer as an actor although it is often the customer who initiates a use case. We could have modelled the system as in Figure 3.14.

The choice of actors is to a large extent dictated by where we choose to draw the system boundary. If we are producing a high-level model of a whole business system with, for example, the purpose of making the business or company more efficient, the actors will be people outside the company, in the environment. In the case of the Wheels system this would be the Customer and possibly also the Supplier. From this point of view the employees of the company are viewed as resources inside the system boundary and are not modelled as actors. If, on the other hand, we are talking about the automation boundary of a computer system that is part of the overall business system, the actors will be the people who

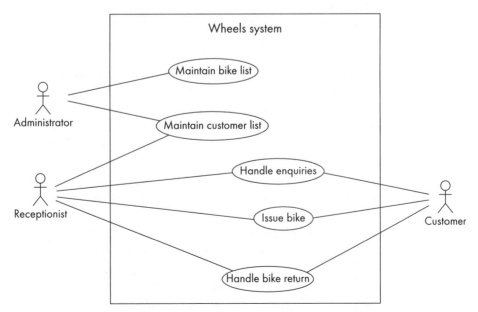

Figure 3.14   *Use case diagram with Customer actor*

use the system, the employees of the company. The modelling we describe in this book is aimed at the design of computer systems and the boundaries we draw are automation boundaries; our actors are therefore the people who use the system. In the Wheels system this would be the Receptionist and the Administrator.

The important thing to remember is that what we really want to know about, at the stage where we are designing the use case model, are the use cases themselves. In the early stages of software development the identification of actors is done principally as a means of finding out about the use cases. Later on, when considering security aspects and when designing the user interface, we might like to think some more about the actors involved so that we can specify user privileges and design interfaces that are appropriate for each user.

We find that it really is not worth losing sleep over who the actors are – it's a bit of a red herring. The actors we show in this book are the ones who physically use the system, e.g. put their hands on the keyboard, read the screen or receive a report. This is because, when we move on to doing the interaction diagrams, these actors are the only ones providing input directly to the system and reading the output from the screen. Our preferred use case model for the Wheels system, therefore, is that shown in Figures 3.2 and 3.9, not that shown in Figure 3.14.

Essential and real use cases. It is worth understanding the difference between essential and real use cases (again without getting lost in the jargon). An essential use case is one that is completely free of implementation or detailed design decisions. A use case will be in essential form in the early stages of software development before these decisions have been made. It is important to keep use cases free of implementation detail in the early stages so as not to constrain subsequent design decisions. Real use cases, by contrast, do show detail of design and implementation decisions insofar as they affect the user. A real use case will show, for example, detail about the user interface. Implementation decisions that do not directly affect the user's view of the system such as choice of programming language, data storage structures or programming algorithms are not specified in a use case.

The use case descriptions in Figures 3.5 and 3.6 are free of implementation information and are therefore essential use case descriptions. The use case description in Figure 3.15 has some implementation decisions added (e.g. that the bike details will be displayed in report format) and is therefore a real use case description.

Use case: Issue bike
Preconditions: 'Maintain bike list' must have been executed
Actors: Receptionist
Goal: To hire out a bike

Overview:
When a customer comes into the shop they choose a bike to hire. The Receptionist looks up the bike on the system and tells the customer how much it will cost to hire the bike for a specified period. The customer pays, is issued with a receipt, then leaves with the bike.

Cross-reference:
R3, R4, R5, R6, R7, R8, R9, R10

Typical course of events:

Actor action	System response
1 The customer chooses a bike	
2 The Receptionist keys in the bike number	3 Displays the bike details including the daily hire rate and deposit. Information will be displayed in report format
4 Customer specifies length of hire	
5 Receptionist keys this in	6 Displays total hire cost in ££.pp format
7 Customer agrees the price	
8 Receptionist keys in the customer identification	9 Displays customer details
10 Customer pays the total cost	
11 Receptionist records amount paid	12 Prints a receipt

Alternative courses:

Steps 8 and 9 The customer details are already in the system so the Receptionist needs only to key in an identifier and the system will display the customer details.

Steps 7–12 The customer may not be happy with the price and may terminate the transaction

Figure 3.15   A real use case description of the 'Issue bike' use case

Stereotypes. We have already come across several uses of stereotypes without identifying them as such. Knowing about stereotypes is not essential to successful modelling, but it is useful to know what they are because you may come across them in your reading. CASE tools, for example, often use the term.

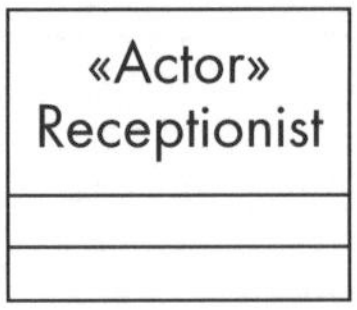

Figure 3.16   Receptionist as actor drawn as a stereotyped class

A stereotype is a specialized use of a modelling element. A stereotype is usually identified by a label inside a pair of guillemets « » such as «include» and «extend». The relationships «include» and «extend» are stereotyped association relationships. This means that they are relationships used in a highly specific way. Sometimes you will see «communication» added to a normal association link between an actor and a use case. This is not strictly necessary as the relationship between an actor and a use case can only be a communication association. However, associations between use cases can be «include» or «extend» relationships and so must be labelled.

Strictly speaking the actor icon is a stereotyped class. Instead of using the stick figure to model an actor such as the Receptionist, we could equally well use the UML class icon and label it as an actor stereotype (see Figure 3.16).

Subsystems and packages. If we are modelling large systems we very soon get to the stage, when drawing the use case diagram, where we can no longer fit all of our use cases on one screen. UML has a grouping notation known as a package to cope with this. Packages are simply a convenient notation for managing our models, they do not represent anything in the system, but are used to group elements that do represent things in the system. We can use packages to group any set of modelling elements: classes, use cases or an entire set of models, e.g. the use case model, the object model, and the interaction diagrams relating to a subsystem. We can use packages simply as a way of managing models that get too big by grouping elements in convenient bundles, or we can use packages to represent specific logical units, e.g. a subsystem or a collaboration (see below). For example, a mail ordering system might be split into three subsystems: customer order processing, accounting and stock control. We would then place all the model elements relating to customer order processing into a customer order processing package, those to do with accounting in an accounting package, those to do with stock control into a stock control package (see Figure 3.17). Packages are discussed in more detail in Chapter 5.

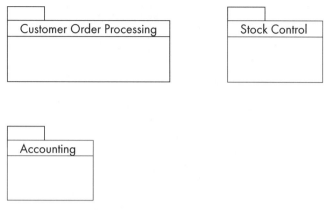

Figure 3.17   Packages of use cases

Use case realization. The development of a use case from the its initial identification during requirements elicitation to its implementation is known as use case realization. In other words, use case realization for a single use case requires a complete iteration through all of the development activities. RUP (see Chapter 1) is essentially use case driven which means that the software is developed incrementally by use case realization. During use case realization, once all the use cases have been identified and documented, each use case is analysed separately to identify the classes required by it. The group of classes involved in a particular use case is known as a collaboration. The classes in a particular collaboration are often grouped into a package. The unified class diagram for the whole system is compiled from an analysis of the complete set of collaborations. Sometimes the same class will appear in more than one collaboration.

In this book we are not going to adopt a use case realization approach to developing the Wheels system simply because the Wheels system is too small to warrant it.

Common problems

1   Can more than one actor be associated with a use case?

It is quite common for more than one actor to be associated with a use case in the sense that more than one actor can perform that particular task. For example, in Figure 3.18 we can see both the Administrator and the Receptionist may be associated with 'Maintain customer list'. This is because, although the job of maintaining the customer list is normally part of the Administrator's role, sometimes when dealing with a bike issue, the Receptionist may have to update the customer list.

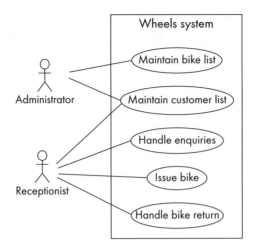

Figure 3.18   *Use case diagram for Wheels (Figure 3.2 repeated)*

However, what the question often means is: on any given occasion can more than one actor be involved in a use case? For example, in the Wheels system could we model the customer as an actor and then have both Customer and Receptionist involved in the use cases 'Issue bike', 'Handle enquiries' and 'Handle bike return'. The answer is that it is really a question of style (see the discussion in the section on initiating and participating actors). In this book our boundaries represent the automation boundary, i.e. include only the computer hardware and software inside the system. The actors, therefore, are the people who use the system directly, i.e. the Receptionist and the Administrator. Our models, therefore, do not show the Customer as an actor. If we made Wheels a more sophisticated system, where the Customer could make enquiries and hire a bike online, then Customer would also be modelled as an actor.

2 What dictates the granularity of use cases, i.e. how do we know how big or how small to make them?

The first and principal rule that dictates the size of a use case, i.e. what activities are included in it, is what the user sees as a complete job. A use case should represent a complete process; one end-to-end pass through the system, a job that the user sits down at the computer to achieve at one go. Don't confuse steps or stages in a process with the whole use case. For example, we have modelled 'Customer pays amount due (deposit plus rental charge)' as part of the use case 'Issue bike'. This is because we found that making a payment was never an event that was done in isolation: it was always done as part of the hiring process. With 'Handle enquiries', however, we found that, although this

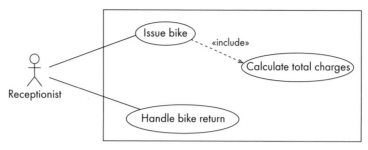

Figure 3.19   *Unnecessary use of «include»*

was sometimes part of the 'Issue bike' process, it was often something that was done on its own. Customers frequently phone up requiring information about the types of bike available and about the deposit and rental charges. For this reason we have modelled it as a separate use case.

From a practical point of view, the developer should beware of making use cases too small. Each use case spawns a large number of other models. Each use case will potentially have associated with it a use case description, a number of scenarios and several interaction diagrams. If each use case models only a small amount of functionality we need more of them to model the whole system and the number of models spawned increases exponentially.

3 How do I know when it is appropriate to use an «include» relationship?

It is very easy to make mistakes when using both «include» and «extend» relationships. One common error, on discovery of the technique, is to use it over enthusiastically. In Figure 3.19 a use case 'Calculate total charges' has been introduced and linked to 'Issue bike'. 'Calculate total charges' works out the rental charges for a bike for a given number of days and adds it to the deposit. The point of using «include» is to save effort by identifying behaviour common to more than one use case. However, the behaviour specified in 'Calculate total charges' would only ever be used by the 'Issue bike' use case; it is therefore unnecessary to model it as a separate use case.

Chapter summary

Use cases model the user's view of the functionality of a system. The use case model consists of a use case diagram, supported by textual descriptions, use case and actor descriptions, and scenarios. Both the diagrams and the supporting text are simple and intuitive which makes them an ideal vehicle for discussions with the user and for clarifying the developer's understanding of the users' requirements. Actors identified in the use case diagram represent users who interact with the system in some way, who use the system to achieve a particular task. Each use case represents a task or major chunk of functionality. The use case description describes the task in more detail. The description views the task from the user's perspective, it does not attempt to provide a program specification.

There are several different ways of describing alternative paths through a use case. All routes through the use case – what normally happens, minor variations and significant alternatives – can be illustrated in detail using scenarios. Minor variations can be documented as alternative courses in the use case description. More significant differences can be modelled as separate use cases linked to the original by an «extend» relationship. Alternatively, a specialized use case can be used to model different behaviour within a use case. Common functionality can be extracted into a separate use case linked by an «include» relationship to any use case that needs this functionality.

The use case model is a useful starting point for identifying classes and forms the basis of the interaction diagrams. It is also useful as a guide for project management, for checking requirements and for system testing.

Bibliography

Bennett, S., McRobb, S. and Farmer, R. (2002) *Object-Oriented Systems Analysis and Design Using UML* (2nd edition), McGraw-Hill, London.

Brown, D. (1997) *Object-Oriented Analysis: objects in plain English*, John Wiley, NY.

Fowler, M. (2000) *UML Distilled: A Brief Guide to the Standard Object Modeling Language* (2nd edition), Addison-Wesley, Reading, MA.

Jacobson, I. (1992) *Object-Oriented Software Engineering: A Use Case Driven Approach*, Addison-Wesley, Wokingham, England.

Larman, C. (1998) *Applying UML and Patterns: An Introduction to Object-Oriented Analysis and Design*, Prentice Hall, NJ.

Stevens, P., with Pooley, R. (2000) *Using UML. Software Engineering with Objects and Components* (updated edition), Addison-Wesley, Harlow.

Quick check questions

You can find the answers to these in the chapter.

a What aspect of a system does the use case model?

b The use case model consists of a set of complementary elements. Can you name them?

c Suggest two ways of identifying use cases.

d What is the relationship between scenarios and use cases?

e It would be impracticable to write scenarios for every possible sequence of events. What would be a sensible set of scenarios for a developer to write?

f Describe the typical contents of a high-level use case description and an expanded use case description.

g What is the relationship between an actor and a use case?

h You can use four types of relationship on a use case diagram; list them and give a brief description of each one.

i Apart from its main purpose (outlined in your answer to question a), what other use can the developer make of the use case model?

Exercises

3.1 Below are some scenarios from a library system. For each scenario work out its use case and actor, then draw the use case diagram for the whole library system.

A
- A library member chooses three books and takes them to the librarian on the loans desk
- The librarian checks how many books the member has out on loan
- The member has no books already out on loan
- The librarian registers the loans on the system and issues the books to the member.

B
- A library member chooses six books and takes them to the librarian on the loans desk
- The librarian checks how many books the member has out on loan
- The member has three books already out on loan
- The librarian says that the member can only borrow a total of six books

- The member puts three back
- The librarian registers the three new book loans on the system and issues the books to the member.

C

- A library member chooses four books and takes them to the librarian on the loans desk
- The librarian checks how many books the member has out on loan
- The member has six books already out on loan
- The librarian will not allow the member to borrow any more books until she brings some back.

D

- A library member brings back three books to the library
- She takes then to the returns desk
- The librarian registers the returns on the system.

E

- A library member looks up the online catalogue for a book She finds the title she wants
- She checks the title availability and finds that there is a copy in the library
- She notes down the library reference number for the book.

F

- A library member looks up the online catalogue for a book She finds the title she wants
- She checks the title availability and finds that all copies are out on loan
- She makes an online reservation for the book.

G

- New books arrive in the library
- The librarian allocates to each a library reference number
- She updates the online library catalogue with the new titles.

3.2   In the use case diagram for the library system, Figure E.3 on page 353, the use cases 'Search catalogue' and 'Reserve book' share common functionality. To confirm this read their associated scenarios described in Question 1 (e) and (f). Using an «include» relationship, amend the diagram in Figure E.3 so that the use case 'Reserve book' does not duplicate the functionality of 'Search catalogue'?

3.3   Below are some scenarios from a hairdresser's system. For each scenario work out its use case and actors, then draw the use case diagram for the whole hairdresser's system.

A
- Annie rings the hairdressers Cool Cuts for an appointment for a cut and blow dry
- Jenni, one of the trainees, asks her who normally cuts her hair
- Annie says Jason or Phil
- Jenni asks when she would like to come
- Annie says Saturday
- Jenni says that Phil has a free slot on Saturday at 11.15
- Annie says that would be fine.

B
- Ed rings Cool Cuts for an appointment for a hair cut
- Jasmine, the part-time receptionist, asks him who normally cuts his hair
- Ed says he hasn't been before
- Jasmine asks when he would like to come
- Ed says Thursday afternoon
- Jasmine says Antonia has a free slot at 5.10 on Thursday
- Ed says that would be fine.

C
- Jo rings Cool Cuts for an appointment to have highlights put in plus a cut and blow dry
- Michael, the manager, asks her who normally does her highlights
- Jo says she would like Diana do her highlights and Michael to cut her hair
- Michael says he can't find a time when both are free until three weeks on Monday at 10.25
- Jo says she will take that slot.

D
- Michael, the manager of Cool Cuts, takes on a new haircutter called Rudolph
- Rudolph's day off will be Tuesday
- Michael enters these details into the computer system.

E
- After her cut and blow dry Annie comes to the reception desk to pay
- Jasmine, the part-time receptionist, says that will be £20
- The customer pays the amount due
- Jasmine registers the amount paid on the system

F
- Jenni accepts a new delivery of hairdressing products (shampoo etc.)

- She notices that the price of several of the items has increased
- She updates the relevant prices on the system
- She also updates the stock levels for those items that have been delivered.

3.4 Further investigation reveals extra information about the Cool Cuts system (see Exercise 3.3). When customers come to the till to pay for their haircut, they sometimes also buy hairdressing products (shampoo, conditioner etc.). The junior on the till enters the product code and the system looks up the price of the product. The use case 'Handle customer payments' (see Figure E.5 on page 354), therefore, sometimes involves looking on the system to find a product and its price. The use case 'Maintain product list' always involves doing this. Using «include» and «extend» relationships, amend the use case diagram in Figure E.5 to show this extra information.

3.5 On further investigation you find that sometimes customers come into Cool Cuts just to buy shampoo or conditioner. The diagram in Figure E.6 on page 354 assumes that customers always pay for hairdressing products in conjunction with paying for their haircut – it's a single transaction. However, these off-the-street customers want to pay for the products as a separate transaction. How would you alter the diagram in Figure E.6 to model this new information?

3.6 Mr Major, the town's only dentist, has a computer system to help him keep track of patients' appointments and dental treatment. Mr Major's receptionist makes appointments with patients either when they phone up or when they are back in the waiting room after treatment. Sometimes patients phone to cancel appointments or to change them. Mr Major keeps notes on the system about his patients' treatments – these are updated each time he sees a patient. The receptionist also makes out bills for patients and records payments on the system.

a Draw a use case diagram of the dentist's system.

b One of the use cases in Figure E.8 on page 355 is 'Maintain appointments'. Write scenarios for this use case, recording sequences of events that might occur when:

i A patient phones up for an appointment on a specific date. The Receptionist tells her what times are available on that date and she picks one.

ii A patient phones up for an appointment and is offered a choice of available date and time slots. She picks one.

iii A patient comes into the waiting room after having a filling. He wants to make another appointment. The Receptionist offers him a list of possible slots. None are suitable so he doesn't make an appointment.

3.7 In the Dentist's system (see Exercise 3.6) you discover that sometimes patients phone up to talk to the receptionist about their treatment or to complain of toothache. In these cases the receptionist adds comments to the patient's notes and advises Mr Major that she has done so. You also discover that on the receptionist's day off Mr Major makes the appointments. How would you amend the diagram in Figure E.8 on page 355 to model this new information?

3.8 Your local railway station is going to install automatic ticket dispensing machines. Each machine will be able to give passengers up-to-date train timetable and ticket price information. The machines must also issue tickets and transfer statistics about ticket sales to a central computer system. Railway staff must be able to update ticket prices and timetable information.

Draw a use case diagram to model what the ticket machines must do.

3.9 Quick Bites is a fast food restaurant. They use a computer system to deal with taking customer orders, assembling the order and then paying for it. Customers find a table and a waiter takes their order. The waiter goes to the nearest till and keys in the order using a touch screen with icons on it showing possible food combinations. The table number is used to identify the order. In the kitchens a cook reads the order on his screen, assembles the meal on a tray, and prints a chit with the table number on it plus the details of the order. The tray is put in the food lift and the cook presses a key to indicate that the order is ready. A large screen in the restaurant displays a list of orders that are ready, identified by table number. The waiter collects the tray from the food lift and takes it to the customer. He also removes the order from the large order screen. When customers have finished their meal the waiter keys the table number into the system and the bill is printed. The waiter takes the customer's payment and records the bill as paid.

Draw a use case diagram of this system.

3.10 Once you have got a basic set of use cases reflecting the main tasks in the system, what might make you decide to create a new use case linked to one of the basic use cases by an «include» relationship?

3.11 Under what circumstances would you consider creating a new use case and linking it to an existing use case with an «extend» relationship?

3.12 James Barlow is a recently graduated software developer. He and his wife, Caitlin, have just set up their own business, Barlow & Barlow. They have been asked by a video rental company, View Us, to convert their rather antiquated computer system to something more modern. Barlow & Barlow have decided that an object-oriented system will be just the ticket. James has just spent a morning rather nervously observing what goes on at View Us as customers and employees go about their normal business. James jotted down the sequence of events that he observed, hoping to make sense of it later.

a James' notes are written as a long undivided list of events. Your first job is to separate the list of events into scenarios. Having done that, work out what the use cases will be. Finally, draw a use case diagram to model what happens at the video rental business, View Us.

- Lucy comes into the shop
- She finds two videos she wants to borrow
- She takes the empty video covers to the counter and says she wants to borrow them tonight
- She presents her membership card
- Phil, the assistant, finds the videos
- He scans the barcode on the membership card
- Lucy's details come up on the screen
- Phil checks that Lucy still lives at 6 Privet Drive
- He sees that she has no videos outstanding and does not owe View Us any money
- He scans the barcodes on the videos and hands them to Lucy
- Phil takes the money for the rental and says Lucy must return the videos by 8pm the next evening
- Lucy leaves the shop with the videos
- Ian comes into the shop
- He finds a video he wants to borrow for one night
- He takes the video case to the counter
- Phil asks for his membership card

- Ian says he isn't a member but he'd like to become one
- Phil takes details of his name, address, telephone number and bank account number and sort code
- He prints out a membership card for Ian
- He scans the video barcode
- Phil takes the money for the rental and says Ian must return the video by 8pm the next evening
- Ian leaves with the video and his new membership card
- Rachel comes into the video shop with three videos she borrowed the previous day
- She hands them to Phil
- Phil scans the video barcodes
- He checks that the videos are back in time and that Rachel doesn't owe them any money
- Rachel leaves the shop
- Hannah comes into the shop and says she wants to become a member
- Phil takes details of her name, address, telephone number and bank account number and sort code
- He prints out a membership card for Hannah
- He asks Hannah if she wants to borrow a video now
- She says 'No'
- She leaves with her new membership card
- Andy comes into the shop with two videos to return
- The videos are a day late
- Phil is busy with another customer
- Andy puts the videos into the returned video box and leaves
- When Phil has finished with his customer he retrieves the videos and scans the barcodes
- He notices that they are a day late and checks that the system has registered this against Andy's name
- Kim, the View Us manager, arrives with a box of new videos
- Phil and Kim sort through the videos allocating barcodes and prices: newly released videos are more expensive to rent than older ones
- Kim enters the details of the new videos on to the system
- Tony comes into the shop
- He chooses three videos
- Phil swipes his membership card
- He notices that Tony still has two videos out; they are three days overdue

- He says he cannot let Tony borrow any more videos until he returns those still out.

b Based on his observations, James produces the use case diagram shown in Figure E.12 on page 361. Ten days after his original visit he returns to View Us, this time accompanied by Caitlin. While James discusses his model with Kim, Caitlin notices a customer complaining to Phil that all of the copies of the video he wants to borrow are out on loan. Phil says that he can reserve that video for the customer. On further enquiry she finds that reserving videos is quite common. What happens is that a video is marked on the system as reserved, then as soon as any copy of that video is returned it is put under the counter and a postcard sent to the member who reserved it. When the reserving member comes in he presents the postcard and is issued with the video in the normal way.

Kim and Phil also remember that another thing they use the system for is to respond to customer enquiries about what videos they stock. Usually customers know the title of the video they want to borrow but sometimes these enquiries take the form of questions like 'Have you got a video of that film with Leonardo DiCaprio and Kate Winslet in it?'; 'Which films have you got starring Brad Pitt?'; or even 'Have you got any videos about the sea?'

Redraw your use case diagram incorporating this extra information.

c Caitlin comes up with the revised diagram shown in Figure E.13 on page 361. She and James study the diagram and decide that there is probably some duplicated functionality in the use cases. To test this theory they need use case descriptions for the use cases 'Find video details', 'Loan a video' and 'Reserve video'. Write high-level use case descriptions for these use cases.

d Caitlin and James write the use case descriptions reproduced in Figure E.14 on page 362. As they suspected, there is some duplication. Redraw the use case diagram shown in Figure E.13 on page 361 to avoid having duplicated functionality in the use cases.

e James is having trouble with Caitlin's diagram (Figure E.13); he is not sure what is implied by the «extend» relationship between the use cases 'Print ready card' and 'Return a video'. Write expanded use case descriptions for these two use cases.

f Scenarios 1 and 2 and 7 (see answer to Question 3.12a.) are all descriptions of sequences of events that can happen in the 'Loan a video' use case. There are significant differences between these sequences. Write an expanded use case description that identifies a typical sequence of events and incorporates the differences as alternative courses.

4 Objects and classes: the basic concepts

Learning outcomes

The material and exercises in this chapter will enable you to:

- Recognize some of the problems associated with traditional ways of developing software systems

- Explain how the object-oriented approach addresses these problems

- Describe the main features of an object and why it is effective as a software construct

- Apply the concept of a class and explain the relationship between objects and classes

- Identify the object relationships: association, aggregation and composition

- Apply inheritance and polymorphism.

Key words you will find in the glossary:

- aggregation
- association
- attribute
- class
- client–server
- cohesion
- composition
- data hiding
- dynamic binding
- encapsulation
- inheritance
- instantiation
- message
- method
- multiplicity
- object
- operation
- over-riding
- polymorphism
- public interface
- substitutability

Introduction

In this chapter we start by looking at the problems associated with traditional approaches to developing software and at how object-orientation addresses these problems. We introduce the object as the fundamental building block of object-oriented software, i.e. as the basis of the software architecture. We briefly summarize why the object-oriented community base their software decomposition on the object rather than on traditional top-down functional decomposition. We explain the concept of a class and the relationship between objects and classes. Finally, we examine the different relationships that may exist between objects and explain what they mean in the context of the developing system.

Why a new development method was needed

Problems with the structured approach to software development

This section looks at the way in which systems were developed before object-orientation, and at some of the problems that resulted from using the traditional approach.

Functional decomposition. For many years, software systems were developed using a structured approach based on functional decomposition. This meant that developers decomposed and then constructed the system according to the main areas of activity – in other words, the subsystems that were identified corresponded directly to tasks that the system had to carry out. For example, in a bike hire system, such as the one used in this book, the system would probably be based on subsystems or processes dealing with issuing a bike, returning a bike, maintaining records for bikes and for customers etc. Each of these processes would perform a separate function, and the data about bikes, transactions and customers would be passed freely between them. In functional decomposition, there was a clear separation between data and process, and data items could frequently be accessed by any part of the program. Figure 4.1 shows data about bikes being transferred between a data store that holds records about bikes and the processes that deal with issuing and returning bikes to customers. This is a potential source of problems, because the bike details are accessible to other parts of the system with no protection from processes that may access and modify them in error.

Maintenance. Structured software designed using functional decomposition brought with it big maintenance problems. Changes to the code frequently introduced new bugs; a change in one place

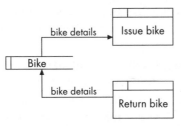

Figure 4.1   *In functional decomposition data (here details about bikes) flows unprotected round the system*

caused unexpected side-effects elsewhere: the infamous 'ripple effect'. Software developers became aware that if the data in the system was accessible to all parts of the code, it could be accidentally corrupted and this was what was causing the ripple effect. Software developers realized that to prevent this, data needed to be encapsulated (protected from unauthorized access).

Poor modularity. However a system is decomposed, it is very important that each separate component or module is self-contained, with a well-defined purpose, and as independent as possible from other modules. Unfortunately, decomposing a system using functional decomposition did not lead to modules with these characteristics. A module in a system based on functional decomposition often was not internally cohesive and was heavily dependent on other modules in the program.

With functional decomposition, making changes to code, either to correct software bugs or implement changes in the user requirements, was a very slow process. In order to understand enough of the code to make the change, preferably without causing side effects, the maintaining programmer had to read a great deal of the code. This was because of poor modularity, the code modules were not independent enough, they were not autonomous. The maintaining programmer could not understand them in isolation, he had to read many peripheral modules to make sense of the one he was changing. This implied that there were hidden dependencies between the modules. What was needed were cohesive (internally coherent) modules that could function either independently or via well-defined interfaces to other modules.

Testing. Software systems based on functional decomposition were still being delivered with errors in the code; they were perceived as unreliable and not sufficiently well tested. It was thought that this might be partly because it was difficult to test units in isolation and manage rigorous integrated testing. This was again partly because units of code were too interdependent. Software developers wanted software units that could be both easily tested in isolation and logically incorporated into an integration testing schedule.

Software reuse. Reuse of software had never taken off as it was expected to do. One of the principal reasons for this was that a suitable software construct didn't exist. A module that is heavily dependent on other software modules cannot easily be put in a software library – all the bits it depends on have to be in the library also. To be reused, modules need to be independent. Useful library modules must also have a clear single purpose that is general enough to be useful in more than one system.

Data versus function. The structured approach built systems based on their functionality – what the system had to do, the tasks that it had to carry out. The problem with this was that typically the functionality of a system is much more volatile and subject to change than its data. Extensive studies have shown that the most common changes in user requirements are to the functionality of the system. Let us consider, for example, a system for allocating patients and staff to wards in a hospital. We can imagine that over time the ways in which patients are assigned to beds in a ward and the way that the nurses' rota is worked out may change. In addition, it is likely that the system will be required to produce more and different reports for its users. Whatever these changes may be, however, the system will still be dealing with patients, beds, nurses and wards – in other words, the data remains the same. The data is much more stable than the functionality, and is a much sounder basis on which to build a system. In functional decomposition the software architecture (the way the system was divided up) was based on its functionality, and over time the whole structure of the system eventually became unstable. The data in the system, however, remained relatively unchanged over the life-time of a system; it eventually became obvious to the software development community that a system based on data would be more robust.

Advantages of object-oriented development

In order to address the problems associated with functional decomposition, developers needed a software construct that was:

- Autonomous, i.e. did not depend heavily on other modules either explicitly or in obscure ways

- Cohesive with a single, well-defined purpose

- Easy to understand

- Easily adapted to accommodate new or changed requirements

- Based on data.

In addition to these characteristics, the software construct should also have:

- encapsulated data

- a well-defined public interface.

This type of unit would be easier to test thoroughly both in isolation and as part of an integrated test plan. It would more likely be reusable and could be included in a software library.

The object-oriented community proposed the *object* as a software construct which had the characteristics listed above. Objects, although they provide functionality, are based on the data in the system. This provides a structure that is less subject to change. As we shall see later in this chapter, an object protects (or encapsulates) its data by making the data accessible only by using the object's publicly declared operations. Well-designed objects are independent and autonomous, making them easy to test in isolation before being integrated into the system. A good object is cohesive, i.e. concerned with a single idea, which makes it suitable for inclusion in a software library for possible reuse.

Use case decomposition and object-oriented decomposition

Although objects are based on the data in the system, this does not mean that object-oriented software ignores the required functionality. We have seen in Chapter 3 that the use case model specifies, from the user's point of view, what the system must do. The objects we define must be capable of delivering that functionality. The use case model provides one decomposition of the system, based on the required functionality. However, the software structure of an object-oriented system is based on the object. In other words when we come to build the software and divide it up into separate parts we don't split it up according to use cases but by objects and groups of objects.

Another advantage of the object-oriented approach is that it provides a seamless development process. The objects we identify as part of the analysis stage persist through the development stages to the code. This thread of continuity means the software objects have a certain predictability – we have expectations, for example, of what an object representing a customer will look like and what it will do. In well-designed object-oriented code our expectations will not be disappointed. This makes the code easier to understand and therefore easier to maintain.

The seamless development also provides traceability of user requirements from initial identification through to the code. In the traditional structured approach to development some of the models that were used to capture user requirements (such as the data flow diagram) were abandoned at the design stage where a new modelling technique was used to specify the structure of the code (for example, structure charts). This made it hard to ensure that all of the user requirements were incorporated in the final implementation: it was easy to lose features in the changeover of models. In the object-oriented approach we identify objects which represent things in the problem domain and about which we need to store information. Later in the development process we add objects to provide the software structure we want to implement (for example, control and boundary objects) and objects that are to do with how the software will work (buttons, windows, mouse-listeners etc.). However, the original objects, although they may gather some extra features in the development process, will still be identifiable in the code.

What is an object?

The object is the most important concept in object-oriented software development; object-oriented systems are based on the object. At its simplest, an object is a representation of something in the application area about which we need to store data to enable the system to do what the users want it to. In the Wheels system, for example, we will undoubtedly want to store data about bikes. Bikes, therefore, would be objects in our model of the Wheels system and eventually in the code. The bits of data we need to store about these bikes, such as the type, the daily hire rate and the deposit, are known as the *attributes* of the bike object.

In the UML an object is represented as shown in Figure 4.2 as a rectangle with two sections. The top section is for the name of the object, and the second section is used for the object's attribute values.

In the case of Figure 4.2 the name of the object is aBike :Bike. Object names are always underlined and can have two parts, either of which can be used on its own. The first part of the name, aBike, labels the object; the second part, :Bike, identifies it as an object of the Bike class. There are a number of ways in which we can refer to an object: we can talk about 'an object of the Bike class', 'a Bike object', or ':Bike' – all of these names mean the same thing in this context.

Every object belongs to a *class* which is a template or factory for producing objects. All of the objects of a class have the same

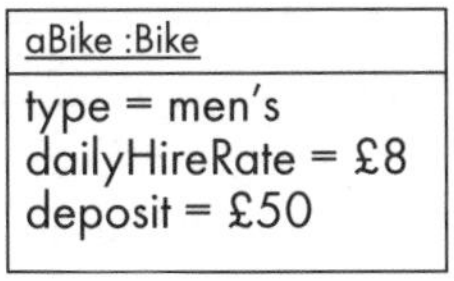

aBike :Bike
type = men's dailyHireRate = £8 deposit = £50

Figure 4.2   *A bike object*

attributes, the same behaviour and the same relationships. Classes are discussed in detail later in this chapter.

Object diagrams can be drawn with attributes and their values displayed as in Figure 4.2, or without attributes (as in Figure 4.6). In Figure 4.2 the attributes that are common to all Bike objects are type, dailyHireRate and deposit, and the values for this particular object are 'men's', '£8' and '£50'.

However, there is more to an object than its ability to record data. For the sake of completeness we are now going to give a more detailed definition of an object and discuss what is meant by the terms used in the definition. Some of this discussion will involve concepts that we have not yet met, so don't worry if you do not understand it all at the moment; you might find it useful to return to this section once you have read about classes.

An object is a concept, abstraction, or thing with clear boundaries and meaning in the current application area. We use objects both to model the real world characteristics of the application area and to provide us with a basis for the computer implementation.

An object can represent something concrete in the real world[1] such as this chair, that red bike, Ben's car or a concept such as a financial transaction (e.g. paying for a stamp), a customer order, the transaction of borrowing a book from a library etc. An object is always an abstraction (see Chapter 1) because although we want it to represent a real world thing, we are only interested in certain aspects of the real world thing. For example, a library member object will store information of interest in a library system: the member's name and address but not her passport number or her taste in shoes – we ignore currently irrelevant details. We are only including properties of the real world thing that have meaning for the problem at hand.

Every object in a system has three characteristics: behaviour, state and identity.

---

1. *During design and implementation (see Chapters 9 and 10) we will meet objects that do not represent things in the real world, but artefacts we need for structural and implementation purposes.*

Behaviour. So far the concept of an object will seem quite familiar to anyone used to entities in entity-relationship modelling (see Howe, 2001). However, unlike entities, objects don't just store information, they have behaviour. Historically, the reason that objects have behaviour is they were originally used in computer simulations. An aeroplane in a computer simulation stores information: it knows how high it is, how much fuel is in its tank, how fast it is flying. It can also do certain things: it can take off, ascend, fly forward, turn and land. Objects in an information system are not usually simulations in the same way (our system won't have bikes whizzing round the screen) but they do know certain things and they can do certain things. A bike object knows (stores) its type, daily hire rate and deposit. When we design the bike object we decide what it is able to do. The system will certainly need to be able to store, update and display the values of each bike object's attributes. We will also need to be able to work out the total cost of a hire for a given number of days. In object-oriented development, processes that act on related data items are bundled together with the data. In fact, an object is little more than a bundle of data items and processes that manipulate them. These processes are called *operations*. An object's behaviour is divided into operations, each of which represents something the object can do (e.g. update dailyHireRate, display deposit). An object's behaviour is triggered in response to a message sent from another object asking it to perform one of its operations. We discuss messages later in this chapter.

State. Most objects have attributes; e.g. type, dailyHireRate and deposit (see Figure 4.2). These attributes have values, e.g. type = men's, dailyHireRate = £8 and deposit = £50. Normally attribute values can change – the dailyHireRate might go up or we might change the amount we ask customers to leave as a deposit. The state of an object is determined by the values of its attributes and its links to other objects. We can tell, for example, if a bank account object is in the overdrawn state by looking at the value of the attribute balance. The reason we are interested in the state of an object is that its behaviour may vary depending on what state it is in. An obvious example of this is the type of bank account where the account holder is not allowed to overdraw. In this case, how the account responds when a request is made to withdraw money depends on how much money is in the account. If there is enough money in the account, the withdrawal is allowed. If not, the withdrawal is not allowed. State and its effect on object behaviour are discussed fully in Chapter 7.

Identity. When we say that an object has identity, we mean that each object is unique, it has a separate existence and ultimately a separate space in the computer memory from every other object. Each bike in the Wheels system will be represented by a separate object in the code. Even two objects whose attributes have identical values are totally distinct from one another. In the computer implementation, objects are identified by a unique computer-generated reference (the object-id) which is an internal code not normally visible to the programmer; roughly speaking it corresponds to a memory location. This is quite separate from any business related identifier such as a customer number or a bike number, or any programmer-generated name for an object. Wheels' bikes all have numbers allocated by the bike shop for business purposes. These numbers are recorded as one of the attributes of a bike object, but they are not the way the computer software identifies the bike object. As far as the programmer or other parts of the code are concerned, objects must be named and addressed by their name. For example, if the list of Wheels' 600 bikes is stored in an array wheelsBikes[600] and we want to know the daily hire rate of one of the bikes in the array, we would send a message addressed to that particular bike (say number 105 in the array) asking it to display its daily hire rate – wheelsBikes[105].showDailyHireRate(). wheelsBikes[105] is the name of the bike object we are interested in, showDailyHireRate() is the operation we want it to perform.

Encapsulation and data hiding

One of the advantages of object-oriented software is that objects encapsulate data. Data can be hidden inside an object in such a way that it is protected and cannot be directly accessed by other parts of the program. The big advantage of this is that it cannot be accidentally corrupted. As an example, let us design a counter to keep track of the score in a game of rugby. We shall have an object called blueSide :Counter with an attribute score as in Figure 4.3 – blueSide is the name of the object, Counter is its class.

The scoring system in a game of rugby is that a side gets 3 points for a penalty, 3 for a drop goal, 5 for a try and 2 for a

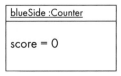

Figure 4.3   *Counter object*

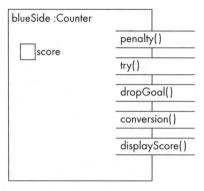

Figure 4.4   *A Counter object showing operations in its public interface*

conversion. If you are not familiar with the game of rugby don't worry about these terms. All we need to understand is that we can only increment the score attribute by 2, 3 or 5. In Figure 4.4 we have depicted the attribute score inside the protective wall of a rectangle representing the blueSide :Counter object.[2] The only way score can be updated is by using one of the operations we have defined for this object: penalty(), try(), dropGoal() or conversion(). This means that no other part of the program can inadvertently (or deliberately!) alter the score by using ordinary integer arithmetic, for example to subtract 10 or multiply by 4. The data is protected by the operations that encapsulate it. In fact the rest of the program need not even know that we have implemented it as an integer. All the rest of the program needs to know is the name of the object and the names of the operations it can use to correctly update or display blueSide's score. This is sometimes known as *data hiding*.

Public interface and messages. In the example in Figure 4.4 the operations penalty(), try(), dropGoal(), conversion() and displayScore() are what is known as the Counter object's public interface – all of these operations are defined as public, i.e. available for use by other parts of the program. Each operation has a *signature*, for example displayScore(), which forms the operation's public interface and must be used when the operation is invoked. The signature consists of the operation's name, parameter list, type of result and an indication of whether it is a private or public operation. An object's public interface is the only thing the rest of the program knows about the object apart from its name. The public interface provides the *services* it makes available to other objects. If another object wants to update blueSide's score – because the blue side have scored a try – it cannot do it directly, it

---

2. *Note that this is not a standard way of modelling objects, we only use it to illustrate encapsulation.*

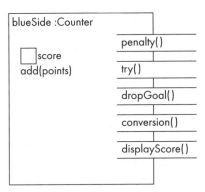

Figure 4.5   *A Counter object showing its public interface and a private operation,*
add(points)

must do it by sending a *message* to the object blueSide, requesting
that it update the score. The message must correctly identify the
object to which it is sent and the operation's signature. It must be in
a specific format: starting with the name of the object, followed by
a full stop, followed by the signature of the operation to be
invoked, for example blueSide.try(). For the message to work, it
must correctly address the object by name and the operation it
specifies must be part of that object's public interface.

Counter may have other operations designed for its own
internal use, for example it might have a operation add(points),
used by most of the operations in the public interface, to add a
specified number of points to the attribute score (see Figure 4.5).
Such internal operations are known as private operations and are
not part of the services that a Counter object makes available to
other objects; they form a private interface for an object to send
messages to itself.

Dependencies. As we have seen, one advantage of using a clearly
defined public interface is that it encapsulates data; another
advantage is that it clarifies *dependencies* between software
constructs and limits the damage that can be done by
dependencies. Two modules are said to be dependent on each other
if one uses the services of the other. This is known as a *client–server*
relationship.

Dependencies between modules can cause problems with
maintenance if they are not carefully controlled. As soon as a
dependency is established it becomes possible, at least in theory,
that changes to one module may affect the other. For example, if we
had designed the counter example above in such a way that score
was visible to other modules and could be directly manipulated by
processes in other modules, we would have to be very careful if we
changed score. If we decided to implement score as a real or a

Figure 4.6   *A Referee object uses the services of a Counter object*

natural number, all the modules that knew that score was an integer would have to be changed. However, if modules communicate with each other by message passing via a public interface, as objects do, then changes to the code that implements the operations do not affect client modules; as long as the interface is not changed, they are not affected. This is true for the actual body of code as well as for data structures involved. For example, if we decide to change the code implementing an operation in order to make it execute faster, so long as we don't change the interface, no client object will be affected. The use of a public interface not only hides the data, it also hides the code.

Dependencies can also complicate the reuse of modules. For example, let us suppose the Counter object is used in a simulation of a game of rugby where a Referee object uses the Counter object to keep the score up to date as in Figure 4.6. The Referee object uses the services of, i.e. is a client of, the Counter object.

This would mean that, if we wanted to reuse the Referee object in another program, we would also have to use the Counter object. In this case there is not really a problem, because we know about the dependency, it is clearly declared. If we want to store away Referee for possible reuse, we can store it bundled together with Counter in a package. You can read about packages in Chapter 5.

Problems arise if two modules are dependent on each other in undeclared ways. In programs written in early programming languages it was possible to jump without restriction to another part of the program or to another module, execute a few lines of code or access some data when you got there, then jump back. Such jumps made it very difficult to read through the code and understand what was happening. If a maintaining programmer had to change one part of the code it was hard to work out how the rest of the program would be affected. Unless he read right through all the code, he could not see which parts of the program might use the section he had just changed: this was the problem of side-effects. Declaring a public interface and using a programming language that enforces it (such as Java or C++) therefore has two big advantages for maintenance.

- It makes it much more obvious to someone reading the code that a client–server relationship exists. That makes the job of changing the code quicker, both because it is easier to

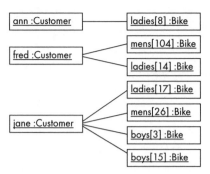

Figure 4.7   *Partial object diagram showing Customer objects and the Bike objects they hired*

understand and because the maintainer does not have to read the entire program to check for dependencies, just the modules affected.

- Unless the interface itself is changed, the internal code of a module can be changed without affecting any client modules. In this sense the internal code of a module (as well as any data) is encapsulated, it is hidden from the rest of the program.

What is a class?

So far our discussion has been entirely about objects and object diagrams. On an object diagram each object is represented by a rectangle, as in Figure 4.7.

Figure 4.7 represents three customers and the bikes they hired; this might model the hire transactions that took place in one hour at the Wheels bike shop. In this diagram we are using simple strings (e.g. ann) for the Customer object names, and array references (e.g. ladies[8]) for the names of the Bike objects.

We can see that, using an object diagram like this, we would very quickly run out of space if we tried to model all the hire transactions that took place in the course of a week; to model all the transactions that took place in a year would be out of the question. The problem with object diagrams is that they take up a lot of space. They are useful for exploring complicated or confused areas of the system, but they are not an efficient way to model the complete set of objects in a system. Wheels have 600 bikes; if they hired them to 5000 customers over the course of a year, we would not attempt to model all of these hires on one object diagram. It is more efficient and convenient to think in terms of classes of objects.

| Customer | 0..* | hires | 1..* | Bike |

Figure 4.8   *Class diagram showing the relationship between the classes Customer and Bike*

A class of objects is a group of objects with the same set of attributes, the same relationships and the same behaviour. When we study a problem domain, we will probably start by finding the objects in it and, once we have done that, work out what classes we need. In the Wheels system, we know we have 600 bike objects to represent. The next step is to agree upon a set of attributes those bikes have in common. Then we need to work out what we want our bike objects to be able to do. Once we have done that a Bike class can be defined with the agreed set of attributes, and operations that can deliver the required behaviour. We can then think and model in terms of classes of objects and their relationships to each other. To represent the hiring of Wheels' 600 bikes by 5000 customers, instead of having an object diagram with several thousand objects on it, we can summarise the information on a class diagram as shown in Figure 4.8. The notation is explained later in the chapter.

Although we start by identifying objects, it is the class that determines the structure and behaviour of its objects. We can compare a class to a scone cutter, or one of those animal-shaped cutters that children use to cut figures out of playdough. One cutter can be used to produce an infinite number of scones or animal figures. A class is used, like the scone cutter, as a template for creating objects in its form. Producing objects is a class's main role in life; a class is an object factory, it can produce hundreds of objects, all with exactly the same structure and behaviour. When we define a class we define the structure and the public interface for all objects of that class.

In object-oriented software, all objects belong to a class. Well-designed object-oriented code consists entirely of objects (and their classes); all of the system functionality is produced by the operations we define for the classes. In the software, the code that implements the operations is situated in the class. Objects of the class know about and access these operations, but don't carry round their own copy of them. For example, a Bike object knows that it can display its number and work out the cost of hiring it (or rather the bike it represents) for a given number of days. However, the code for these operations is part of the Bike class.

Objects are sometimes called instances of classes; the process of creating a new object belonging to a class is called *instantiation*.

Bike
bike#
type
dailyHireRate
deposit
getCharges(no.Days)
findBike(bike#)

Figure 4.9   *The Bike class from the Wheels system*

Every object of a given class will have the same set of attributes and the same set of operations. However, although they have the same information structure and the same set of possible behaviours, each will have its own set of values for its attributes, and each will have its own identity. In the Wheels system every bike owned by the shop and every customer who hires a bike will be represented by an object in the software.

Figure 4.9 shows the Bike class from the Wheels system.

The UML symbol for a class is a rectangle divided into three sections. The top section is used for the class name, the middle section for the attributes and the bottom section for the operations. The UML does not have any naming rules; in this book we use a naming convention, used by most object-oriented practitioners, that is based on object-oriented programming style. Class names begin with a capital letter with the rest of the name in lower case. If a class name comprises two or more words the words are run together without spaces and the first letter of each word is capitalized, e.g. BikeList, FlowerArrangingTalk. Class names are always singular.

Notice that attribute names are written in lower case. If an attribute name comprises two or more words the words are run together without spaces and the first letter of each word, except the first one, is capitalised, e.g. dailyHireRate. Operations use the same notation, e.g. getCharges( ).

Relationships between classes

There are three types of relationship between classes: association, aggregation and inheritance.

Association. One of the main characteristics of an object-oriented system is that its objects co-operate to achieve the required functionality. For this to happen, they have to be able to communicate with one another. They do this by message passing. Objects will not be able to pass messages to each other unless we build in links between classes, a route for them to talk to one another – a navigable path.

Figure 4.10   *Object diagram showing a customer hiring a bike*

Figure 4.10 is an object diagram showing a :Customer[3] linked to a :Bike. It models the real-life relationship of a customer hiring a bike. By contrast, in a class diagram (like the one in Figure 4.11) association relationships simply build into the model the possibility for objects to be linked; so that a :Customer can be linked to a :Bike as required. The association does not tell us which :Customers are actually linked to which :Bikes, as the object diagram in Figure 4.7 does, just that they can be linked. An association represents a group of links between objects in much the same way as a class represents a group of objects.

In the early stages of modelling, we don't yet know in detail how objects will need to communicate. At this stage, when we model an association between classes of objects, we are not saying much more than that a real-life connection exists between these objects, and can be used by the objects when needed.

Figure 4.11 shows the association relationship between the Customer and Bike classes.

We can see from Figure 4.11 that an association can be named: a customer *hires* a bike. An association has two ends, each attached to a class. Each association end can have a role name: on the association between Customer and Bike the association end next to Customer is *hirer*, next to Bike is *hired*. The default name for an association end is the name of the class it is attached to; for example, in Figure 4.11 the default name for the association end attached to Customer would be *customer*. In practice, both association names and role names are omitted, unless they significantly aid understanding.

Association ends also have multiplicity. Multiplicity is indicated by the numbers and asterisks on the line. The multiplicity of an association indicates limits on the number of objects allowed to participate in the

Figure 4.11   *Association between the Customer and Bike classes in the Wheels system*

3.   *Remember – this notation means an object of the Customer class.*

Table 4.1:   *UML association notation*

Meaning	Example	Notation
an exact number	exactly one exactly six	1 (or may be omitted) 6
many	zero or more one or more, lots of	0..* 1..*, *
a specific range	one to four, zero to six	1..4, 0..6,
a choice	two or four or five	2, 4, 5

relationship. We must read multiplicity separately for each association end. To interpret the association between Customer and Bike in Figure 4.11 we first look at how many :Bikes a :Customer may hire, then at how many :Customers a :Bike may be hired by. To work out how many :Bikes one :Customer may hire we look along the association from the Customer class end to the number specified at the Bike class end. In this case the number is 1..*. This means one customer may hire 1 or many bikes. In object terms the diagram specifies that one :Customer may be linked to 1 or many :Bikes. Interpreting the multiplicity in the other direction, the diagram specifies that any one :Bike may be hired by 0, 1 or many (0..*) :Customers. We assume this means over a period of time. The multiplicity is always specified from the point of view of a single object.

The UML multiplicity notation allows us to specify degrees of association as shown in Table 4.1

Aggregation is often thought of as a tighter form of association; it models a whole-part relationship between classes, e.g. wheels, doors and an engine are parts of a car. An aggregation relationship can be identified:

- If a phrase such as 'consists of', 'has a', or 'is a part of' is used to describe the relationship

- If one class in the relationship (the whole) is more important than the other (the part)

- If some operations apply to the whole and its parts.

Figure 4.12 shows the aggregation relationship between a car and its parts: wheel, door and engine.

In the UML notation, aggregation is shown as a line joining the two classes with a diamond next to the whole class, see Figure 4.12. Notice that multiplicity can be specified at the part end of the

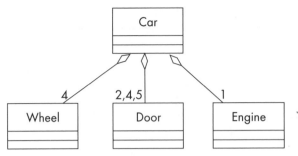

Figure 4.12   *Aggregation relationship: the classes Wheel, Door and Engine are part of the Car class*

relationship, using the same notation as for association. The whole end is always assumed to be one, a wheel object, for example, is only part of one car. In Figure 4.12, one car has four wheels, two, four or five doors, and one engine.

In the days before the UML was published, there was much heated debate about the importance and the meaning of aggregation. The UML includes aggregation, but without a precise definition. There is little to distinguish an aggregation relationship from an association relationship. Since this is the case, we feel that aggregation often adds little to the meaning of a model and does not have to be included. The UML includes a stronger form of aggregation, known as composition. Composition is useful because it does have a precisely defined meaning; it is discussed in the Technical points section of this chapter.

Inheritance and generalization. If we notice, while modelling classes, that some of them share some common attributes and operations, it can be useful to introduce a new class for the shared bits, leaving only the distinguishing features in the original classes. This process is known as *generalization*. For example, in Figure 4.13 we have two classes we might find in a system for an art gallery: Photograph and Painting. These two classes both have the attributes title and price and the operation updatePrice().

We can create a new general class, Picture, in which we can place these common features; this is shown in Figure 4.14. Photograph and Painting retain their distinctive features and share those of Picture.

In the structure in Figure 4.14, the classes Photograph and Painting are *specializations* of the general class, Painting. The relationship between a general class and its specializations is known as an *inheritance* relationship. The inheritance mechanism allows the specialized classes to share or inherit the features of the general class. The UML notation for an inheritance relationship is an open-headed arrow which points from the specialized class to the general class.

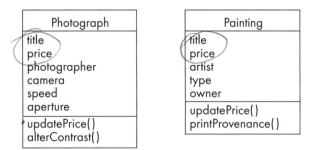

Figure 4.13   *The art gallery classes Photograph and Painting have attributes and an operation in common*

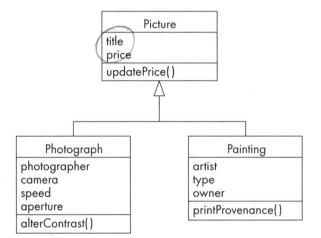

Figure 4.14   *The Picture class stores the features common to the Photograph and Painting classes*

There are various ways of describing the inheritance relationship:

- A specialized class inherits from a general class

- A subclass inherits from a superclass

- A child class inherits from a parent class

- A derived class inherits from a base class.

Looking at the process the other way round, it is also useful to be able to create new classes from existing classes; instead of starting from scratch, we can refine ones we already have. This permits the reuse of classes from another system or perhaps from a class library. The specialized class can tailor the more general class to suit the new system by adding attributes or operations. Inherited operations can be *overridden*, i.e. the inherited code can be replaced with new code that implements the operation in a different way.

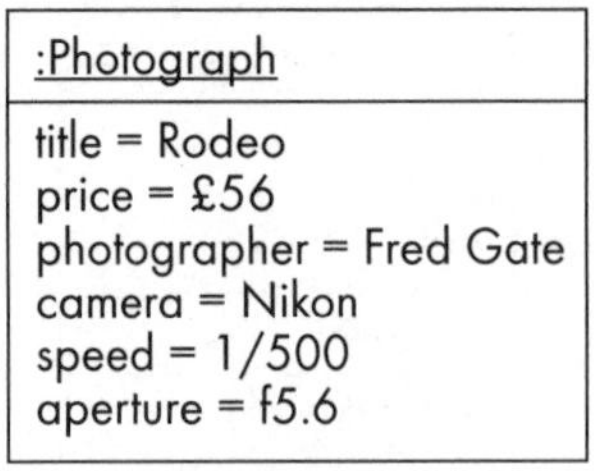

:Photograph
title = Rodeo price = £56 photographer = Fred Gate camera = Nikon speed = 1/500 aperture = f5.6

Figure 4.15   *Photograph object showing its own and its inherited attributes*

When we create a specialized class, it inherits all the attributes, operations and relationships of the parent class. In Figure 4.14, the specialized classes Photograph and Painting inherit the attributes title and price and the operation updatePrice() from the Picture class; they also each have attributes and operations that are relevant only for objects of their specialized class. Notice that the inherited characteristics are not shown in the subclasses; these are the shared features that justify the generalization. This economy of representation simplifies the diagram. However, inherited features do form part of the structure of the inheriting object. A Photograph object would have the attributes: title and price (inherited from Picture) as well as photographer, camera, speed and aperture (see Figure 4.15). It will know about the inherited operation updatePrice() as well as the operation alterContrast().

When we create a set of subclasses we must have some basis for differentiating the subclasses from each other; this is known as the *discriminator*. In the art gallery classes in Figure 4.14 the basis for the differentiation is the type of picture. Usually there will be one subclass for each possible value of the discriminator. As another example, in Figure 4.16 the discriminator is the type of publication; in this case there are three types of publication, therefore there are three subclasses.

It is easy to misuse inheritance; it is a useful technique only if used correctly. In the past programmers have been tempted to introduce a class from another system and specialize it simply so that they can use one if its methods.[4] The reused class might have nothing in common with the new system except for a useful algorithm. This can be confusing for those reading the code; their expectations of the inheritance relationship are confounded. Classes should not be linked by inheritance unless there is an *is-a* or *is-a-kind-of* relationship between them: in the art gallery example photograph and painting are both *a-kind-of* picture.

---

4. *A method is the way that an operation is implemented; this is discussed later in this chapter.*

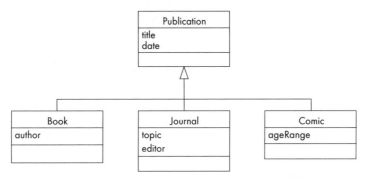

Figure 4.16   *The Publication class and three subclasses*

A generalization/inheritance relationship can be identified:

- If phrases such as 'is-a' or 'is-a-kind-of' can be used to describe the relationship between classes, e.g. a journal is a-kind-of publication, a horse is-a mammal

- Where one or more classes have very similar attributes and operations and the introduction of a general class would simplify the model.

Theoretically, there is no limit to the number of levels allowed in an inheritance hierarchy; in practice, it has been found that a hierarchy with more than about six levels becomes unmanageable.

Generalization and inheritance are useful techniques because, as we have seen, they allow reuse of existing classes. Classifying classes into an inheritance hierarchy also means that we avoid repeating code. Inherited operations reside in the superclass; subclasses do not need to carry around their own version, unless they are going to specialize the operation (see polymorphism below). This means if we alter the code that implements an operation we need only alter it once, in the superclass.

Classifying classes into an inheritance hierarchy also helps organise and simplify our understanding of the classes in the system. Classes suitable for such classification have both similarities and differences; an inheritance hierarchy emphasizes both. To avoid unnecessary repetition and clarify our understanding of the classes, attributes and operations are defined at the highest applicable level in the hierarchy. Differences are reflected in attributes and operations that are added or redefined as the distinguishing features of the specialized classes.

Abstract classes. Inheritance is a relationship between classes, not between objects; it is a mechanism for organizing and simplifying the classes in the system and the relationships between them. Some classes are only used for purposes of classification and are never

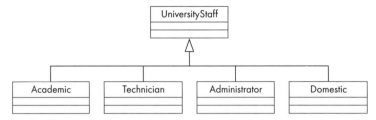

Figure 4.17   *UniversityStaff is an abstract class that is never instantiated*

instantiated in other words no objects of the class exist in the system. In the art gallery example in Figure 4.14, if we assume that a picture must be either a painting or a photograph, there will never be objects that are just pictures. Similarly, in the hierarchy in Figure 4.17, the class UniversityStaff is never instantiated; all employees of the university have to be either academics, technicians, administrators or domestics.

Classes that are never instantiated are known as *abstract* classes; the opposite is a *concrete* or *instantiated* class. The UML notation for an abstract class is {abstract} placed below the class name – see Figure 4.18.

Abstract classes are often very useful candidates for class libraries; their generality means they capture the essence of their type of class without any taint of the specific system for which they were designed.

Polymorphism. To discuss polymorphism, we must first understand the difference between operations and methods. The two terms are generally used as if they were interchangeable, but this is not quite the case. We have described an operation as a process that an object can perform, part of its behaviour. Strictly speaking the word *operation* refers to the interface of the process; the operation must be invoked (by message passing) when a client module wants the process to be executed. The code that implements the process is known as the *method*.[5]

Picture {abstract}
title price
updatePrice( )

Figure 4.18   *The UML notation for an abstract class*

---

5. *Programmers often refer to operations as* method signatures.

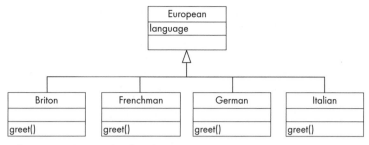

Figure 4.19   Inheritance hierarchy for the European class

```
1   public class Frenchman extends European
2   {
3   // 'String language' does not need to be declared as it is inherited
4
5       Frenchman()
6       {
7       language = "French";
8       }
9
10      void greet()
11      {
12      System.out.println(" Bonjour");
13      }
14  }
```

Figure 4.20   The Java code for the Frenchman class

Figure 4.19 shows a simple inheritance hierarchy for a European class, and Figure 4.20 contains the Java code for Frenchman, one of the subclasses in the hierarchy.

In Figure 4.20, line 10 is the operation part of the process greet(). Line 12 is the method.

Notice in the inheritance hierarchy in Figure 4.19 that, although it is inherited, the greet() operation appears in all the classes in the hierarchy. This is not because we have forgotten that inherited features can be omitted from the diagram, it is because greet() is redefined (i.e. is implemented by a different method) in all of the subclasses.

The significance of the distinction between operation and method is that, in an inheritance hierarchy, it becomes possible for one operation to be implemented by many methods. When a subclass inherits an operation, as long as it doesn't alter the interface, it can change the method to suit its own specialization. Altering a method is called *over-riding,* and an operation that is

Table 4.2:   *How the different classes in the European hierarchy implement the greet() operation*

Class	Method specification for greet()
European	undefined
Briton	Good morning
Frenchman	Bonjour
German	Guten Tag
Italian	Buongiorno

implemented by a number of different methods is called *polymorphic*.

Polymorphic operations are used in the context of an inheritance hierarchy where the same operation may be implemented differently in each subclass. A single message will produce a different response depending on the class of the object to which it is sent. For example, in the inheritance hierarchy shown in Figure 4.19 the operation greet() appears in all of the classes in the hierarchy. The method for greet() is undefined in the class European.[6] Each of the other classes in the hierarchy has a different method for greet() (see Table 4.2).

To illustrate polymorphism in action, let us create an object called pierre of the Frenchman class with French as his language. If we send him the message pierre.greet() he will respond by saying 'Bonjour', see Table 4.3 which also shows the response of hans, a :German. We have set you an exercise to work out the responses of george, a :Briton, and antonio, an :Italian (see Exercise 4.9)

To understand a bit more how polymorphism works, we create an array of four European objects, named nationality[4]. We can populate this with objects of all of the instantiable classes in the European hierarchy as in Figure 4.21.

We can iterate through the array sending the greet() message to each of the objects in turn (see Figure 4.22); each will respond according to the method implementation of their class, and the

6. *The reason for putting any undefined operation into a superclass (as we have done with greet()) is to try to build some future-proofing into the model; we are guessing that if new classes are introduced to the hierarchy, they will need this operation. If a new class is introduced it will inherit this operation and define it to suit its purpose. This should simplify the process of modifying the system.*

Table 4.3:   *Attributes and responses to the greet() message of some objects from the European hierarchy*

Object name	Class	Attributes	Response to greet() message
pierre	Frenchman	language: French	Bonjour
hans	German	language: German	Guten Tag

```
European nationality[ ];
  int i;
  nationality = new European[4];

  nationality [0] = new Briton();
  nationality [1] = new Frenchman();
  nationality [2] = new German();
  nationality [3] = new Italian();
```

Figure 4.21   *Java code for the array of European objects*

```
for (i=0;i<4;i++)
   {
   nationality[i].greet();
   }
```

Figure 4.22   *Java code for the array of European objects*

output will be: 'Good morning', 'Bonjour', 'Guten Tag', 'Buongiorno'.

These sections of code illustrate three points:

- A subclass object can always be substituted for an object of the class above it in the hierarchy, or indeed for an object of any ancestor class. The array is declared to be of type European, but we have populated it with objects of the subclasses, Briton, Frenchman, etc. This is known as substitutability. It does not work the other way round, we could not declare an array of type Frenchman and populate it with objects from its superclass, European (even if European were instantiable). This is because objects of subclasses usually have added attributes and operations that the superclass objects don't know about.

- It is easy to extend an inheritance hierarchy to suit changes in user requirements. A new class can be added to the hierarchy without much change to the code or the class model. To convince yourself that this is the case, try doing this as an exercise – see Exercise 4.14 based on the Robot hierarchy that is described in the Technical points section of this chapter.

- The program does not know in advance which classes are involved in the processing of the array; as far as it is concerned it is dealing with an array of European objects. As the program works its way through the array, it only knows which methods will be executed when it gets to the next object and works out which class it belongs to. This is known as *late or dynamic binding*.

You will find a more complex example of polymorphism, the Robot hierarchy, in the Technical points section of this chapter.

Technical points

What makes a good class?

Knowing what makes a good class comes with experience, but we can offer a few pointers.

Problem domain. During analysis, classes should correspond to things in the real world of the problem domain – Bike, Customer, Hire and Payment all correspond to things in the Wheels problem domain that the user would know about and understand.

Functionality. A class (at least during analysis) usually has both attributes and behaviour. Be suspicious of a class that seems to be just one big function and has no attributes; it might turn out to be just an operation on some other class. Similarly, a class that has only attributes and basic set and get[7] operations sounds like a badly designed class. The functionality of the system is shared between the classes, so they should be doing more than just maintaining and displaying the values of their attributes.

Cohesion. One of the qualities of a good software construct, listed at the beginning of this chapter, is cohesion. A class is cohesive if it is concerned with only one thing, if all its attributes and operations relate to the same topic. For example, Figure 4.23 shows a version of the art gallery Painting, one of the classes from the hierarchy that we mentioned earlier in the chapter (we have omitted the rest of the classes for simplicity).

---

7. *A set operation sets or modifies the value of an attribute. A get operation displays or retrieves the value of an attribute. Set and get operations are not normally shown on a class diagram.*

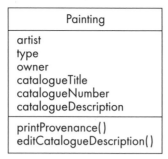

Figure 4.23   *Adding attributes and operations relating to a catalogue destroys the cohesion of the Painting class*

Figure 4.24   *The Painting and Catalogue classes are linked by association*

In the version of the Painting class in Figure 4.23 we have added the attributes catalogueTitle, catalogueNumber and catalogueDescription, and the operation editCatalogueDescription(). This makes the Painting class unbalanced; it is no longer cohesive because these three attributes and the operation belong in a different class, one concerned with catalogues. The two separate classes could be linked by association as in Figure 4.24.

Substitutability. In an inheritance hierarchy, objects of descendant classes should always be substitutable for objects above them in the hierarchy. This is what we saw happening in the European example that we used to illustrate polymorphism. We declared an array of European objects and populated it with objects of European subclasses (see Figure 4.21). The subclass objects could all be treated as if they were European objects; any message that could be understood by a European object could be understood by its descendants. For this to happen we need to construct our inheritance hierarchies with care.

As an example of how not to construct an inheritance tree, we will revisit the art gallery example (see Figure 4.14). We started with the two classes in Figure 4.13, reproduced here in Figure 4.25.

Photograph
title
price
photographer
camera
speed
aperture
updatePrice()
alterContrast()

Painting
title
price
artist
type
owner
updatePrice()
printProvenance()

Figure 4.25   *Photograph and Painting have attributes and an operation in common*

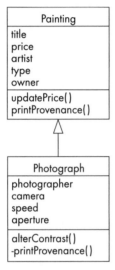

Figure 4.26   *Incorrect use of inheritance*

We could have tried to make Photograph inherit directly from Painting, as in Figure 4.26, but in this case we would have created a subclass whose objects could not be substituted for objects of its superclass.

In Photograph the printProvenance() operation has been effectively disabled by being made private; a client object can send the printProvenance() message to Painting objects but not to Photograph objects. Photograph also inherits the attributes artist, type and owner which it does not use.

A better way to introduce inheritance in this situation is shown in Figure 4.27 (repeated from Figure 4.14). We have introduced a new class, Picture, in which we can place common features. Photograph and Painting retain their distinctive features and share those of Picture.

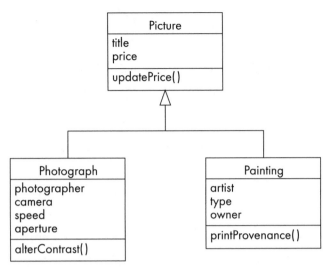

Figure 4.27 *Picture, Painting and Photograph classes restructured to conform to the principle of substitutability*

Composition

The UML has a stronger form of aggregation known as composition (it is also sometimes referred to as aggregation containment). Composition is like aggregation in that it models a whole–part relationship between objects, but unlike aggregation in that it has a very precise meaning. In a composition relationship:

- The whole object has exclusive ownership of its parts, i.e. the part object can only participate in one aggregation

- Part objects, therefore, have no separate existence from the whole

- The parts live and die with the whole, i.e.

  - the whole creates its parts and

  - when the whole is deleted, its parts are deleted (a cascading delete).

Part objects are hidden (contained) within the whole in that they are not visible to the rest of the program. In the same way that operations forming the interface of an object encapsulate and hide the object's data, the interface of the whole object encapsulates and hides its part objects. The rest of the program can communicate only with the whole; any communication with the parts is done by the whole object. The notation for a composition relationship is the same as for aggregation, but with a black diamond instead of a white one. This is shown in Figure 4.28, which illustrates a composition relationship between a Robot and its parts.

If we want to get the Robot to pick up a glass, we send the message to the Robot object, not to its hand.

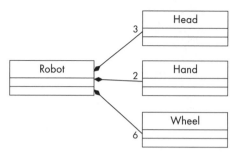

Figure 4.28   Composition relationship between a Robot and its parts

A more complex example of polymorphism

Figure 4.29 shows an inheritance hierarchy of the Robot class, and Figure 4.30 shows the Java code for ButlerRobot, one of the subclasses in the hierarchy.

In this code line 12 is the operation part of the process perform(). Line 14 is the method.

In the inheritance hierarchy shown in Figure 4.29 the perform() operation appears in all of the classes in the hierarchy. The method for perform() is undefined in the classes Robot, Humanoid, DomesticRobot and AlienRobot. Each of the other classes in the hierarchy has a different method for perform() (see Table 4.4).

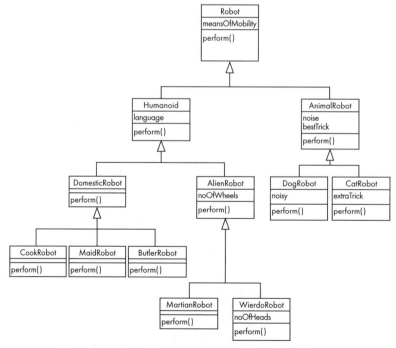

Figure 4.29   The Robot hierarchy

```
1   class ButlerRobot extends DomesticRobot
2   {
3       // 'String meansOfMobility' not required because inherited
4       // 'String language' not required because inherited
5
6       Butler()
7       {
8       meansOfMobility = "two legs";
9       language = "English";
10      }
11
12      void perform()
13      {
14      System.out.println(" I answer the door");
15      }
16  }
```

Figure 4.30   *The Java code for the Butler class in the Robot hierarchy*

Table 4.4:   *Method implementations for classes in the Robot hierarchy*

Class	Method specification for perform()
Robot	undefined
Humanoid	undefined
DomesticRobot	undefined
AlienRobot	undefined
CookRobot	prepare meal
MaidRobot	clean stairs
ButlerRobot	answer door
MartianRobot	transmit reports to earth in *language*
WierdoRobot	converse with other heads in *language*
AnimalRobot	do *bestTrick* and make *noise*
DogRobot	If noisy: do *bestTrick* and make *noise, noise, noise, noise*; Else do *bestTrick* and make *noise*
CatRobot	do *bestTrick* and make *noise*; do *extraTrick*

To illustrate polymorphism in action, we will create an object called jeeves of the ButlerRobot class with two legs as his meansOfMobility and English as his language. If we send him the message jeeves.perform() he will respond by answering the door, see Table 4.5. The responses of mart, a :MartianRobot, and pat, a :DogRobot, are also shown in Table 4.5; we have set you an exercise to work out the responses of objects of the rest of the classes, see Exercise 4.11.

To illustrate again how polymorphism works in the code, let us create an array of seven Robot objects, named automaton[7]. We can populate this with objects of all of the instantiable classes in the Robot hierarchy as in Figure 4.31.

We can iterate through the array sending the perform() message to each of the objects in turn (see Figure 4.32); each will respond according to the method implementation of their class.

Reuse

Software developers, unlike their colleagues in most forms of hardware development and indeed most other industries, have never really gone in for component reuse. The most frequently documented reasons for this seem to be as follows.

- Programmers don't seem to like using code written by other people – the 'Not Invented Here' syndrome.

- Problems are caused if components that might be suitable for reuse are written in a different programming language, or for a different hardware platform from that used by the new system.

- There are many libraries of software components both commercial and in-house. However, library components are often either too specific or too general. In both cases they don't quite do what is required. Software libraries are not always well documented and it can be hard to find out exactly what a module does.

The object-oriented approach offers some help.

- Libraries of classes now exist and are widely used.

- The inheritance mechanism allows programmers to tailor library classes to meet the requirements of a new system.

- Often a group of related classes is more useful than a single class as a component for reuse. Classes related by composition form a coherent software unit with a clearly defined public interface.

- Well designed classes and compositions of classes are cohesive and easy to understand; they have a clear and easily identifiable

Table 4.5:   *Attributes and responses to the perform() message of some objects from the Robot hierarchy*

Object name	Class	Attributes	Response to perform( ) message
jeeves	ButlerRobot	meansOfMobility: two legs language: English	answer door
mart	MartianRobot	meansOfMobility: wheels language: Martian noOfWheels: 8	transmit reports to earth in Martian
pat	DogRobot	meansOfMobility: four legs noise: Woof bestTrick: fetch stick noisy: True	fetch stick and say 'Woof, Woof, Woof, Woof'

```
Robot automaton[];
 int i;
 automaton = new Robot[7];

 automaton[0] = new CookRobot();
 automaton[1] = new MaidRobot();
 automaton[2] = new ButlerRobot();
 automaton[3] = new MartianRobot();
 automaton[4] = new WierdoRobot();
 automaton[5] = new DogRobot();
 automaton[6] = new CatRobot();
```

Figure 4.31   *Java code for the array of Robot objects*

```
for (i=0;i<7;i++)
 {
 automaton[i].perform();
 }
```

Figure 4.32   *Java code for the array of Robot objects*

purpose. Programmers searching a library are able to readily identify software components to meet their needs.

• Classes and compositions of classes encapsulate their internal details so that all that a client component needs to know about is the interface. This helps with the problem of using components originally written for different systems in different languages.

Common problems

1 When I look at objects that seem to be the same sort of thing but have quite different values, how do I know whether they should be modelled as different classes or as different objects of the same class? For example, if I have a father, mother and several children, should I create a new class for each or are they all of objects of a general class like Person?

It depends on what your system needs to record about these objects and what it wants them to do. In a library system they would all just be objects of a class such as FamilyMember. In a school system the children would all be objects of the Student class and the parents might just feature as attributes. However, if you were writing a system that simulates the behaviour of families you might model them as separate classes. For entities to warrant being modelled as different classes, they must have distinguishing features, i.e. distinctive behaviour or attributes, not just different values for their attributes.

2 I have two classes, Customer and Employee. Both Customer and Employee need to record title, forename and surname; can I make them subclasses of a class Name so that they inherit name details, as in Figure 4.33.

This would be a totally incorrect use of inheritance. Customer and Employee should not be modelled as specializations of Name as there is not an is-a relationship between them; neither customers nor employees are kinds of name. A better way to model this would be to use an association relationship as shown in Figure 4.34.

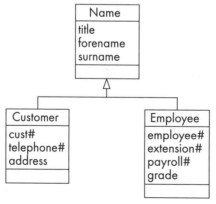

Figure 4.33   Incorrect inheritance from Name class

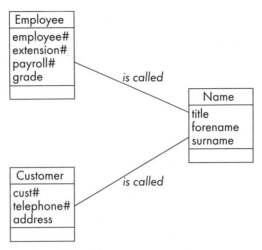

Figure 4.34   Improved model of the Name example

3   When I am dealing with an inheritance hierarchy, I sometimes can't tell whether one class should be a subclass of another or if I am looking at two members of the same class. For example, is Shetland pony a subclass of Horse?

For something to qualify as a subclass it must have at least one extra attribute or operation or over-ride an inherited operation.

4   Organizing classes into an inheritance hierarchy seems like a lot of extra work; is it always worth doing?

Organizing classes into an inheritance hierarchy does involve extra effort. It is worth doing if it simplifies your model and clarifies your thinking. It is also worthwhile if it seems quite likely that you will need to introduce new classes in the future and an inheritance hierarchy would simplify the process. Another factor is whether you are thinking of reusing any of your classes. The more general they are, the easier they are to reuse.

5   Do subclasses always inherit all the features of the parent class?

Yes, for all practical purposes. Some object-oriented programming languages allow inherited features to be suppressed, but this is generally considered to be bad practice.

6   How can I recognize an abstract class?

Technically, an abstract class is one that has no method defined for one or more of its operations; this means that there can be no instances of the class in a system.

Chapter summary

Software produced using a structured development approach still has many problems particularly relating to maintenance, reuse and testing. These failings are perceived to be due to the lack of a suitable software construct. The object-oriented approach is based on the object, a software construct which should overcome the problems suffered by structured software.

Objects are based on the data in a system, but are also able to provide the required functionality. Every object belongs to a class, which determines its attributes, behaviour and relationships. A good class should demonstrate the qualities listed in the chapter. It should produce objects that are autonomous, cohesive and easy to understand. We have discussed how objects encapsulate data, together with operations to manipulate it, in a single construct, and hide the data behind a public interface of operations. We have also seen that abstract classes can be used to build some future proofing into the system.

There are three main ways in which classes can be linked: association, aggregation and inheritance. Inheritance is a powerful technique that allows us to create new classes by specializing existing ones; it is therefore an important tool in reuse of software. Inheritance also allows polymorphism, where an operation can be implemented in different ways by different classes.

Bibliography

Bennett, S., McRobb, S. and Farmer, R. (2002) *Object-Oriented Systems Analysis and Design Using UML* (2nd edition), McGraw-Hill, London.

Britton, C. and Doake, J. (2000) *Object-Oriented Systems Development: A Gentle Introduction,* McGraw-Hill, London.

Brown, D. (1997) *Object-Oriented Analysis: objects in plain English,* John Wiley, New York.

Fowler, M. (2000) *UML Distilled: A Brief Guide to the Standard Object Modeling Language* (2nd edition), Addison-Wesley, Reading, MA.

Howe, D. (2001) *Data Analysis for Database Design* (3rd edition), Butterworth-Heinemann, Oxford.

Larman, C. (1998) *Applying UML and Patterns: An Introduction to Object-Oriented Analysis and Design,* Prentice Hall, New Jersey.

Quatrani, T. (1998) *Visual Modeling with Rational Rose and UML,* Addison-Wesley, Reading, MA.

Rumbaugh, J., Blaha, M., Premerlani, W., Eddy, F. and Lorensen, W. (1991) *Object-Oriented Modeling and Design,* Prentice-Hall, Englewood Cliffs, NJ.

Stevens, P., with Pooley, R. (2000) *Using UML. Software Engineering with Objects and Components* (updated edition), Addison-Wesley, Harlow.

Quick check questions

You can find the answers to these in the chapter.

a   Developing systems using a structured approach can result in problematic software. List three problems associated with the structured approach.

b   List four qualities that are desirable in a software construct.

c   What is meant by the term *seamless development*?

d   What is the difference between a class and an object?

e   What is the difference in the UML diagrammatic notation for a class and an object?

f   What do we mean when we refer to the behaviour of an object?

g   How does the state of an object affect its behaviour?

h   What is meant by the term *encapsulation*?

i   How do objects communicate?

j   What do we mean when we talk about the public interface of an object?

k   What is instantiation?

l   List three types of relationships between classes. Briefly describe each.

m   Why might you decide to model one class as a subclass of another?

n   What is an abstract class? Why do we use them?

o   What is the difference between an operation and a method? What is the significance of this for polymorphism?

p   What is dynamic binding?

q   What is the difference between aggregation and composition?

Exercises

4.1 This is an exercise to do in tutorial groups. Each group should be supplied with a large piece of paper such as one from a flip chart and a couple of marker pens.

a Get into groups of three or four students.

b Place the contents of your pockets and bags on the desk in front of you.

c Arrange the items in categories such as stationery (pens, notebooks, etc.), communication (mobile phones, etc.), garments (hats, gloves, etc.).

d Study the categories and try to refine them into subcategories, e.g. within the stationery group there might be writing implements, electronic devices, etc.

e Repeat d) until you can refine no longer.

f See if any of the items on the desk can be taken apart (without breaking them). For example, a pen can have its top taken off, a pair of gloves can be split into the right-hand glove and the left-hand glove.

g On the large piece of paper or a board draw a diagram to represent your categories such as the one in Figure 4.35. The categories are arranged in a hierarchy with the top rectangle representing the original group of items, the next down your initial categorization, etc. Draw a line

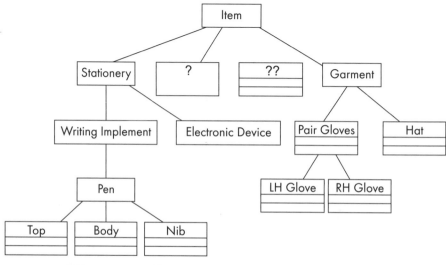

Figure 4.35   Object category diagram

joining each subcategory to the category above it. Draw the final categorization (the one where you took items apart) in a different colour.

h Discuss how your diagram relates to what you know about objects and classes.

4.2 Identify class and attribute names for the following groups of objects.

a

Sarah Porter 039777657 Systems Modelling CS20045 53%	Rakesh Patel 039765869 Programming 2 CS20046 65%	Lyn Michaels 039654344 Programming 2 CS20046 41%

b

WM073COC Linen Trousers Cocoa 8,10,12,14,16,18 £55	WL123YLW Floral Cardigan Yellow 8,10,12,14,16,18 £23	MA023BL Friday Shirt Blue 15,16,17,18 £39

c

0333695275 Into Thin Air Jon Krakauer Macmillan 1997	0434287466 Grace Maggie Gee Heinemann 1998	0099268558 Music & Silence Rose Tremain Vintage 2000

4.3 Suggest classes you would expect to find in the following systems:

a A banking system.

b A drawing package.

c A library.

d University human resource department.

e Mail order.

4.4 Objects and classes come in different categories: people, organizations, physical things, conceptual things. Identify the categories of the classes you suggested in your answer to Question 4.3.

4.5 Items a–n in Table 4.6 list object-oriented concepts. Items 1–14 list short definitions. Match the concept to the definition that best describes it.

Table 4.6:   Items and concepts for Exercise 4.5

Concept	Definition
a aggregation	1 a relationship between two classes where one is a specialization of another
b association	2 the ability of one operation to be implemented by different methods
c attribute	3 abstracting common features into a superclass
d class	4 code implementing an operation
e data hiding	5 concealing internal details of an object
f encapsulation	6 creation of an object
g generalization	7 data item defined as part of a class or object
h inheritance	8 instance of a class
a instatiation	9 interface of a method
b message	10 packaging together data and operations
c method	11 relationship between classes
d object	12 request for a service to be executed
e operation	13 template for objects
f polymorphism	14 whole-part relationship

4.6   This question relates to the rugby counter example in the section on encapsulation and data hiding. Give a list of all the messages that the object blueSide :Counter can understand.

4.7   Draw diagrams to link the following classes using association, aggregation, inheritance and multiplicity where appropriate.

a   hotel room, booking, guest

b   club member, adult member, junior member

c   exam paper, instruction, question, solution

d   animal, mammal, bird, reptile, dog, horse, parrot

e   sentence, word, letter, punctuation

f   academic staff, lecturer, professor, student.

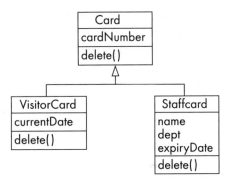

Figure 4.36   Card class hierarchy

4.8   a   In the diagram in Figure 4.36, what will be the attributes of a StaffCard object?

b   In the diagram in Figure 4.37, what will be the attributes of a WholesaleCustomer object?

4.9   Complete in Table 4.3 (relating to the European hierarchy) which shows object names, classes, attribute values and responses to the greet() message. As well as the information in Table 4.2, you can assume the following:

◆ the Briton object is called george

◆ the Italian object is called antonio

◆ all Britons speak English

◆ all Italians speak Italian.

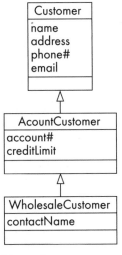

Figure 4.37   Customer class hierarchy

4.10 If a CatRobot object, from the Robot hierarchy defined in the Technical points section on polymorphism, is called jojo, what message would you send to get him to perform? Hint: remember you have to address the object as well as the operation.

4.11 Complete Table 4.5 (relating to the Robot hierarchy) which shows object names, classes, attribute values and responses to the perform() message.

As well as the information in Table 4.4, you can assume the following:

• all DomesticRobots and their descendants have 2 legs

• all AlienRobots and their descendants have wheels

• all WierdoRobots have several heads

• all AnimalRobots and their descendants have 4 legs.

Where attribute values are unspecified (e.g. names, languages, no.OfWheels, noise, etc.) you can choose whatever value you like for the objects.

4.12 Which of the classes in the Robot hierarchy are abstract and why? (Hint: Table 4.4 will help you here.)

4.13 What would the output be from the code sections in Figures 4.31 and 4.32? (Hint: Table 4.4 and the answers to Question 4.11 will also help you here.)

4.14 Amend the Robot hierarchy in Figure 4.29 by adding a class HorseRobot as a subclass of AnimalRobot; do not redefine the perform() method. (Hint: remember that for a class to be a specialization of its parent, it must have some distinguishing feature.)

i What attributes would the HorseRobot class inherit?

ii What implementation of perform() would it inherit?

4.15 a Add an object of the HorseRobot class to the array of Robot objects in Figure 4.31 and adjust the code to accommodate it.

b Adjust the code in Figure 4.32 to process the updated array.

5 The class diagram

Learning outcomes

The material and exercises in this chapter will enable you to:

- Explain the role and purpose of the class diagram in the early phases of development

- Recognize different stages in building a class diagram

- Identify the objects and classes in a system and their attributes

- Construct a class diagram

- Write a data dictionary to support the class diagram

- Use packages to group related classes.

Key words you will find in the glossary:

- aggregation
- application domain
- association
- attribute
- class
- collaboration
- data dictionary
- domain model
- inheritance
- multiplicity
- noun analysis
- object
- operation
- package
- problem domain
- use case realization

Introduction

The class diagram is central to object-oriented analysis and design, it defines both the software architecture, i.e. the overall structure of the system, and the structure of every object in the system. We use it to model classes and the relationships between classes, and also to model higher-level structures comprising collections of classes grouped into packages. The class diagram appears through successive iterations at every stage in the development process. It is

Figure 5.1   *A first attempt to model classes in the Wheels system in a class diagram*

used first to model things in the application domain as part of requirements capture. Subsequently, with classes added which are part of the solution not the problem domain (e.g. interface classes), it is used to design a solution. Finally, with classes added to facilitate the implementation (e.g. buttons, windows, mouse-listeners, etc.), it is used to design the program code.

The UML notation for a class diagram. Figure 5.1 (repeated from Figure 4.11) shows a first attempt to model the classes in the Wheels system using the UML notation. The diagram shows which attributes all Customer and Bike objects should have; as we work through the stages of building a class diagram, we will uncover more.

Stages in building a class diagram

There are many different approaches to building a class diagram. What is an appropriate approach will depend on factors such as the size and type of system being developed, the experience and ability of the team, the working practices and procedures of the organization concerned. One way to approach the class diagram is by *use case realization*. In use case realization we look at each use case in turn and decide what classes we would need to provide the functionality modelled in the use case. The group of classes required by a use case is called a *collaboration*. When each use case has been analysed, the resulting collaborations are amalgamated into a unified class diagram. We will look at collaborations in Chapter 6, but for the moment we are going to use a different approach to developing the class diagram. We will develop a *domain model*, i.e. a class diagram that sets out to model all of the classes in the problem domain in one go, not use case by use case. Both approaches should eventually arrive at the same model.

Building a class diagram is essentially an iterative process; no one, no matter how experienced, gets it right first time. However, to begin with, it is useful to identify stages in the process of building the model and to approach the process sequentially, even if we know that in fact we will repeat some of the stages many times and do some of them in parallel. The stages listed below were originally proposed by Rumbaugh *et al.*, (1991) and have been widely used with minor adaptations ever since:

- Identify the objects and derive classes

- Identify attributes

- Identify relationships between the classes

- Write a data dictionary to support the class diagram

- Identify class responsibilities using CRC cards

- Separate responsibilities into operations and attributes

- Write process specifications to describe the operations.

In this chapter we will concentrate on the first four stages in this list; responsibilities and operations are covered in Chapter 6.

Identify the objects and derive classes

Class diagrams are a very useful way of modelling the structure of the objects in a system and the links between them. However, when we are trying to design a new software application, we don't know what the classes are in advance and we will often start by looking for objects before making decisions about what their class will be.

Objects come in different categories; being aware of the categories gives us an idea of the sorts of things to look for. Objects at the analysis stage will be things that have meaning in the application domain. They can be:

- People (such as customers, employees, students, librarians)

- Organizations (such as companies, universities, libraries)

- Physical things (such as books, bikes, products)

- Conceptual things (such as book loans and returns, customer orders, seating plans).

Various techniques can be used for object identification, none of them are foolproof, none can be guaranteed to produce a definitive list of objects and classes; they are just guidelines that might help. A good starting point is to look at the documentation about the system produced so far and to search for nouns in any description of the system requirements, preferably one that is complete and concise. It is a good idea to discuss your choice of objects with users who understand the application domain, and with colleagues who have experience in object analysis.

Object identification using noun analysis. Noun analysis is a rather long-winded technique for identifying objects. However, it is straightforward and reassuringly mundane if you are a bit unsure of what you are trying to do. The steps are as follows.

- First, find a complete but concise description of the system requirements. The Problem Definition (see Chapter 2) is often a good place to look. Use case descriptions are also useful for this purpose, although for a complete description of the system you would have to look at all of the use case descriptions.

- Pick out all of the nouns and noun phrases and underline them. This usually provides a rather long list of possible (or candidate) objects, many of which are obviously unsuitable and some of which are unsuitable in more subtle ways.

- Reject unsuitable candidates by applying a list of rejection criteria.

For our object analysis we will use the list of requirements produced at the end of Chapter 2, reproduced in Figure 5.2.

The new Wheels system must:

R1 keep a complete list of all bikes and their details including bike number, type, size, make, model, daily charge rate, deposit (this is already on the Wheels system)

R2 keep a record of all customers and their past hire transactions

R3 work out automatically how much it will cost to hire a given bike for a given number of days

R4 record the details of a hire transaction including the start date, estimated duration, customer and bike, in such a way that it is easy to find the relevant transaction details when a bike is returned

R5 keep track of how many bikes a customer is hiring so that the customer gets one unified receipt not a separate one for each bike

R6 cope with a customer who hires more than one bike, each for different amounts of time

R7 work out automatically, on the return of a bike, how long it was hired for, how many days were originally paid for, how much extra is due

R8 record the total amount due and how much has been paid

R9 print a receipt for each customer

R10 keep track of the state of each bike, e.g. whether it is in stock, hired out or being repaired

R11 provide the means to record extra details about specialist bikes.

Figure 5.2   Requirements for the Wheels system

The next step is to underline the nouns and noun phrases.[1]

R1   keep a complete <u>list of all bikes</u> and their <u>details</u> including <u>bike number, type, size, make, model, daily charge rate, deposit</u>; (this is already on the <u>Wheels system</u>)

R2   keep a <u>record of all customers</u> and their <u>past hire transactions</u>;

R3   work out automatically how much it will cost to hire a given <u>bike</u> for a given <u>number of days</u>

R4   record the <u>details of a hire transaction</u> including the <u>start date</u>, <u>estimated duration</u>, <u>customer</u> and bike, in such a way that it is easy to find the relevant transaction details when a bike is returned

R5   keep track of how many bikes a customer is hiring so that the customer gets one unified <u>receipt</u> not a separate one for each bike

R6   cope with a customer who hires more than one bike, each for <u>different amounts of time</u>

R7   work out automatically, on the <u>return of a bike</u>, how long it was hired for, how many days were originally paid for, how much extra is due

R8   record the <u>total amount due</u> and how much has been paid

R9   print a receipt for each customer

R10   keep track of the <u>state of each bike,</u> e.g. whether it is in stock, hired out or being repaired

R11   provide the means to record <u>extra details about specialist bikes</u>.

The candidate objects that result from this exercise are:

- list of bikes

- details of bikes: bike number, type, size, make, model, daily charge rate, deposit

- Wheels system

- record of customers

- past hire transactions

- bike

- number of days

- details of a hire transaction: start date, estimated duration

- customer

- receipt

---

1. *For simplicity, nouns are only underlined once, even if they appear several times.*

- different amounts of time

- return of a bike

- total amount due

- state of each bike

- extra details about specialist bikes.

We now examine the list of candidate objects and reject those that are unsuitable. Objects should be rejected if they are:

- *Attributes.* Sometimes it is clear that a noun is an attribute of an object rather than an object itself. *Bike number, type, size, make, model, daily charge rate and deposit* are clearly attributes of a bike object rather than objects in their own right. Similarly, hire transaction sounds like a possible object, with *start date* and *estimated duration* as its attributes. *Number of days* also sounds like an attribute as do *different amounts of time, total amount due* and *extra details about specialist bikes. Specialist bike,* however, sounds like an object. If in doubt ask yourself whether the noun you are considering would be likely to have attributes of its own. Would it have behaviour?

- *Redundant.* Sometimes the same concept appears in the text in different guises. Here *past hire transactions* and *hire transaction* are probably the same thing. *Different amounts of time, number of days* and *estimated duration* are probably the same thing – all three refer to the length of a hire (in any case they are attributes, not objects).

- *Too vague.* If we don't know exactly what is meant by a term it is unlikely to make a good class. For this reason we reject *return of a bike* as an object. Return of bike is really an event and features in our use case model. Any data we might need to store about bike returns (e.g. date of return) can probably be bundled with the data about hires.

- *Too tied up with physical inputs and outputs.* This refers to something that exists in the real world but is a product of the system or data input to the system and not an object in its own right. For example, a bill exists in the real world, but is something the system outputs from data it already stores and as such would not be modelled as a class. *Receipt* qualifies for rejection under this heading. *Receipt* is an output; it is also redundant as we either store or can calculate the details we would print on it. *List of bikes* also requires some consideration. If we have an object to represent each bike, we can use these objects to produce a list. *Bike,* therefore, is a good candidate object, but we can drop the list at this stage. The same applies to *record of customers* and *customer*.

- *Associations.* In the class diagram in Figure 5.1 *hires* is modelled as an association between Customer and Bike. Whether hires is an object or an association raises some interesting issues and we will postpone that decision until later. The general rule in this situation is that if there is data associated with the relationship (and in this case there is), then we probably want to model it as an object.

- *Outside the scope of the system.* In this category would be anything we have decided to be beyond the system boundary. For example, according to the Problem Definition in Chapter 2 the system will not cover payroll, personnel or general accounting.

- *Really an operation or event.* This criterion is quite confusing and should be treated with care. If a candidate object seems to have no data associated with it, then it might be better modelled as an operation on another class. Quite often, however, operations and events are modelled as objects. For example, hiring a bike might be described as an event but as there is associated data, start date and number of days, we are more likely to want to model it as an object (see below).

- *Represent the whole system.* It is not normally a good idea to have an object that represents the whole system; we want to divide the system into separate objects. *Wheels system* should be rejected for this reason.

That leaves us with the candidate objects:

- bike
- customer
- hire transaction
- specialist bikes.

We can use these objects to form the basis of our class diagram. Remember that class names are always singular – see Figure 5.3.

Figure 5.3   *Four candidate classes derived from noun analysis*

Figure 5.4   *Initial class diagram for the Wheels system*

Noun analysis gives us a good start, but it is important to remember that it is only a starting point and is very unlikely to produce a complete or satisfactory set of classes. Some objects simply may not appear in the requirements description in the guise of a noun. Iterations and further modelling will uncover other classes or might get rid of some of the classes. Just remember that at this stage the list of candidate classes is not cast in stone; common sense and an understanding of the application domain should never be abandoned.

It is interesting to compare this with our initial attempt at a class diagram in Figure 5.1 reproduced in Figure 5.4 for ease of comparison.

In Figure 5.4 *hires* is shown as a relationship, not a class. Object-oriented system developers are often faced with a decision about whether something is a class or an association; indeed, we have listed it above as one of the criteria for rejecting candidate objects. The reason we have not rejected hire as an object is that there is data associated with it. The requirements list in Figure 5.2 mentions *details of a hire transaction including the start date, estimated duration.* If there is data associated with an object, i.e. details about the object that we need to store for the system to work, then that is a good enough reason to make it a class at this stage.

There is another compelling reason for keeping Hire as a class. Wheels' customers pay for their hires in advance but sometimes keep the bikes longer than they paid for. To calculate how much they owe when they return the bike we need to store both the start date of a hire transaction and its estimated duration. If we store this information in the Customer object we will have to cater for storing multiple sets of dates because a customer may hire several bikes for different durations. If we store the data in the Bike object we might also find we are storing multiple dates as we want to keep a record of past hire transactions. Storing multiple sets of dates is difficult because we have to make messy decisions about how many attributes we need to design into a class. If we decide to store the dates in the Customer class we need to make a decision about the maximum number of bikes a customer is likely to hire. If we store

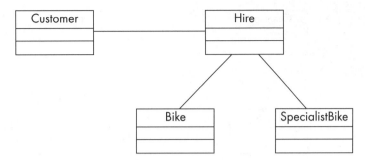

Figure 5.5   *Wheels class diagram with a Hire class included[a]*

a.   *We are only guessing about relationships at this stage, we will consider them later in the chapter.*

the dates in Bike we will have to decide how many times a bike is likely to be hired and how many past transactions we need to keep track of. If we get our estimates wrong we will be either wasting storage space or finding that we have to explain to an irate user why their brand new expensive system won't allow a customer who wants to hire 20 bikes for a birthday party to hire more than six bikes.

It is much simpler and less messy to store the dates in a Hire class associated with both the Customer class and the Bike class as in Figure 5.5. Each hire object will contain the attributes relating to only one bike and one customer.

The requirements list in Figure 5.2 indicates that our system is going to have to cope with customers who hire several bikes at once. A father may wish to hire two bikes for his two sons for the week at half-term, and two adult bikes for himself and his wife for the weekend only. We don't want the system to treat this as four separate transactions – see requirement R5 in Figure 5.2. The customer will expect to pay for all four bikes at once and have a single receipt. With the classes we have so far it's hard to see where to put data about payments and an operation to work out totals. The most obvious place is in Customer. However, Wheels have told us they want to store past transactions both for auditing purposes and so that, if a customer wants to hire the same bikes he had last time, we have a record of it (requirement R2). This would mean storing multiple sets of data about payments in Customer. It would be better to have a separate Payment class and store details about financial transactions there, as in Figure 5.6.

Identify the attributes

Many attributes will appear as nouns in the text being analysed. Sometimes we have to make difficult decisions about where to put

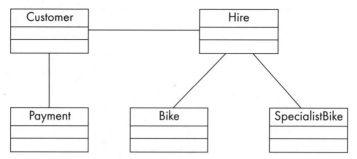

Figure 5.6   *Wheels class diagram with a Payment class added*

them. The simple rule is that attributes belong in the class that they describe.

Bike class. We have already decided that *bike number, type, size, make, model, daily hire rate* and *deposit* belong in the Bike class. The requirements list (R10) specifies that the system 'keep track of the state of each bike, e.g. whether it is in stock, hired out or being repaired'. We need to add an attribute *available* that can take these bike states as its values. This gives us the Bike class in Figure 5.7.

SpecialistBike class. The SpecialistBike class needs more or less the same attributes as Bike with the 'extra details about specialist bikes' mentioned in R11 of the requirements list. This refers to the type of specialist bike, e.g. penny farthing, tandem, unicycle etc., and the approximate date that this type of bike was used – its epoch, e.g. Victorian, early twentieth century, etc. Wheels make an insurance charge for specialist bikes; this amount must be recorded. This gives us the SpecialistBike class in Figure 5.8.

Hire class. We decided earlier that *start date* and *estimated duration* are attributes of Hire. If a bike is returned late, the cost of the extra time is deducted from the deposit; if the bike is returned damaged, a mechanic estimates the cost of the repair and this amount is

Bike
bike#
available
type
size
make
model
dailyHireRate
deposit

Figure 5.7   *Bike class*

SpecialistBike

bike#
available
type
size
make
model
dailyHireRate
deposit
specialistType
epoch
insurance

Figure 5.8   *SpecialistBike class*

deducted from the deposit. The amounts recorded are *latenessDeduction* and *damageDeduction*. It is not a good idea to store this information in Bike as we will have the problem of multiple sets of data – the bike may be returned late or damaged more than once. We would also have no way of knowing which customer they related to. If we store them in Customer, we potentially have multiple sets of data. The best place therefore is in Hire. It would be wise also to store the date the bike was actually returned as we know bikes are sometimes returned late. Storing this date will signal that the hire is no longer active. This gives us the Hire class in Figure 5.9, with the estimated duration represented as the attribute numberDays.

Hire

startDate
numberDays
dateReturned
latenessDeduction
damageDeduction

Figure 5.9   *Hire class*

Customer class. The requirements list makes no mention of attributes to be stored in the Customer class, but common sense would suggest we store at least a name, address and telephone number. Experience of other systems such as banking systems, library systems and store credit systems suggest that it will be useful for Wheels to have a unique identification number for each customer – a customer Id – see Figure 5.10.

Figure 5.10   *Customer class*

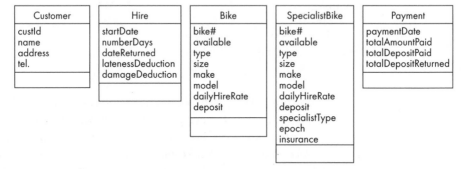

Figure 5.11   *Wheels class diagram with attributes but without operations or relationships*

Payment class. As far as the Payment class is concerned, it would seem sensible to record at least a payment date and the actual payments made: i.e. the total amount of deposit paid and the total amount paid for the hires. As Wheels deduct money from the deposit if a bike is damaged or late, we could also store the amount of deposit returned to the customer. This would give us the classes shown in Figure 5.11. It is not strictly necessary to store any of these totals, as they can all be calculated, but it seems sensible to keep some record of what was actually paid to facilitate any queries in the future.

Identify relationships between the classes

During analysis we have not yet got an exact notion of how objects will need to communicate with each other; the relationships that we include at this stage model real-life relationships that we think might be useful. We will not have an exact idea of the navigable paths we need to build in until after we have done the interaction diagrams (see Chapter 6).

Associations and multiplicity. As we have decided that we need a Hire class and that an object of this class holds data about the hiring of a bike, we will need an association between the Hire class and the Bike class. The multiplicity of the association needs a bit of

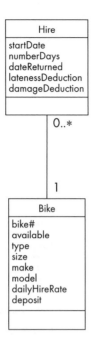

Figure 5.12   *One to many relationship between the Bike and Hire classes*

care; is the Hire object (:Hire[2]) for one Bike object (:Bike) or many? Requirement R6 (Figure 5.2) states that the system must 'cope with a customer who hires more than one bike, each for different amounts of time', therefore we might be dealing with more than one set of dates, but we only want one set per :Hire. Also the damageDeduction attribute in the Hire class relates to a specific bike. Therefore a :Hire is for one :Bike only. A :Bike, on the other hand, can be hired many times or may not be hired at all. The same applies to a SpecialistBike object. The relationship between Bike and Hire will therefore be one to many, as in Figure 5.12.

A :Customer can make many :Hires, but a :Hire is a specific transaction relating to just one :Customer. A :Payment is made by just one :Customer, but a :Customer can make many :Payments. There is no suggestion that one class is part of another one here, so there does not seem to be a reason to make any of these relationships aggregations. This gives us the associations shown in Figure 5.13.

Generalization and inheritance. When we are looking for generalization relationships in a diagram, we look for classes that share attributes and behaviour. Looking at the diagram in Figure 5.13, we can see that Bike and SpecialistBike share the

---

2. *Remember that an object of a class can be referred to in a number of ways, for example: a Hire object; an object of the Hire class; or :Hire.*

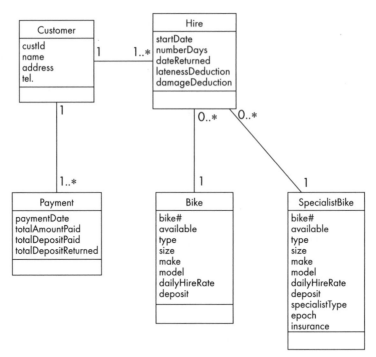

Figure 5.13   *Wheels class diagram with initial associations*

attributes: bike#, available, type, size, make, model, dailyHireRate and deposit. If we make SpecialistBike a subclass of Bike, it will inherit all of these attributes and add its distinctive attributes: specialistType, epoch and insurance. Examination of the possible values of type (mountain bike, racer, tourer, etc.) and specialistType (penny farthing, tandem, unicycle, etc.) show that they are just different sets of values for the same attribute, so we can keep type and get rid of specialistType, see Figure 5.14.

If we incorporate this inheritance relationship into the Wheels model, we get the class diagram in Figure 5.15. Notice that SpecialistBike inherits not only Bike's attributes and operations, but also its relationships to other classes. SpecialistBike therefore has a one to many relationship with Hire.

Write a data dictionary to support the class diagram

The UML does not provide a specific notation for constructing a data dictionary, but it is nonetheless important in any development project to have some agreed way of documenting the data and operations in the system. In the main UML models (such as the class, interaction and state diagrams) labels have to be short and detail about the data kept to a minimum, so that the model as a whole is uncluttered and readable. Detailed information about classes and their attributes is recorded in the data dictionary,

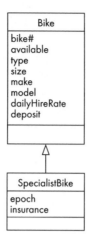

Figure 5.14   Inheritance relationship between Bike and SpecialistBike

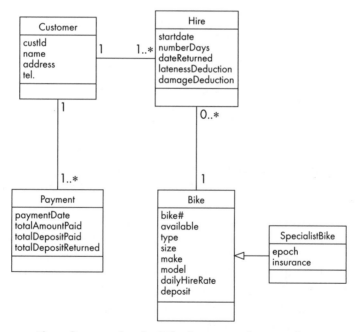

Figure 5.15   Class diagram for the Wheels system showing classes, attributes and relationships

which acts as a central repository with agreed terms and their meanings expressed in a standardized notation.

The data dictionary is constructed in parallel with the other models. Details are added to the dictionary definitions as more information becomes available in the same way that the class and other diagrams are enhanced and refined as development progresses. The main UML models are cross-referenced via entries in the data dictionary, which thus provides a valuable means of ensuring consistency between them.

The data dictionary notation that we use in this book is semi-formal, and suitable for documenting the data of a small information system, such as the Wheels case study. In this section we only cover classes and their attributes; describing operations is discussed in Chapter 6.

We want to be able to define classes in terms of their attributes including:

- The order in which they are listed (e.g. name, address, phone number)

- Whether an attribute is repeated (e.g. a customer may have more than one phone number)

- Any restrictions on the number of repetitions

- Whether an attribute is optional (e.g. a customer may or may not have an email address)

- The set of possible values for an attribute (e.g. in some businesses a customer may be individual or wholesale)

- Selection between alternative values for an attribute (e.g. a customer is either individual or wholesale).

We also want to be able to include comments where needed to explain some aspect of the definition.

One notation that allows us to do all these things is shown in Table 5.1.

Notice that in this notation most items are in lower case. An initial capital for the first word indicates that a class is being described (e.g. Customer). Where a description consists of more than one word, the words are run together with no spaces but with a capital letter at the start of the second and every subsequent new word, e.g. houseNumber. As an example, let us look at a simple definition of a customer.

$$\text{Customer} = \text{customerID} + \text{name} + \text{address} + \{\text{phone}\}_2 + (\text{email})$$

Notice that there is a restriction of two on the possible number of phone numbers; this is indicated by the subscript after the second curly bracket. If we want to indicate a minimum number of phone numbers, we can do this with a subscript before the first curly bracket. For example, $_1\{\text{phone}\}_2$ would mean that there had to be at least one phone number.

Table 5.1:   *Data dictionary notation*

Meaning	Symbol	Description	Example
consists of	=	introduces the definition of a data item	Customer ≐
and	+	joins components of the definition in sequence	Customer = name + address
one or more	{ }	attributes may be repeated; any restrictions on number of repetitions are shown by a subscript	Customer = name + address + {phone}$_2$
zero or one	( )	attribute is optional	Customer = name + address + {phone}$_2$ + (email)
alternatives	[ ]	selection is indicated by enclosing the alternatives in square brackets [ ]	Name = [initial | firstname] + surname
either..or	|	alternatives for selection in [ ] are separated by a vertical bar	
specific value	" "	indicates specific values	"individual", "wholesale"
...	comment	comments are enclosed between asterisks	Customer = name + address + {phone}$_2$ + (email) + ["individual" | "wholesale"] *Wholesale customers are entitled to special discounts*

Initially definitions are written at a high level, simply listing the attributes of the class, but as development progresses more details are added, as shown below.

Customer = customerID + name + address + {phone}$_2$ + (email)
customerID = {digit}6 *A customer ID is a 6 digit number*
name = title + [initial | firstName] + surname
address = (houseName) + houseNumber + street + town + county
          + postcode
phone = areacode + number
email = *if customer has an email address*

You can see from this example that a data dictionary is structured in the same way as a standard language dictionary. We could have included the extra details as part of the original definition of Customer as follows:

Customer = customerID + title + [initial | firstName] + surname +
        (houseName) + houseNumber + street + town +
        county + postcode + {areacode + number}$_2$ + (email)

However, this is clumsy and difficult to read; the structured approach that we showed above is much clearer.

There is still one more refinement that we may wish to make to the definition. The expression [initial | firstName] allows the system to record a single initial or first name for a customer, but not both. However, some businesses may wish to record customer names in different ways, for example: Lee Jones, L. Jones, Lee M. Jones, L. M. Jones, etc. We can cater for this in our definition by changing [initial | firstName] to {[initial | firstName]}. This allows a choice between either an initial or a name any number of times, and will allow all the variations that we need.

It is often useful to write data dictionary definitions of documents provided by clients during the early phases of development. This allows the developer to separate the information held in the document from the way it is presented. Figure 5.16 shows a receipt form as used in the current Wheels system.

When documenting something like this, it is best to divide it up into separate sections and then describe each of these in turn. This produces a definition that is clearly structured and easy to follow. For example, we can divide the Wheels receipt into the sections: title, customer details, hire details, and total as shown below.

Receipt = title + customerDetails + {hireDetails} *a customer may
        hire more than one bike at a time* + total
title = "Wheels Bikes Receipt for Hire" + receiptDate
customerDetails = customerName + customerAddress
hireDetails = bike# + bikeDescription + ratePerDay + no.OfDays
        + hireCost + deposit + totalCost
total = amountDue + "Paid with thanks"

We can decompose to further levels as needed, for example we could add:

bikeDescription = make + model + type + size

In general, the closer we get to implementation, the more details we need in the data dictionary.

Wheels Bikes

Receipt for Hire

Date _____

Customer name _____

Address   _____

            _____

Bike no.	Bike description	Rate per day	No. of days	Hire cost	Deposit	Total cost
Paid with thanks					Amount due	

Figure 5.16   Receipt form used in the current Wheels system

Packages

All but the simplest of systems are likely to have more classes than we can handle on one class diagram. *Packages* provide a mechanism for managing our models by grouping modelling elements. In Chapter 3 we saw that packages can be used to group use cases. Packages can also be used to group classes. We can use packages to assemble a related set of classes into a higher-level construct. The complete class diagram, therefore, can have many levels; where each level except the bottom one (which will have classes only) can consist of just packages or a mixture of packages and classes. Our

Figure 5.17   *A package representing the Wheels system*

Figure 5.18   *Package of classes in the 'Maintain bike list' collaboration*

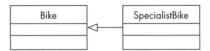

Figure 5.19   *Classes inside the 'Maintain bike list' package forming the 'Maintain bike list' collaboration*

top-level class diagram might consist only of packages. For a small system like Wheels, classes found at analysis can be grouped into one package, the system (see Figure 5.17).

Inside the system package would be all classes shown in the Wheels class diagram in Figure 5.15.

Classes should be grouped into packages on a logical basis. For example, classes are often grouped into collaborations: a collaboration consists of the classes used by a single use case (see Chapter 3). Figure 5.18 shows a package consisting of the classes in the 'Maintain bike list' collaboration.

Figure 5.19 shows the classes that are grouped inside the package.

Other logical groupings of classes are by subsystems, or by class type, e.g. interface classes, domain classes, control classes. These are discussed in Chapters 9 and 10.

Using the class diagram in system development

The class diagram is central to the development of an object-oriented system because it forms the basis for the structure of the software. Objects and classes are the basic building blocks of any object-oriented system. During analysis, the class diagram models classes in the problem domain. Features of the real-life objects that are of relevance to the system are modelled as attributes, and real-life links are modelled as relationships. During design activities we begin to think in terms of a software solution rather than just modelling the real-world situation. We add classes required by the logic of the solution that are not part of the real world, for example interface and control classes. The implementation model will add classes required to implement it, for example classes from the programming language's library such as mouse listeners, buttons and windows. However, the classes identified during analysis will still be in the code that implements the system.

The class diagram is the basis of the overall analysis model. Interaction diagrams (see Chapter 6) cannot be attempted until the class diagram has been constructed. Interaction diagrams identify the classes involved in producing the functionality of each use case. They specify, scenario by scenario, the messaging between objects that is required in the execution of the use cases. State diagrams (see Chapter 7) are also based on the class diagram. The state diagram models, class by class, all the things that can happen to an object and all its possible reactions. It focuses on one class of objects at a time and shows how all the scenarios affect it.

Common problems

1   Do the stages of building a class diagram have to be carried out in the same order as in the list?

As we said at the beginning of the chapter, there are many ways of building a class diagram. The list of stages is only a guideline, but it helps beginners to the subject to get started. Once you have constructed a number of class diagrams, your own experience will be the best guide as to how to proceed.

2   The Wheels class diagram does not contain any aggregation – why is that?

It is not compulsory to use aggregation, or any of the relationship constructs, in a class diagram. Aggregation is really only useful when there is an obvious 'consists-of' or 'is-made-up-of' relationship and it is important to document this. For example, in a restaurant system it might be useful to document that a set meal consists of three food courses and a drink. In the Wheels system there are no obvious aggregation relationships that it is important to record, so we have used association only.

3   How do I know what level of detail to go down to in a data dictionary?

This depends on how the data dictionary will be used. If it is to be used simply to document the system developer's understanding of the current system and to support discussions with the client, labels such as 'name' or 'date' will be self-explanatory; no more detail is required. During design, however, the developer is thinking ahead to the detail required in an automated system. Decisions have to be made that were unnecessary earlier, for example, about input and output formats for dates and how they are going to be represented internally.

Chapter summary

The class diagram defines the software architecture and the internal structure of the objects in an object-oriented system; the classes we model in the class diagram form the basis of the classes in the code. In this chapter we limit the discussion to the analysis class diagram; this only models classes which have meaning in the application domain. Classes relating to the design and implementation of the solution will be discussed in Chapters 9 and 10. The association relationships we identify in the analysis diagram model real-life relationships between objects and evolve through various iterations of the model to define the navigable paths between the objects. The inheritance relationships we identify clarify and simplify the model and allow us to build in some future-proofing of our system.

The stages in the construction of a class diagram are identifying objects and deriving classes, identifying attributes, identifying relationships, writing a data dictionary, identifying operations and writing operation specifications. In this chapter we cover the first four of these stages, relating to classes, attributes, relationships and the data dictionary. We also show how managing the model in larger systems can be facilitated by using a package to split classes into logical groups.

Bibliography

Bennett, S., McRobb, S. and Farmer, R. (2002) *Object-Oriented Systems Analysis and Design Using UML* (2nd edition), McGraw-Hill, London.

Britton, C. and Doake, J. (2000) *Object-Oriented Systems Development: A Gentle Introduction,* McGraw-Hill, London.

Fowler, M. (2000) *UML Distilled: A Brief Guide to the Standard Object Modeling Language* (2nd edition), Addison-Wesley, Reading, MA.

Larman, C. (1998) *Applying UML and Patterns: An Introduction to Object-Oriented Analysis and Design*, Prentice Hall, New Jersey.

Quatrani, T. (1998) *Visual Modeling with Rational Rose and UML*, Addison-Wesley, Reading, MA.

Rumbaugh, J., Blaha, M., Premerlani, W., Eddy, F. and Lorensen, W. (1991) *Object-Oriented Modeling and Design,* Prentice-Hall, Englewood Cliffs, NJ.

Stevens, P., with Pooley, R. (2000) *Using UML. Software Engineering with Objects and Components* (updated edition), Addison-Wesley, Harlow.

Quick check questions

You can find the answers to these in the chapter.

a The class diagram starts with classes that are part of the application domain. What sorts of classes are added during later phases of development?

b What is use case realization?

c What are the main stages in building a class diagram?

d List four categories of objects.

e List eight reasons for rejecting candidate objects when looking for classes.

f Give one reason for modelling a concept such as Hire as a class rather than as a relationship.

g What is the purpose of a data dictionary?

h What are packages? What are they used for?

Exercises

5.1 Suggest objects you would expect to find in the following systems:

a A system for a medical centre.

b A system for a video hire shop.

c A system for a car park which allows entry with an ID card.

d A system allocating equipment to local schools.

5.2   Identify the categories (people, organizations, physical things, conceptual things) of the objects you suggested in your answer to Question 5.1.

5.3   From the case study descriptions below, prepare a list of nouns for consideration as candidate objects. Reject those that would not form suitable objects, giving reasons for your rejection. List the remaining objects.

a   Mr Major, the town's only dentist, has a computer system to help him keep track of patients' appointments and dental treatment. Mr Major's receptionist makes appointments with patients either when they phone up or when they are back in the waiting room after treatment. Sometimes patients phone to cancel appointments or to change them. Mr Major keeps notes on the system about his patients' treatments – these are updated each time he sees a patient. The receptionist also makes out bills for patients and records payments on the system.

b   Your local railway station is going to install automatic ticket dispensing machines. Each machine will be able to give passengers up-to-date train timetable and ticket price information. The machines must also issue tickets and transfer statistics about ticket sales to a central computer system. Railway staff must be able to update ticket prices and timetable information.

5.4   Suggest attributes for the following classes:

a   A Customer in a banking system.

b   A library Member.

c   A university Lecturer in a system for a university human resources department.

d   A Student in a university enrolment system.

e   A Patient in a dentist's system.

5.5   Items a–f in Table 5.2 list object-oriented concepts. Items 1–6 list short definitions. Match the concept to the definition that best describes it.

5.6   What information appears on an object diagram (such as the one in Figure 4.7 in Chapter 4) that is not shown on a class diagram such as the one in Figure 5.15 (in this chapter)?

Table 5.2:   *Concepts and definitions for Exercise 5.5*

Concept	Definition
a) application domain	1. mechanism for grouping modelling items, e.g. classes
b) multiplicity	2. area of study, e.g. business application
c) domain model	3. group of classes relating to a single use case
d) collaboration	4. a class diagram that sets out to model all of the classes in the problem domain together (not in separate use cases)
e) noun analysis	5. describes the number of instances allowed to participate in an association or aggregation relationship
f) package	6. identifying objects and classes from nouns in a written description of the problem

5.7   This exercise will help you to revise aggregation and inheritance.

An art gallery organizes exhibitions that consist of exhibits. An exhibit may be an oil painting, a watercolour, a piece of sculpture or a photograph. Draw a class diagram to represent this information.

5.8   Study the class diagram in Figure 5.20 and answer the questions that follow it.

a   Does a customer have to place an order?

b   What does an order consist of?

c   Can a payment be for more than one order?

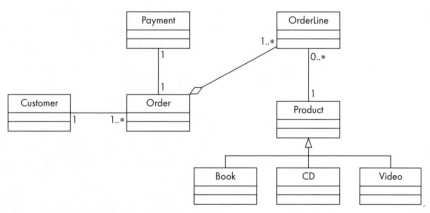

Figure 5.20   *Class diagram for Exercise 5.8*

d   How many products are there in an order line?

e   What is the relationship between a CD and a product?

f   Can a product appear on more than one order line?

5.9   This exercise will help you to construct a class diagram. Build up the diagram by drawing the separate parts according to the information given below.

a   A football club has two grounds.

b   Each ground consists of two or three pitches and a club-house.

c   The football club has lots of members.

d   A member may be a playing member or a social member, and a playing member may be an adult member or a junior member.

e   A playing member may be chosen to play for one or more teams, and each team has 11 playing members.

f   Each team plays a number of fixtures.

5.10   A large film organization has several cinemas, which each consists of up to ten separate screens. Filmgoers can book seats in person, by phone or on the Internet. The organization keeps a record of the names and addresses of regular filmgoers for marketing purposes. Draw a class diagram to represent this information.

5.11   a   The Keep Well Medical Centre is run by five doctors with three practice nurses. When a patient calls for an appointment, he or she usually sees the same doctor, but at busy times patients may see any of the doctors or nurses. Once a patient has been seen by the doctor or nurse, the medical records are updated and the doctor may also write out a prescription for the patient. Draw a class diagram to represent this information.

b   Sometimes the doctor considers that the patient needs further tests. These tests may be routine or intensive; they are carried out at one of the local hospitals. Extend the diagram that you drew for part (a) to include this extra information.

5.12   Study the class diagram in Figure 5.21 and answer the questions that follow it.

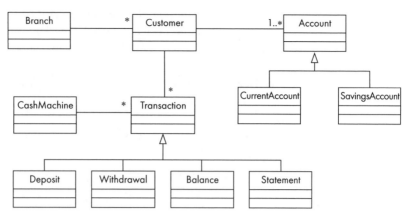

Figure 5.21   *Class diagram for Exercise 5.12[a]*

    a. Remember that where the multiplicity is one only, the '1' symbol may be omitted (see Chapter 4).

a   Does a customer have to have at least one account?

b   Can a customer have both current and savings accounts?

c   Is a deposit part of a transaction or a kind of transaction?

d How is a cash machine related to a branch?

5.13 Oscar's Films is a shop that rents out films on video and DVD. Oscar has a large number of customers and keeps a record of the name and address of everyone who hires a video or DVD. Regular customers can become members of the shop; this entitles them to certain privileges, such as being able to take out more films at one time. In the case of members, Oscar also keeps a record of their membership number, phone number and the types of film they like to watch. He also keeps records of all films and the copies he stocks of each.

a   Draw a class diagram to represent this information.

b   Write a data dictionary description for Member.

5.14 Study the data dictionary definition below and answer the questions that follow it.

Order = orderHeader + {orderLine} + total
orderHeader = customerDetails + (deliveryAddress)
          +dateRequired
customerDetails = (title) + 1{[firstName | initial]}$_2$ +
            surname + customerAddress + phone + (email)

orderLine = product# + productDescription + quantity +
productCost + costOfLine
total = costOfOrder + (deliveryCharge) + amountOwing

a   Does a delivery address have to be recorded?

b   Does the date required have to be recorded?

c   How many first names or initials are recorded for each customer?

d   Can an order have more than one order line?

e   The delivery charge only applies if a customer lives more than ten miles away. How would you document this in the definition?

f   It has been decided to modify the order line part of the definition to include product category. This can take one of five values: men's, women's, children's, outdoor, sport. Add this information to the data dictionary definition.

5.15   A textbook consists of a preface, between six and ten chapters, an optional glossary and a bibliography. Each chapter has an introduction, several sections and a summary, and the glossary contains lots of terms with their definitions. Write a data dictionary definition for a textbook as described here.

5.16   Figure 5.22 shows an example card used to record details of offers for properties in an estate agent's business. Write a data dictionary definition of the information held on the cards.

Find-a-Home Estate Agents

Vendor name: _____ .

Vendor address: _____

_____

Vendor phone no: _____

Property address: _____

Property type: detached   semi   terraced   bungalow   flat

Property price: _____

Offers:

Name	Contact phone	Offer price	Outcome

Figure 5.22   *Estate agent's card for recording offers on properties*

6 Identifying functionality: CRC cards and interaction diagrams

Learning outcomes

The material and exercises in this chapter will enable you to:

- Describe the role of CRC cards in identifying responsibilities and allocating them to classes

- Identify separate operations within a class responsibility

- Explain the purpose of interaction diagrams

- Draw a simple sequence diagram

- Draw a simple collaboration diagram

- Write a process specification to describe the functionality delivered by an operation.

Key words you will find in the glossary:

- algorithm
- class-responsibility-collaboration (CRC) card
- collaboration
- collaboration diagram
- constructor
- decision table
- decision tree
- interaction diagram
- lifeline
- message
- multiobject
- object activation
- operation specification
- package
- reflexive message
- responsibility
- return
- scenario
- sequence diagram
- signature

Introduction

In Chapter 3 we discussed how use case analysis can help identify and document, from the user's perspective, what the system has to do. In Chapters 4 and 5 we discussed how to identify objects and classes and their attributes using noun analysis and how to model relationships between classes. We made a list of the stages in the development of a class diagram and applied the first four stages to the Wheels system. The remaining three stages are: to identify class responsibilities using CRC cards, to separate responsibilities into operations and attributes, and to write process specifications to describe the operations.

In this chapter we discuss how to use the CRC technique to allocate responsibilities to classes and work out the interaction between classes that is required to implement the use case scenarios. We then discuss how to turn these high-level responsibilities into operations on classes and how to describe the functionality of the operations using process specifications. We introduce interaction diagrams and discuss how they are used to document the details of the interactions we identified using the CRC technique. Interaction diagrams also give us a much more precise idea of the associations between classes that are necessary to allow the requisite message passing between objects. In this chapter we also explain the difference between the two types of interaction diagram, sequence and collaboration, and discuss where to use each.

Identifying operations using the CRC card technique

As we saw in Chapter 5, objects can be identified from nouns in a description of the problem domain. In the same way it is possible to identify operations on classes by picking out verbs and verb phrases from the problem description. Phrases that occur in the requirements for the Wheels system (see Figure 5.2), such as 'keep a record of all customers' or 'work out automatically how much it will cost to hire a given bike', tell us that operations will be needed to fulfil these functions. However, analysing verb phrases in this way turns out to be an inefficient method of uncovering operations and allocating them to classes – a more effective and popular approach is to use CRC cards.

CRC (class-responsibility-collaboration) cards are not officially part of the UML, but are regarded as a valuable technique that works extremely well with it. CRC was popularized by a development method called Responsibility Driven Design. The method and the book that describes it (Wirfs-Brock *et al.*, 1990) are both quite old now, but the idea of thinking about a class in terms of the responsibilities it has to fulfil and the technique of CRC cards are both well regarded and widely used in object-oriented development today. We will look first at the concept of a responsibility and how this leads to identifying operations, and we will then describe how the CRC card technique works in practice.

Class responsibilities and operations

At this stage of constructing a class diagram, our aim is to look at the overall functionality of the system, as identified in the use cases, and divide it up between the classes that we have identified in the class diagram. Each class is regarded as having certain responsibilities to provide services to the user of the system (such as maintaining a customer record) or to another class (such as supplying data for a calculation). Each responsibility identifies something that a class is expected to do; it is an obligation on the class to provide some kind of service.

CRC cards

The aim of the CRC card technique is to divide the overall functionality of the system into responsibilities which are then allocated to the most appropriate classes. Once we know the responsibilities of a class, we can see whether it can fulfil them on its own, or whether it will need to collaborate with other classes to do this.

The actual CRC cards are usually index cards about 10 cm × 15 cm in size, and each card represents one class in the system. The size of the card is important because it restricts the amount that can be written on it. On the front of the card is a high-level description of the class, and the back of the card records the class name, responsibilities and collaborations (if any). An example of a CRC card for the Customer class in the Wheels system is shown in Figure 6.1. We can see from the figure that the Customer class has two responsibilities; it is able to carry out the first of these (Provide customer information) on its own, but in order to carry out the second responsibility (Keep track of hire transactions) it will have to collaborate with the Hire class.

Customer	
Responsibility	Collaborator
Provide customer information	
Keep track of hire transactions	Hire

Figure 6.1   *CRC card for the Customer class in the Wheels system*

This size of card is used rather than a sheet of A4 paper to encourage system developers to restrict the size of each class in terms of the number of its responsibilities. Good object-oriented design depends on having small cohesive classes, each of which has limited, but well-defined functionality. The CRC card also encourages developers to specify responsibilities at a high level rather than write lots of low-level operations. The general rule is that no class should have more than three or four responsibilities.

One of the most effective ways of using CRC cards is in group role-play. Each member takes the role of an object of one of the classes in the system, and the group then enacts the events that take place during a typical scenario. As each responsibility arising from the scenario is identified, it is allocated to the most suitable object. If a responsibility cannot be fulfilled by the existing objects, a new object (and therefore class) will have to be identified. The aim is to minimize the number and complexity of the messages that need to be passed between the objects, and ultimately to produce classes that have a clear purpose and are internally coherent. This method of using CRC cards is popular with both developers and clients as it tends to promote ideas and facilitate discussions. CRC cards do not involve any special notation and so are easily accessible to clients and users of the system.

Figure 6.2 (repeated from Chapter 3) shows a typical scenario from the 'Issue bike' use case. In this figure, where we identify a responsibility of the system, we have added the object (in bold, e.g. **:Bike**) that will carry it out. This illustrates how the overall functionality of the 'Issue bike' use case will be divided up between the classes in the system.

Although it does not feature in this scenario, which models only the user's view of the system, we also know that we need a :Hire object to record details about the hire transaction (see requirement R4 in Figure 5.2: record the details of a hire transaction including the start date, estimated duration, customer and bike). Collectively, the objects that interact to execute a use case are known as a collaboration; the collaboration for the 'Issue bike' use case is shown in Figure 6.3.

Software developers find that the simplicity of CRC cards, their lack of detail, make them an ideal tool for exploring alternative ways of dividing responsibilities between classes. It's easy to scrap one design and start again without agonizing about the amount of work that is being discarded. Another way of exploring alternatives is to use sequence diagrams, which are discussed later in this chapter. In practice, however, sequence diagrams show too much detail and are too slow to draw to be useful for this purpose. They are much more useful for documenting the detail of design decisions once these have been reached using CRCs.

- Stephanie arrives at the shop at 9.00am one Saturday and chooses a mountain bike

- Annie sees that its number is 468

- Annie enters this number into the system

- The system confirms that this is a woman's mountain bike and displays the daily rate (£2) and the deposit (£60) (**:Bike**)

- Stephanie says she wants to hire the bike for a week

- Annie enters this and the system displays the total cost £14 + £60 = £74 (**:Bike**)

- Stephanie agrees this

- Annie enters Stephanie's name, address and telephone number into the system (**:Customer**)

- Stephanie pays the £74

- Annie records this on the system and the system prints out a receipt (**:Payment collaborating with :Customer**)

- Stephanie agrees to bring the bike back by 5.00pm on the following Saturday.

Figure 6.2   *Scenario for the 'Issue bike' use case showing the objects that will carry out the different responsibilities*

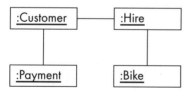

Figure 6.3   *Collaboration of objects required by the 'Issue bike' use case scenario in Figure 6.2*

Applying the CRC method to the Wheels classes in Figure 6.3 yields the set of responsibilities shown in Figure 6.4.

Deriving operations from CRC responsibilities

As we start to move from analysis to design we need more detail about how class responsibilities are going to be carried out. This means that we need to specify the responsibilities in terms of individual operations and attributes; we must ensure that each class has the data and operations needed to fulfil its responsibilities in the way that the user requires. We demonstrate this for the

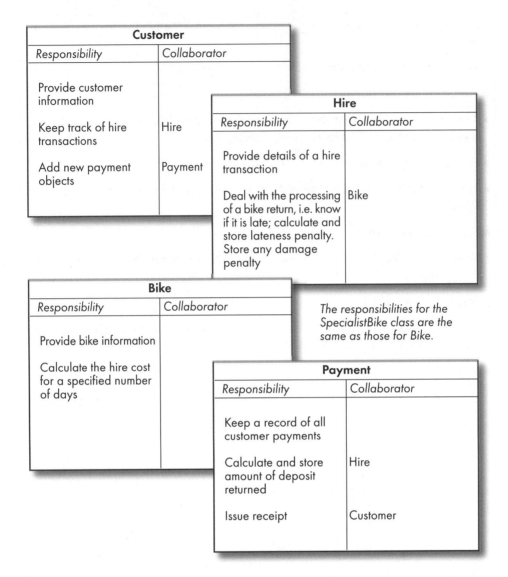

The responsibilities for the SpecialistBike class are the same as those for Bike.

Figure 6.4   CRC cards for the Wheels system

'Issue bike' use case, using the use case description to guide us (see Figure 6.5), as it is more general than the scenario.

From the use case description in Figure 6.5, we can see that issuing a bike involves the following tasks.

1   We need to be able to input to the system a bike number (all numbers are stencilled on the bikes) and retrieve the details of this bike to confirm that it is the bike the customer has chosen and to inform the customer of the hire and deposit charges. To do this, we need an operation findBike(), which takes bike number as a parameter, findBike(bike#). We know from the CRC analysis that

Use case: Issue bike
Preconditions: 'Maintain bike list' must have been executed
Actors: Receptionist
Goal: To hire out a bike

Overview:
When a customer comes into the shop they choose a bike to hire. The
Receptionist looks up the bike on the system and tells the customer how
much it will cost to hire the bike for a specified period. The customer pays,
is issued with a receipt, then leaves with the bike.

Cross-reference:
R3, R4, R5, R6, R7, R8, R9, R10

Typical course of events:

Actor action	System response
1 The customer chooses a bike	
2 The Receptionist keys in the bike number	3 Displays the bike details including the daily hire rate and deposit
4 Customer specifies length of hire	
5 Receptionist keys this in	6 Displays total hire cost
7 Customer agrees the price	
8 Receptionist keys in the customer details	9 Displays customer details
10 Customer pays the total cost	
11 Receptionist records amount paid	12 Prints a receipt

Alternative courses:

Steps 8 and 9   The customer details are already in the system so the
Receptionist needs only to key in an identifier and the
system will display the customer details.

Steps 7–12   The customer may not be happy with the price and may
terminate the transaction

Figure 6.5   *Use case description for 'Issue bike'*

providing information about bikes is the responsibility of the Bike
class, so findBike() should be an operation on Bike, allowing us to
retrieve information from the appropriate bike object.

2 We then want to be able to find out the hire cost for a specific
number of days' hire. This again is the responsibility of the Bike
class, so we need another operation on Bike, getCharges(no.Days).

3 The next step is to record the customer details. Knowing about
customers is the responsibility of the Customer class. We
need an operation recordDetails(custID, name, address, tel).

Alternatively, we could do this by using a constructor, which is an operation that creates a new object of a class.

4 The system is required to record what the customer has paid, both in hire charges and as a deposit. The system must also print out a receipt, sometimes for more than one bike. These are both the responsibility of the Payment class. We need an operation on Payment, calcTotalPayment(), which will add up all the hire fees and put them in the Payment attribute totalAmountPaid, and add up all the deposits due and put them all in totalDepositPaid. We also need an operation issueReceipt() that will print out a receipt in the required format. If we want to print the customer's name and address on the receipt, we need to retrieve these from the relevant Customer object.

5 Requirement R4 (see Figure 5.2) states that we must record the details of a hire transaction including the start date and estimated duration. This is not part of the user's view of the system, so is not mentioned in the use case description. However, it should be done at an appropriate point in the proceedings. It is the responsibility of the Hire class to record these details; we need an operation to create a new Hire object and record the details. This could be done by a constructor Hire() with the parameters startDate, no.Days.

By working through the responsibilities identified from the CRC cards, we have identified the operations needed to fulfil the functionality of the 'Issue bike' use case and allocated them to the appropriate classes.

At this stage, the classes and operations are as follows. We have added constructors for all of the classes.

Bike	findBike(bike#)
	getCharges(no.Days)
	Bike()
Customer	recordDetails(custID, name, address, tel)
	Customer()
Payment	calcTotalPayment()
	issueReceipt()
	Payment()
Hire	Hire(startDate, no.Days)

We now need to work through all the other use cases in the same way to identify all the operations required to fulfil the functionality of the system and then add these to the class diagram that we drew in Chapter 5 (see Figure 5.15). The class diagram with all the attributes and operations is shown in Figure 6.6.

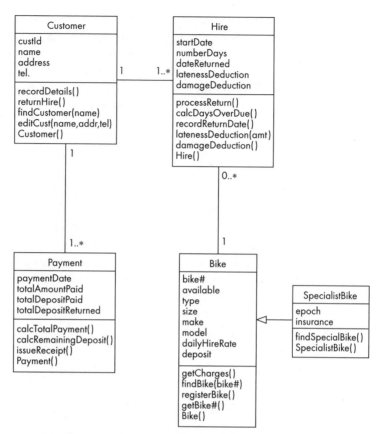

Figure 6.6   *Completed class diagram with attributes and operations*

Interaction diagrams

We have already mentioned in Chapter 4 that objects collaborate to achieve the functionality required of them by sending messages. Interaction diagrams model the messaging between a collaboration of objects that will take place in the execution of a specific scenario.

By the time we come to do the interaction diagrams we have already done a lot of analysis: we know what the system has to do, we know about the classes and attributes, and we have had our first real ideas about the nature of the relationships between classes – they have to be able to support the collaborations between objects that we specified in the CRC analysis. We have also refined the broad outlines of the class responsibilities into a set of operations and attributes that enable the classes to fulfil their responsibilities.

However, although we now have an idea of which objects are needed to produce the required behaviour and a high-level view of how objects need to collaborate to do this, we have no real idea of the sequence of messages this involves. Use case scenarios describe the functionality of a use case in terms of a sequence of events. We need to revisit the sequence of events in each scenario, this time looking at them in terms of the messages between objects spawned by each event. This is what interaction diagrams do. There are two types of interaction diagram: sequence and collaboration. Each shows more or less the same information, but with a different emphasis. We shall describe each in turn.

Sequence diagrams

When students who are new to object-oriented technology, especially those who have been trained in procedural methods, first meet object-oriented code, they are staggered by the way the flow of control jumps about on the page. In procedural programming, the sequence of execution proceeds in an orderly fashion from the top of a page of code to the bottom, with only the odd jump off to a procedure. Quite the opposite happens in the execution of an object-oriented program; the sequence of control jumps from object to object in an apparently random manner. This is because, while the code is structured into classes, the sequence of events is dictated by the use case scenarios. Even for those experienced in object technology, it is very hard to follow the overall flow of control in object-oriented code. Programmers, maintainers and developers need a route map to guide them; this is provided by the sequence diagram. The specification of the functionality in a sequence diagram is literally a sequence of messages, but the object-oriented code underlying the sequence of functionality in the diagram jumps about because the code is structured into classes not functions.

Sequence diagrams show clearly and simply the flow of control between objects required to execute a scenario. A scenario outlines the sequence of steps in one instance of a use case from the user's side of the computer screen, a sequence diagram shows how these steps translate into messaging between objects on the computer's side of the screen. We will illustrate this by walking through a simple scenario, Figure 6.7 (repeated from Figure 6.2), translating it into a sequence diagram.

As we saw in Figure 6.3 the objects required by the 'Issue bike' use case are :Bike, :Customer, :Hire and :Payment. The sequence diagram displays this collaboration horizontally across the page as in Figure 6.8.

The order in which the objects appear is not important. The Receptionist icon is the actor involved in the 'Issue bike' use case. As far as interaction diagrams are concerned, actor is treated as a special sort of object. On a sequence diagram produced during analysis she represents the system interface – she inputs information and receives the output from the system. The dashed vertical line below each object symbol is called the object's *lifeline*. It represents the object's life for the duration of the scenario we are enacting. A message is represented as a labelled arrow from one

- Stephanie arrives at the shop at 9.00am one Saturday and chooses a mountain bike

- Annie sees that its number is 468

- Annie enters this number into the system

- The system confirms that this is a woman's mountain bike and displays the daily rate (£2) and the deposit (£60)

- Stephanie says she wants to hire the bike for a week

- Annie enters this and the system displays the total cost £14 + £60 = £74

- Stephanie agrees this

- Annie enters Stephanie's name, address and telephone number into the system

- Stephanie pays the £74

- Annie records this on the system and the system prints out a receipt

- Stephanie agrees to bring the bike back by 5.00pm on the following Saturday.

Figure 6.7   Successful scenario for the use case 'Issue bike'

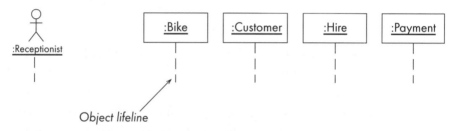

Figure 6.8   Collaboration objects for 'Issue bike' in sequence diagram format

object lifeline (the sender) to another (the recipient). The sequence of messages is read from the top of the page to the bottom, i.e. the time ordering of the messages goes from top to bottom.

The convention for object labelling is the same as for object diagrams (see Chapter 4), i.e. objectName :ClassName where either objectName or :ClassName may be omitted.

As an example, we will now convert the scenario in Figure 6.7 into a sequence diagram. This process is described in the steps below.

1   Stephanie arrives at the shop at 9.00am one Saturday and chooses a mountain bike

2   Annie sees that its number is 468

3   Annie enters this number into the system

4   The system confirms that this is a woman's mountain bike and displays the daily rate (£2) and the deposit (£60).

- Steps 1 and 2 do not require the system to do anything.

- In step 3 Annie, in her role as Receptionist, enters the bike number into the system. We represent this step in a sequence diagram (Figure 6.9) using the findBike() operation we identified from the class responsibilities.

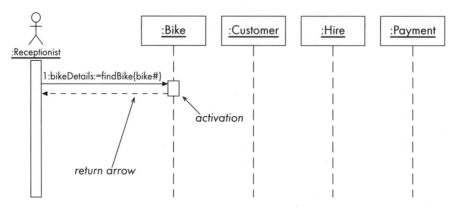

Figure 6.9   *Fragment of sequence diagram*

- The Receptionist sends the message findBike(bike#) to the relevant bike object, the one whose bike number matches the one she has input.

- For this to work, the target object, :Bike, must understand the message. This means that it must correspond to an operation on the Bike class.

- Sometimes we want to show the value that is returned in response to a message. Returned values are usually shown on the message line. The returned value is assigned to a variable. In this case the value returned by findBike() is assigned to bikeDetails (see step 4).

- The message has a number. On sequence diagrams the numbers are optional as the order is implicit in the sequence in which messages are drawn.

- Return of control can be indicated in UML by a dashed arrow. Return arrows are optional. Notice that the return arrow does not have a number, it is not a new message but models the return of control to the sending object.

- Object *activation* is shown by a thin rectangle on the object's lifeline. An object becomes active as soon as it receives a message. This means that the object is computing; processing is taking place in the object as the invoked operation executes. The activation continues until the operation finishes processing when control returns to the object that sent the message. If an active object, in turn, sends a message, it remains active while it waits for a response. While it waits for a response it cannot, itself, do any computing. Showing activation is an optional feature of sequence diagrams.

- A lot of detail is omitted on a diagram that is drawn during analysis. It says nothing about how the Receptionist manages to send a message to the :Bike. In fact when we get to the design version of this diagram, we will use an interface object, which will offer options to the user and translate them into messages to objects.

- The analysis diagram also omits any detail about how the matching bike object is found. At this stage we can take it on trust that it is found and leave the detail of how this happens to the designer (see Chapter 9).

The next two steps are:

5   Stephanie says she wants to hire the bike for a week

6   Annie enters this and the system displays the total cost £14 + £60 = £74.

Using the getCharges() operation with the parameter (no.Days) (see Figure 6.10) we can ask :Bike to work out the cost for the required period. The system is organized in such a way that the customer has the opportunity to see the total cost before being committed to the transaction. Only once the customer has agreed to the cost do we record details about the customer and the hire.

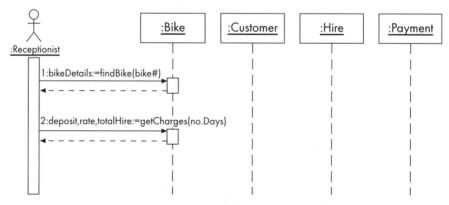

Figure 6.10   Fragment of sequence diagram

The getCharges() operation calculates and returns the deposit, daily hire rate and total amount to be paid (deposit + (no.Days * dailyHireRate)). deposit and dailyHireRate are attributes of :Bike.

The next few steps in the scenario:

7   Stephanie agrees this

8   Annie enters Stephanie's name, address and telephone number into the system.

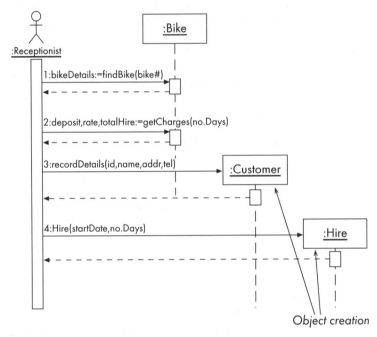

Figure 6.11   Fragment of sequence diagram with :Customer and :Hire added

- Once Stephanie has agreed to hire the bike at the rates quoted (which does not affect the system), we can start recording her details.

- Stephanie is a new customer, so the system must create a new Customer object and send it details about Stephanie (see Figure 6.11). We use the recordDetails() operation to do this with the arguments: id, name, addr, tel.

- The UML notation for a new object is to show the creating operation being sent to the object symbol rather than its lifeline.

- Although this is not mentioned in the scenario, we also have to record the details about the hire. This means we need to create a new Hire object and record the start date of the hire and its duration in days. We can do this using the Hire class constructor, Hire(startDate, no.Days).

- Again, a lot of detail is omitted from the diagram. We are not saying anything about where the parameters for the hire constructor come from. We wouldn't want the Receptionist to have to enter the number of days again, so presumably, some sort of interface or control object will deal with holding on to these details when they were entered the first time.

The last three steps in the scenario are: .

9 Stephanie pays the £74

10 Annie records this on the system and the system prints out a receipt

11 Stephanie agrees to bring the bike back by 5.00pm on the following Saturday

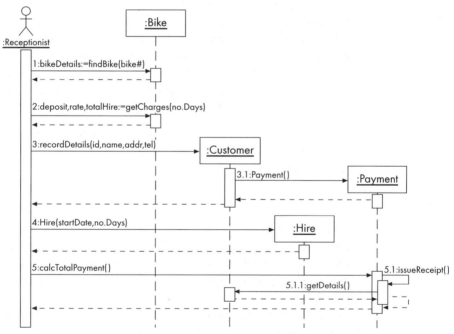

Figure 6.12   *Complete sequence diagram for the 'Issue bike' scenario*

- The system is required to record what the customer has paid, both in hire charges and as a deposit. A Payment object will calculate how much the customer owes and record these figures. It makes sense to create a Payment object from the Customer object, so that they are permanently linked, see Figure 6.12.

- Notice that the message from :Customer to :Payment is numbered 3.1 rather than 4. The UML numbering style for interaction diagrams emphasizes the nesting of the messages, rather than the numerical sequence. This is to make it clear which object is calling which.

- calcTotalPayment() will scoop up the total hire fees and total deposits paid and record them in totalAmountPaid and totalDepositPaid. How it does this is left to the designer.

- As it executes, the calcTotalPayment() operation calls issueReceipt() which is another operation on the Payment class; this is known as a *reflexive message*. The Payment object is already active, so this second activation is shown as a new activation box on top of the existing one.

- As the issueReceipt() operation is executing, it sends a message to :Customer to retrieve the customer name and address so that it can print them on the receipt.

- In Figure 6.12 all returns are shown so that you can clearly see the nesting of operations and how control returns eventually to the sending objects. In fact return arrows are usually omitted unless they add meaning to the diagram. Control is always returned to the sending object as soon as the receiving object ceases to be active. The activation boxes tell us how long an object is active, so we can assume the returns. Figure 6.13 shows us the same diagram without the return arrows.

- Notice that :Customer remains active while it sends a message to :Payment. It ceases to be active only when it returns control to the interface.

Collaboration diagrams

Collaboration diagrams show pretty much the same information as sequence diagrams. In fact most CASE tools will automatically generate a collaboration diagram from a sequence diagram or vice versa.

The collaboration diagram version of Figure 6.13 is shown in Figure 6.14.

Although this diagram contains much the same information as the diagram in Figure 6.13, it is obviously different in a number of ways.

- Messages are not shown in time sequence, so numbering becomes essential to indicate the order of the messages

- Links between objects are explicitly modelled, which is not the case with the sequence diagram

- Messages are grouped together on the object links

- Messages are shown as text labels with an arrow that points from the client (the object sending the message) to the server (the object providing the response)

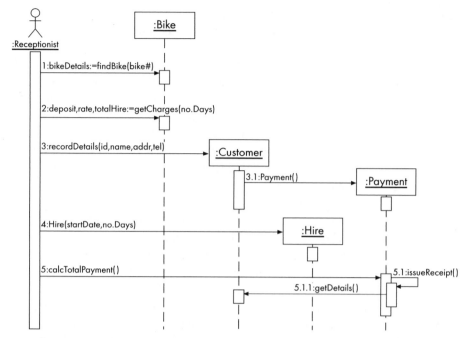

Figure 6.13   *Complete sequence diagram for the 'Issue bike' scenario without returns*

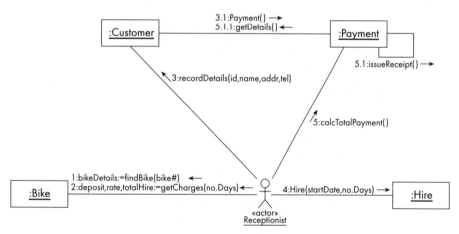

Figure 6.14   *Collaboration diagram for the 'Issue bike' scenario*

- Unlike sequence diagrams, returns are never modelled in a collaboration diagram

- In Figure 6.14, the message issueReceipt() is a reflexive message, i.e. a message from :Payment to itself. A link is modelled from :Payment to itself and the message goes along the link. On the sequence diagram this is shown as a nested activation.

Using sequence and collaboration diagrams

As sequence and collaboration diagrams are logically equivalent (they display the same information), there is no point in drawing both at any given stage. Both types of diagram convert a textual scenario into a graphical view of the flow of events, and both can be shown at varying levels of detail. If either diagram gets too cluttered with messages we can choose to model only the main flow of messages. Both diagrams can be used to represent the functionality of the system at different levels, for example to illustrate how a use case is realized or to show the workings of a complicated operation.

The main advantage of the sequence diagram is its ability to represent the passage of time graphically. The order of messages is very clear: a sequence diagram reads from top to bottom. It is, of course, possible to figure out the sequence of messages from the numbers on a collaboration diagram, but it is not so intuitively clear. Sequence diagrams can also include return arrows; collaboration diagrams never show return arrows. Another feature that can be added to a sequence diagram is object activation, showing when the object is active. Collaboration diagrams don't have the equivalent of activations.

The special feature of collaboration diagrams is that they include explicit links between objects. A message from one object to another means that there should be an association between the classes to which they belong. In a collaboration diagram this association between classes is represented by an explicit link between the objects of the classes (for example, the link between :Customer and :Payment in Figure 6.14). Sequence diagrams do not explicitly show links, although an underlying link can be assumed or the message could not be sent. Collaboration diagrams are also useful when you want to view the complete set of messages from the point of view of one object. This is valuable when you are preparing a state diagram (see Chapter 7), since the state diagram needs to know everything that can happen to a class of objects.

There are no hard and fast rules about whether to use a sequence or a collaboration diagram in any particular situation. Some people like to use sequence diagrams early in the development process, as their layout tends to be easier for users to follow, and collaboration diagrams later on since they map more clearly onto the class diagram, but in the end the type of diagram used is a matter of individual choice.

Model consistency

Interaction diagrams bring together many existing models and modelling elements: from the use case model, the use cases, the actors, use case scenarios and descriptions; from the class

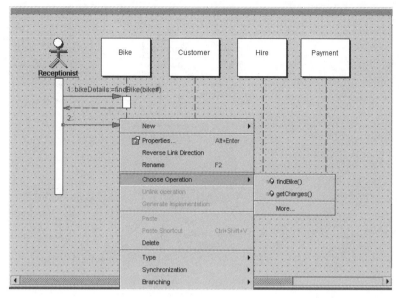

Figure 6.15   *Screen offering developer a choice of known operations for a message label*

diagram, the objects involved in each scenario and the operations on classes. A good CASE tool (see Chapter 1) will support model consistency by allowing the developer to link the objects on the interaction diagram to a list of classes it knows about from the class diagram. Similarly, it allows the developer to choose a label for the message arrow from a list of operations defined on the target object's class. Figure 6.15 shows a CASE tool offering a choice of operations (findBike() and getCharges()) for message number 2. The operations findBike() and getCharges() are defined on the class Bike in the class diagram.

Sequence diagrams are also useful for checking existing models; we may find, when doing the sequence diagrams, that we need an extra operation, or that we never use one that we did specify. A good CASE tool will allow us to add or delete operations and will update models (such as the class diagram) that are affected by our decision.

Using packages in interaction diagrams

On complicated interaction diagrams it is sometimes useful to suppress some of the details. The layout of collaboration diagrams makes it easy to identify groups of tightly coupled objects which can conveniently be regarded as a unit while we concentrate on what is happening in the rest of the diagram. In Figure 6.16a, objects e, f and g show complicated inter-object messaging. They can be grouped into a package and can be treated as a single entity while we concentrate on the interactions between objects a, b, c and d as in Figure 6.16b.

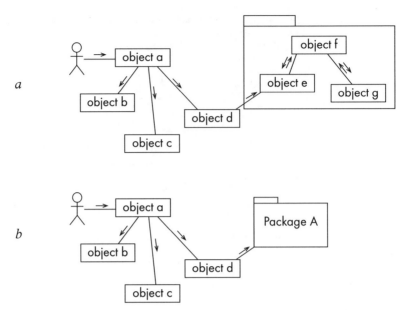

Figure 6.16   a   *Grouping objects into a package in a collaboration diagram*
   b   *A package allows the developer to focus on object interactions in the rest of the diagram*

Specifying operations

In Chapter 5, we saw how a data dictionary notation can be used to document the details of the data in the developing system. However, that notation is restricted to data, and does not provide the means to record details about operations on classes. We have seen in this chapter that interaction diagrams are very useful for specifying the message passing between the group of objects involved in the execution of a use case scenario. However, these diagrams say very little about what happens inside an operation, they don't specify in any detail what an operation does. For this we need operation specifications.

Early on in the development of the system we are not concerned with the details of how an operation works; all we need at that stage is a brief description of what it does, not how it does it. For this sort of description the best tool to use is clear, everyday English or a mixture of English and data dictionary notation. For example, the operation findBike(bike#) in the Bike class can be described as follows:

findBike(bike#)

This operation finds the Bike object whose number corresponds to the bike number input (bike#) and returns details about the bike (bike# + available + type + make + model + size + dailyHireRate + deposit)

We can see a more complex example in the description of the operation calcTotalPayment(amt, deposit) in the Payment class, as shown below:

calcTotalPayment(amt, deposit)

This operation calculates and records the sum of amounts paid as hire fees and the sum of deposits paid. This operation must find all current customer hire objects and for each one calculate the hire fee (Bike.dailyHireRate[1] * Hire.numberOfDays). The hire fees for all of the customer's hires are summed and recorded in Payment.totalAmountPaid. It also finds the deposit for each bike hired, sums them and records the result in Payment.totalDepositPaid.

As development progresses, we need to know more about how each operation carries out its processing. The UML does not provide any particular method for specifying operations, but activity diagrams (see Chapter 8) are an effective way of showing diagrammatically how an operation works.

An alternative approach, known as specification by contract, describes operations in terms of the services they deliver. This type of specification defines:

- The signature of the operation (its name, any arguments, and the type of values it returns)[2]

- The purpose of the operation

- What the client object must provide in order to obtain the required service

- A description of the internal logic of the operation

- Any other operations that are called by this operation

- Any attributes of objects whose values are changed by the operation.

1. *This notation means the attribute dailyHireRate in the class Bike.*
2. *This is a very important part of the specification because the signature of the operation is its public interface; as long as the signature remains unchanged, the internal details of the operation can be modified without affecting the rest of the system.*

As an example, we can use specification by contract to define the getCharges() operation (in the Bike class) which works out the cost of hiring a bike for a given number of days.

- getCharges(no.Days) : (deposit, dailyHireRate, total)

- This operation works out the cost of hiring a particular bike for a given number of days

- The bike details must have been found and the requested number of days of hire known

- The Bike object attribute dailyHireRate is multiplied by the number of days (no.Days). The result is added to the deposit to give the total. The operation returns the deposit, the dailyHireRate and the total

- This operation does not call any others

- This operation does not change the values of any attributes.

The internal logic of an operation can be described in a number of ways depending on the complexity of the algorithm involved. One of the most popular approaches is to use semi-formal, structured English. Structured English is a limited and structured subset of natural language, with a syntax that is similar to that of a block-structured programming language. Structured English generally includes the following constructs:

- A sequence construct:
  e.g. the second statement below is executed immediately after the first statement;
  Get bikeDetails[3]
  Get hireCharges

- Two decision constructs:
  e.g. IF customer is existing customer
       THEN confirm customerDetails
       ELSE record customerDetails
  or: CASE customer is existing customer, confirm customer details

- Two repetition constructs:
  e.g. WHILE more bikes to add DO enter bikeDetails
  or: REPEAT enter bikeDetails UNTIL no more bikes to add

- comments enclosed in parentheses;
  (* this is a comment *)

---

3. *Nouns that are in the data dictionary are written as they appear there.*

As an example of structured English, we will specify the calcDaysOverdue() operation, following the informal description as shown below.

calcDaysOverdue()
This operation uses today's date from the system clock and the attributes Hire.startDate and Hire.numberDays to calculate whether the bike has been returned late and if so by how many days. It calculates the overdue amount (Bike.dailyHireRate multiplied by the number of days late) and records it by executing latenessDeduction(amt).

In structured English this operation could be specified as follows:

> Add numberDays to startDate to give return date
> number of days late = today's date − return date
> IF return date > today's date
>   THEN (*bike is overdue*)
>   latenessDeduction = Bike.dailyHireRate * number of days late
>   ELSE (*bike is not overdue*)
> Display latenessDeduction

When an operation involves a number of decisions, it is often helpful to specify these using a decision table or decision tree. For example, in a more sophisticated bike hire system, the hire charges could depend on the number of bikes a customer has hired in the past year and the number of bikes in the current hire. Let us imagine that Wheels introduce discount hire rates as follows:

> If a customer has already hired at least five bikes during the past year they get a 15% discount, unless the current hire is for three bikes or more, in which case they get a 25% discount.

Figure 6.17 shows how this could be represented in a decision table.

In the decision table all the possible conditions are listed in the top left-hand quarter of the table and all the actions in the bottom left-hand quarter. The top right-hand corner of the table tabulates, in separate columns, all possible combinations of conditions (a dash indicates that the condition is currently irrelevant). This is the Rules section. The appropriate actions are shown below each rule, in the bottom right-hand corner of the table.

Figure 6.18 shows the same information as a decision tree.

Other methods of specifying complex operations include the Object Constraint Language (OCL), which is UML's formal language for specifying constraints on an object model. The Wheels system is not nearly large or complicated enough to justify using OCL, but you can find details about the language in Bennett *et al.*, (2002).

	Rules		
Conditions	*1*	2	3
Customer has hired ≥ 5 bikes during the past year	N	Y	Y
Current hire is for ≥ 3 bikes	–	N	Y
Actions			
No discount	X		
15% discount		X	
25% discount			X

Figure 6.17   Example of a decision table showing hire discounts

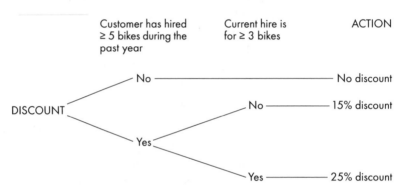

Figure 6.18   Example of a decision tree showing hire discounts

Using the CRC cards and interaction diagrams in system development

CRC cards are used to partition system behaviour between the classes. CRC modelling, by walking through the scenarios, has made us revisit all of our decisions so far – this is part of the iterative nature of object-oriented design. During CRC modelling we may well discover classes and attributes we didn't find doing a noun analysis because we are looking at the classes from a different point of view.

Each class of objects is responsible for some part of the system behaviour. However, for the system to produce a large chunk of required behaviour, for example that specified in a use case, objects must collaborate. The CRC technique is used to discover how classes collaborate to achieve the behaviour of the use cases. Interaction diagrams are used to document in detail the decision arrived at in CRC analysis. CRC cards talk about responsibilities and collaborations. Interaction diagrams talk about messaging between objects.

By the time we come to do the interaction diagrams, we have identified what the system will do and documented it in the use cases and use case scenarios. In the class diagram, we have identified the classes of objects that we think we will probably need, plus some of the attributes, and we have had a guess at what the relationships will be. A message from one object to another means that there should be association between the classes to which they belong. This is a useful check that we have got the associations right. If we find that there is no association on the class diagram between objects that need to message each other in an interaction diagram, then we need to amend the class diagram.

For a message from one object to another to work, the target object must understand the message. It can only do this if we have already defined that operation on its class. Interaction diagrams, therefore, act as a check that we have got the operations right.

Interaction diagrams can be shown at different levels of detail depending on when they are used during development. At their most detailed they can serve as comprehensive specifications of the use cases.

We would not expect an interaction diagram to be drawn for every possible scenario of every use case – a representative selection is enough. Generally these interaction diagrams model what normally happens in the successful execution of a use case (often referred to as the 'happy day' scenario) and the main alternative routes through, including ones where the use case goal is not achieved.

Technical points

Shading. On sequence diagrams we can shade activation boxes to give a more precise indication of when an object is *actively processing*, see Figure 6.19. This is different from when it is *active*. When :Customer sends a message to :Payment, it is still active, but it has passed control to :Payment. At this stage :Payment is doing the processing and :Customer, though still active, is just waiting for a response. :Customer cannot do any processing while it is waiting.

Here is a rather more complicated example that takes place when :Payment receives the calcTotalPayment() message.

- :Payment is active as soon as it receives the calcTotalPayment() message

- The calcTotalPayment() operation starts processing

- calcTotalPayment() stops processing when it sends the issueReceipt() message

- issueReceipt() is also an operation on :Payment, so a separate activation box is opened for the length of time that issueReceipt() is executing

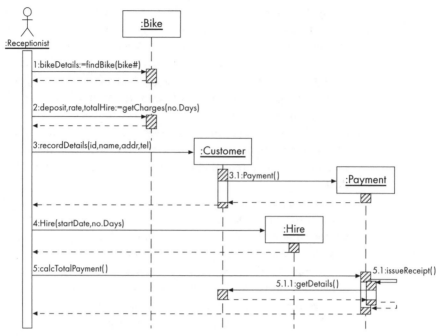

Figure 6.19   *Sequence diagram for the 'Issue bike' scenario with shading to show processing*

- issueReceipt() stops processing when it sends the getDetails() message to :Customer

- Senders regain control as the operations finish processing.

Iteration. The normal assumption on an interaction diagram is that the object icon at the top of a lifeline represents only one object. However, sometimes we want to send the same message to many objects. For example, in the 'Issue bike' use case, when the Receptionist is searching for the details of the bike with a specific bike number, the same message is sent to all of the bike objects until we get a match. This is indicated on the sequence diagram by the iteration marker (*), see Figure 6.20. We can also, optionally, specify how many times the message should be sent. The iteration clause, 'until bike# matched', is shown in square brackets after the asterisk. Bases for iteration are:

- The number of times the message is iterated, e.g. [i = 1..4]

- Repetition while an expression is true, e.g. [while more bikes]

- A for loop, e.g. [for all customers].

On the collaboration diagram, the UML uses a stacked icon to indicate a plurality of :Bike objects, see Figure 6.21. This is known as a *multiobject*.

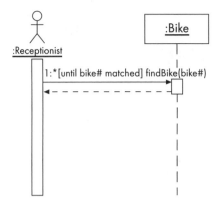

Figure 6.20   *Iteration marker*

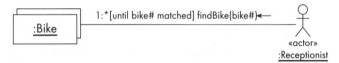

Figure 6.21   *A multiobject*

A multiobject indicates a collection of objects, which may be implemented as an array, a list, a set or some other data structure; the notation allows us to postpone this implementation decision. It is really a shorthand way of modelling the handling of a collection of objects by using a separate collection class. Collection classes are explained in Chapter 10.

Common problems

1   Can I show several actors participating in an interaction diagram? For instance, in the sequence diagram in Figure 6.22, I try to model the behaviour of the Customer and the Receptionist. I think there must be something wrong because the CASE tool would not allow me to call the second actor Customer, so I had to call it Client. I also had to add the messages between the Client and the Receptionist by hand.

There is no reason why you cannot have more than one actor in a sequence diagram, as long as they both participate in the use case and are genuinely inputting information to the system or receiving it directly from the system. However, CASE tools are very good indicators of errors – they understand how object-oriented models should work. Your model is trying to show an

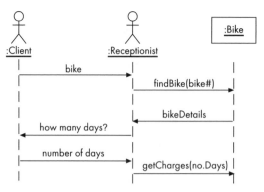

Figure 6.22   Incorrect modelling of the behaviour of two actors

interaction between the customer and the receptionist that is outside the scope of the system. We are not interested in what the customer and the receptionist say to each other, only in how they interact with the system.

The reason your CASE tool would not allow you to have an actor called Customer is probably that you have a Customer class on your class diagram. It is a very common modelling mistake to confuse the real customer with the electronic record of the customer's details.

Your diagram does make two other interesting points. First, it is quite valid to omit object activations. Second, the labels on the message arrows between the actors do not correspond to operations on classes and are therefore invalid. That is why you had to put them in by hand.

2   I can't get my CASE tool to automatically offer me a list of legitimate operations. I want to show that :Bike produces the bike details and the cost information. To get the CASE tool to do this I had to put all the message names in by hand. Is there something wrong with my diagram? See Figure 6.23.

:Bike does produce the items of information that you model, they are its outputs. However, what you have modelled are not messages but operation responses or returns. To get the CASE tool to work, you have to send the right message to :Bike to get it to execute whichever operation produces the outputs you want. Before that can happen you must have specified that this operation is an operation on the Bike class in the class diagram. Once you have done that, when you right-click your message arrow, most CASE tools will list the operations specified on the class of the target object so that you can select the one you want.

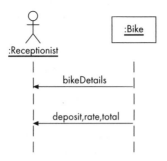

Figure 6.23   *Incorrect modelling of the messages between objects*

Chapter summary

This chapter focuses on the functionality of the system, which we started to look at in Chapter 3 on use cases. We show how to use CRC cards to identify responsibilities and allocate them between the classes in the system, and then discuss how to turn these responsibilities into operations. The two types of interaction diagram (sequence and collaboration) are introduced, and we illustrate how these diagrams model the message passing needed to achieve required functionality. We also look at informal, semi-formal and diagrammatic ways in which we can specify the details of operations. The Technical points and Common problems sections provide further information relating to sequence diagrams.

Bibliography

Bennett, S., McRobb, S. and Farmer, R. (2002) *Object-Oriented Systems Analysis and Design Using UML* (2nd edition), McGraw-Hill, London.

Britton, C. and Doake, J. (2000) *Object-Oriented Systems Development: A Gentle Introduction,* McGraw-Hill, London.

Fowler, M. (2000) *UML Distilled: A Brief Guide to the Standard Object Modeling Language* (2nd edition), Addison-Wesley, Reading, MA.

Lunn, K. (2003) *Software Development with UML,* Palgrave Macmillan, Basingstoke.

Priestly, M. (2000) *Practical Object-Oriented Design with UML,* McGraw-Hill, London.

Quatrani, T. (1998) *Visual Modeling with Rational Rose and UML,* Addison-Wesley, Reading, MA.

Stevens, P., with Pooley, R. (2000) *Using UML. Software Engineering with Objects and Components* (updated edition), Addison-Wesley, Harlow.

Wirfs-Brock, R., Wilkerson, B. and Wiener, L. (1990) *Designing Object-Oriented Software,* Prentice Hall, Englewood Cliffs, NJ.

Quick check questions

You can find the answers to these in the chapter.

a   What aspect of a class is captured on a CRC card?

b   How does a class deal with a responsibility that it cannot fulfil on its own?

c   What are the two types of interaction diagram?

d   What do interaction diagrams model?

e   Apart from the format, what is the difference between a scenario and a sequence diagram?

f   How are messages represented on sequence and collaboration diagrams?

g   What does the thin rectangle on an object's lifeline indicate?

h   List four ways in which collaboration diagrams differ from sequence diagrams.

i   What features of an operation are defined in specification by contract?

j   When is a decision tree or a decision table used to specify an operation?

Exercises

6.1   A mother is planning a birthday party for her son. She wants to invite his friends from school, but doesn't know where they all live, so she asks the form teacher for their addresses and phone numbers. She books a magician and buys lots of food and drink for the birthday tea. She makes the birthday cake herself, but has it iced by the local baker. Draw a CRC card to show the mother's responsibilities and whom she collaborates with to fulfil them.

Use case:	Print ready card
Actors:	Assistant
Goal:	To print a postcard stating that a reserved video is available

Overview:
The Assistant uses the system to find details of the member who reserved the video. A postcard is printed with the member's name and address and the title of the video.

Typical course of events:

Actor action	System response
1 The Assistant asks for details of the reserving member	2 Displays details of the reserving member
3 The Assistant requests a printed postcard	4 Prints a postcard with name and address of reserving member and title of the video

Figure 6.24   Use case description 'Print ready card'

6.2   A mail order company is preparing a new brochure to send out to existing customers and other potential outlets. They will need to get an update on product details from their suppliers and a list of existing customers from the company database. The marketing department will supply them with a new design for the brochure and a list of people and organizations they can send it to. Draw a CRC card for the mail order company showing the responsibilities and collaborations in this situation.

6.3   Figure 6.24 shows the use case description 'Print ready card' from a video rental system (you can find more details about this system in the exercises in Chapter 3).

Following the guidelines given in the section on deriving operations from CRC responsibilities, identify two operations that are needed on the Reservation class.

6.4   Figure 6.25 shows the use case description 'Loan a video' from the video rental system.

Following the guidelines given in the section on deriving operations from CRC responsibilities, identify an operation that is needed on each of the following classes: Member, Video, Loan, and Payment.

Use case: Loan a video
Actors: Assistant
Goal: To lend a video to a customer

Overview:
A customer chooses a video and gives their membership card and the video to the Assistant. The Assistant scans the customer's membership card and checks if they owe any money or have outstanding loans. The system searches for a specific video using the barcode scanned from the video they wish to borrow. The system locates the required video and displays the details on the screen. The Assistant checks that this is the video the customer wants to borrow and looks to see what the rental cost is for this video. The system then registers the loan transaction.

Typical course of events:

Actor action	System response
1 The customer chooses a video	
2 The Assistant scans in the membership card barcode	3 Displays customer details
4 The Assistant agrees the details	
5 The Assistant scans in the video barcode	6 Displays video details including hire cost
7 The Assistant agrees the cost and registers the loan	8 Stores the loan transaction
9 The customer pays for the loan	
10 The Assistant records the payment	11 Prints a receipt

Figure 6.25   Use case description 'Loan a video'

6.5   Figure 6.26 shows the use case description 'Return a video' from the video rental system.

Following the guidelines given in the section on deriving operations from CRC responsibilities, identify two more operations that are needed on the Loan class and one on the Reservation class.

6.6   Describe the operation calcDaysOverdue() using specification by contract as described in the section on specifying operations. The informal description of this operation is as follows.

calcDaysOverdue()
       This operation uses today's date from the system clock and the attributes Loan.startDate and Loan.numberDays

Use case: Return a video
Actors: Assistant
Goal: To register the return of a video by a customer

Overview:
A customer returns a video. The Assistant scans the video barcode and finds the record of the loan transaction. If the video is late back, the system will indicate this and a fine will be registered on the customer's record. The system then checks whether the returned title has been reserved by another member. If so the video is placed on the reserved shelf under the counter and a postcard is printed and sent to the reserving customer.

Typical course of events:

Actor action		System response	
1	A customer returns a video		
2	The Assistant scans in the video barcode	3	Displays the loan transaction
4	The Assistant indicates that the video has been returned	5	Indicates if overdue
7	Assistant returns video to shelves	6	Checks for reservation

Figure 6.26 Use case description 'Return a video'

to calculate whether the video has been returned late and if so by how many days. It calculates the overdue amount (Video.dailyLoanRate multipled by the number of days late) and records it by executing setLatenessFine(amt).

6.7 A nationwide food and clothing store awards loyalty points to its customers in the following ways:

 a If customers use the store's credit card in store, they get 4 points for every pound spent.

 b If customers use the store's credit card at other outlets, they get 2 points for every pound spent.

 c If customers shop in store, but do not use the store credit card, they get 1 point for every pound spent.

 i Express this information in the form of a decision table.

 ii Express the information in the form of a decision tree.

6.8 Figure 6.24 shows the use case description 'Print ready card' (to print a postcard stating that a reserved video is available) from a video rental system. You can find more details about

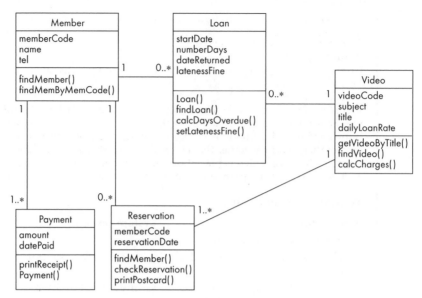

Figure 6.27   Class diagram for the video rental system

this system in the exercises in Chapter 3. Using the class diagram in Figure 6.27:

a Draw a sequence diagram for a successful scenario.

b Draw a collaboration diagram of the same scenario.

6.9   Figure 6.25 shows the use case description 'Loan a video' from the video rental system. Using the class diagram in Figure 6.27 draw a sequence diagram for a successful loan.

6.10 Figure 6.26 shows the use case description 'Return a video' from the video rental system. Using the class diagram in Figure 6.27 draw a sequence diagram for the late return of a video.

7 State Diagrams

Learning outcomes

The material and exercises in this chapter will enable you to:

- Explain the role and purpose of state diagrams in object-oriented systems development
- Use a state diagram to identify how a class behaves in response to events
- Draw a simple state diagram.

Key words that you will find in the glossary:

- action
- event
- state
- transition
- activity
- guard
- superstate

Introduction

So far, we have looked at how to model the organization and structure of data in the system using a class diagram, and at how to model a series of interactions between objects using sequence and collaboration diagrams. In this chapter we examine the system from a different point of view: how a class is affected by the different use cases in the system and how the objects of the class behave in response to events that affect them. The model that illustrates all possible behaviours of a class of objects is called a state diagram. In the chapter we look at the different components of a state diagram, how these are combined, and how the diagrams are used in the development of a system.

State diagrams are an important technique in object-oriented modelling, but they are not widely used in small information systems, such as Wheels. For this reason, most of the examples and exercises in this chapter do not come from the Wheels case study.

BankAccount
accountNo. name address phoneNo. overdraftLimit balance
depositMoney() withdrawMoney()

:BankAccount
accountNo. = 046549370 name = Mr John Bate address = 4 Hill Street, Anytown phoneNo. = 01849 33941 overdraftLimit = £100 balance = 196.73

:BankAccount
accountNo. = 047996047 name = Ms Clare Stevens address = 19 Lime Road, Anytown phoneNo. = 01849 37586 overdraftLimit = £50 balance = −14.50

Figure 7.1   Class BankAccount and two BankAccount objects

States and events

A state diagram models the different states that objects of a class can be in, and the events that cause an object to move from one state to another. In order to be able to draw these diagrams, we therefore need to understand what is meant by state and event in this context.

As we have already seen, a class provides a template or pattern for all the objects of that class. As an example, Figure 7.1 shows a class, BankAccount, and two objects of the class.

Each object of a class such as BankAccount will have the same attributes (although with different values) and the same operations. This means that each object of the class is potentially capable of the same range of behaviours. However, the actual behaviour of an object during the life of the system depends not only on its operations, but also on the events which determine the state that it is in. We can see an example of this if we look at the two BankAccount objects in Figure 7.1. The current balance in John Bate's account is £196.73; it is in the state of being in credit. Clare Stevens' balance, on the other hand, is −£14.50, and her account is therefore in the state of being overdrawn. If John Bate tries to withdraw £40 from his account this will trigger the withdraw money operation and the remaining balance will be £156.73. However, Clare Stevens does not have enough money to withdraw £40 without exceeding her overdraft limit of £50. These two objects are of the same BankAccount class and undergo the same

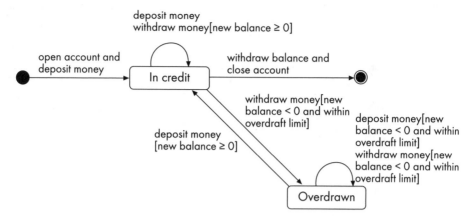

Figure 7.2   Simple state diagram for the BankAccount class

event (the attempt to withdraw £40), but they respond differently to the event because they are in different states at the time.

The state of the object here refers to the situation it is in while satisfying some condition (such as a bank account having some money) or waiting for an event (such as someone trying to withdraw or deposit money). An event is something that happens which has significance for the system and affects an object of at least one of the system's classes. We can tell if an object is in a particular state by looking at the values of some of its attributes and its links to other objects. For example, if a BankAccount object is in credit the value of the balance attribute will be a positive amount or zero, but if it is overdrawn the value of balance will be negative. In the Wheels case study, we can tell if a bike is hired out because there will be a link from the Bike object to an active Hire object.

An example of a simple state diagram

Figure 7.2 shows a simple state diagram for the BankAccount class, illustrating all the different ways in which objects of the class respond to events. The symbols used in state diagrams are illustrated in Figure 7.3

When reading the state diagram in Figure 7.2, we begin from the start state (the filled circle on the left). A state diagram can have only one start state, since all objects of a class are in the same state when created. The event 'open account and deposit money' creates an object of the BankAccount class and causes the object to move from the start state into the 'In credit' state. When a transition between two objects is triggered by an event, the transition is said to fire; it is shown in Figure 7.2 as a labelled arrow between the two states.

While in the 'In credit' state, the object may undergo different types of event, which affect it in different ways; for example as shown in Table 7.1.

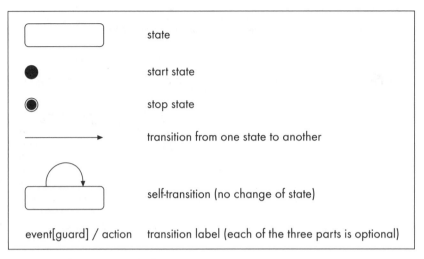

	state
	start state
	stop state
	transition from one state to another
	self-transition (no change of state)
event[guard] / action	transition label (each of the three parts is optional)

Figure 7.3   State diagram symbols

Table 7.1:   *Events in the 'In credit' state*

Event	Result
money is deposited	the account remains in the 'In credit' state
all the money is withdrawn and the account is closed	the account moves into the stop state

While in the 'In credit' state the 'deposit money' event leaves a BankAccount object in the same state. This is known as a self-transition and can be seen as a loop on the 'In credit' state in the diagram in Figure 7.2.

Withdrawing all the money and closing the account causes a BankAccount object to move from the 'In credit' state to the stop state.

Another event which a BankAccount object may undergo while in the 'In credit' state is a 'withdraw money' event. This event can occur with different conditions or guards and therefore may affect the object in different ways (see Table 7.2). It is important to note that the guards relating to an event coming out of a state must be mutually exclusive. This is to ensure that there is no ambiguity about how an object responds to the event. The guards are shown in the state diagram in square brackets.

One of the things that can happen while a BankAccount is in the 'Overdrawn' state is that money may be deposited. This event ('deposit money') can have different conditions or guards and so affect the object in different ways (see Table 7.3).

Table 7.2:   In the 'In credit' state, the event 'withdraw money' can have different results

Event	Guard	Result
money is withdrawn	the new balance is greater than or equal to zero	the account remains in the 'In credit' state
money is withdrawn	the new balance is less than zero and within the overdraft limit	the account moves into the 'Overdrawn' state

Table 7.3:   In the 'Overdrawn' state, the event 'deposit money' can have different results

Event	Guard	Result
deposit money	the new balance is still less than zero	the account remains in the 'Overdrawn' state
deposit money	the new balance is zero or more	the account returns to the 'In credit' state

Another event that can occur in the 'Overdrawn' state is 'withdraw money'. This has a guard '[new balance < 0 and within overdraft limit]', which means that you can still withdraw money while in the 'Overdrawn' state as long as you do not exceed your overdraft limit.

Constructing a state diagram

In our second example we show you how to build a state diagram.[1] You can find a list of all the steps involved in the summary at the end of the chapter. This example concerns a Human Resources system, where one class, Job Application, is complex enough to justify drawing a state diagram. The diagram will illustrate all the different possible behaviours of objects of the Job Application class.

---

1. *It is also possible to draw a state diagram starting from the interaction diagrams; for details of how to do this, see Bennett* et al., *(2002).*

A Job Application object is created when an application form is received and the details recorded. The application will then be read by the manager and may be shortlisted or rejected. If rejected, the application is filed for six months. At the end of this time it is discarded. If it is shortlisted, interview details are sent out and the interview is usually confirmed by the applicant. Once the interview has taken place, the applicant may not be successful; in this case a rejection letter is sent and the application is filed for six months and then discarded. If the applicant is offered the job, an offer letter is sent. If the offer is rejected by the applicant the application is filed for six months, and then discarded; if accepted, the application terminates and other procedures take over. The applicant may withdraw at any time during the application process.

In order to draw a state diagram, we need to sort out the events that can occur and the different states that a Job Application object can be in (see Table 7.4). An object always begins life in the start state, before anything happens to it.

We can see from the list that this diagram will be more complex than the previous BankAccount example, as it not only has more states, but there are three different ways in which a stop state may be reached. Multiple stop states are common in state diagrams, as the way an object ends its life will depend on the specific series of events that it undergoes. In contrast, there is only ever one start state on a state diagram, as all objects of a class are created in the same way.

A number of the events that appear separately in the list are actually the same event, but with different conditions, for example the 'read by manager' event has the conditions 'rejected' and 'shortlisted'. These conditions will be represented in the state diagram in square brackets in the guard section of the relevant transition labels.

We should also check at this stage to see if there are any actions that the system has to perform in response to an event. These will be included in the labels on the relevant transitions. In the Job Application example there are two actions, 'send rejection letter' and 'send offer letter'.

We start to construct the state diagram by beginning with the start state, the event that creates a Job Application object, and the state that the object moves into. Figure 7.4 shows the first stage of the diagram.

We can build up the diagram by deciding what events can happen to a Job Application object while it is in the 'Application logged' state and adding them. Figure 7.5 shows the next stage in the process.

Table 7.4:   *Events and states for objects of the Job Application class*

Event	State
	start state
application form received and details recorded	Application logged
read by manager (rejected)	Filed
read by manager (shortlisted)	Shortlisted
interview details sent	Shortlisted
interview confirmed	Shortlisted
interview (unsuccessful)	Filed
interview (successful)	Job offered
offer rejected	Filed
application discarded (after six months)	stop state
offer accepted	stop state
applicant withdraws	stop state

Figure 7.4   *First stage of the state diagram for the Job Application class*

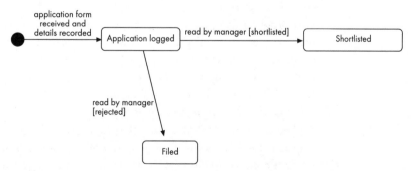

Figure 7.5   *Next stage of the state diagram for the Job Application class*

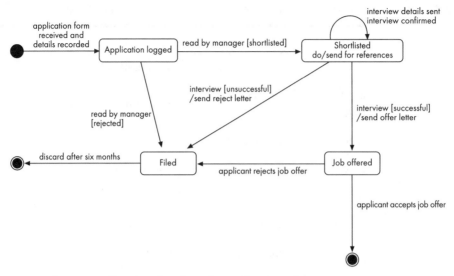

Figure 7.6   State diagram for the Job Application class

We work through the events and states in the list and add them to the diagram, until every item on the list has been included, then we go back to make sure that we have not forgotten any of the guards or actions that should be included in transitions. It is worth noting here that actions can also be contained in states (indicated by the keyword 'do/...' in the state label). This type of action is usually referred to as an activity; it is ongoing (not instantaneous) and can be interrupted by an event. For example, there might be an activity 'send for references' associated with the 'Shortlisted' state.

The state diagram at this stage is shown in Figure 7.6.

There is still one event that we have not included in the diagram. The description of the behaviour of the Job Application class states that an applicant may withdraw at any time. In order to include this in the diagram in Figure 7.6, we would need to add a third stop state and draw transitions to it with the event 'applicant withdraws' from each of the four states on the diagram. This would make the existing diagram cluttered and very difficult to read. In order to avoid clutter, we can draw a superstate round the main body of the diagram, and show a single 'applicant withdraws' transition from it, indicating that an applicant can withdraw at any time during the application process.

Finally, we need to check the completed diagram against the original description of the behaviour of the Job Application class, in order to confirm that it is an accurate representation. The completed diagram with the superstate is shown in Figure 7.7.

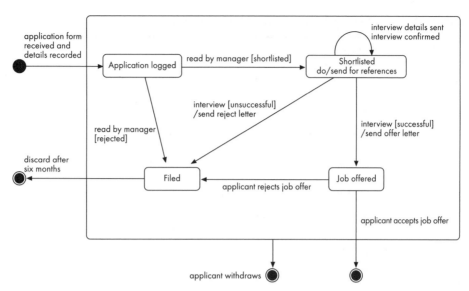

Figure 7.7   Completed state diagram with superstate for the Job Application class

An example from the Wheels case study

For a final example of a state diagram, we return to the Wheels case study. Most of the classes in the Wheels system are relatively simple; the only one where the behaviour is complex enough to merit a state diagram is the Bike class.

As with the previous example, we begin by identifying the events in the system that can affect an object of the Bike class and the different states that an object can be in. The information that we use here to identify the events and states comes from Chapter 2, Requirements for the Wheels case study system.

There may also be some actions that we will need to consider, but we will first construct the basic state diagram. As before, we begin with the start state, the event that creates a Bike object, and the state that the object moves into. Figure 7.8 shows the initial stage of the diagram.

We now build up the diagram as in the previous example, working through the events and states in the list and adding them to the diagram, until every item on the list has been included (see Table 7.5). Some of the events may occur more than once, when the object is in different states; for example, a bike may be sold when it is new or available for hire, but not when it is on hire or under repair. The 'sold' event will appear in the diagram as a transition to a stop state from both the 'New bike' state and the 'Available for hire' state.

We should also take particular note of any events which appear as separate on the list, but which should be represented in the diagram as the same event with different guards. In this case the events 'minor

Table 7.5:   *Events and states for objects of the Bike class*

Event	State
	start state
bike purchased	New bike
bike number is assigned	Available for hire
customer hires bike	On hire
customer returns bike	Available for hire
minor damage to bike	Under repair
major damage to bike	stop state
bike repaired	Available for hire
bike lost or stolen	stop state
bike sold	stop state
bike scrapped	stop state

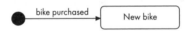

Figure 7.8   *First stage of the state diagram for the Bike class*

damage to bike' and 'major damage to bike' will be represented as one event, 'bike damaged', with guards [reparable] (leading to the 'Under repair' state) and [irreparable] (leading to a stop state).

Figure 7.9 shows the intermediate diagram representing events and states, but without any actions.

The next stage is to check whether we need to include a superstate to cater for events that can occur at any stage in the life of an object. In this example 'bike lost or stolen' is such an event, so we represent this event by a transition from a superstate to a stop state.

Finally, we need to consider whether any actions should be included on the state transitions. For this we will need to look at Chapter 2 again. We discover that the events 'bike damaged/[reparable]' and 'bike damaged/[irreparable]' both have an action 'extra charge to customer', so this action should be added to the relevant transition labels on the diagram.

The completed state diagram for the Bike class is shown in Figure 7.10. This should now be validated against all the information that we have gathered about the behaviour of objects of the Bike class.

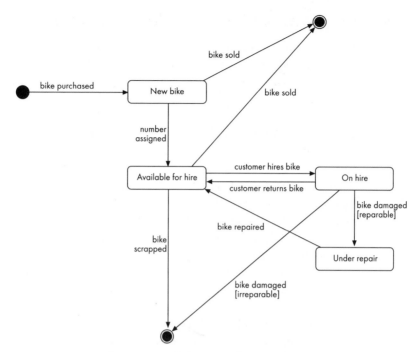

Figure 7.9   Intermediate stage of the state diagram for the Bike class

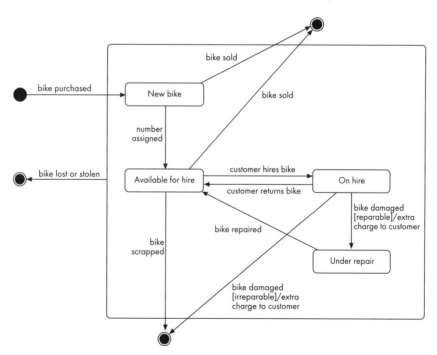

Figure 7.10   Completed state diagram for the Bike class

Using state diagrams in system development

State diagrams model the system from the point of view of a single class and the events that can affect the objects of the class. They show all possible behaviours of objects of a class, and record the ordering of events, for example in the Wheels system a bike must be assigned a number before it can be hired. This information about timing constraints is vital for our understanding of the system, and is not recorded in any of the other system models that we cover in this book.

Although state diagrams are a very useful and important modelling technique, it is not necessary to draw one for every class. In most systems, complexity arises from interaction between objects of different classes, as modelled in sequence and collaboration diagrams (see Chapter 6). It may well be that in any system, particularly an information system, only a few classes will display dynamic behaviour and so need a state diagram to model what happens. This is the case with a system such as Wheels, where most classes have objects that undergo only a restricted set of events and all the objects respond to the same event in the same way. For example, all Customer objects in the Wheels case study system respond to events that happen to them in the same way, although with different values: recording details, finding an associated Hire object, displaying customer details and amending customer details. Their response to events does not depend on what state they are in. For this sort of class which has relatively simple behaviour there is not a lot to show on a state diagram. However, other types of computer system, for example process control or communication systems, frequently have a number of classes whose dynamic behaviour is extremely complex. For this sort of class it is important to document all the possible behaviours of the objects of the class by means of a state diagram.

As with all models that are produced as part of the development process, it is important to check that state diagrams are consistent with other diagrams. A state diagram of a particular class should be checked against interaction diagrams which involve objects of the class to ensure that all the events in the state diagram appear in the interaction diagram as an incoming message to the object. It should also be checked against the class diagram to make certain that every event and action corresponds to an operation on the relevant class.

Technical points

Different types of event. Not all events occur because of outside influences. For example, an event can happen in the course of time. In the state diagram, this is represented by the keyword 'after', for

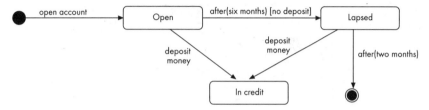

Figure 7.11   Modified BankAccount example showing use of keyword 'after'

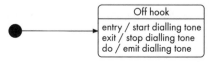

Figure 7.12   Off hook state showing exit and entry events and activity

example 'after (six months)'. In the bank account example we might find, on further investigation, that an account can be opened without a deposit. It is then in the 'Open' state. If a deposit is made it goes into the 'In credit' state. If no deposit is made after six months, it goes into a 'Lapsed' state. It will be deleted two months later unless a deposit is made. This is illustrated in Figure 7.11.

An event can also occur when a certain condition is satisfied; this is represented by the keyword 'when', as for example 'when (all items in stock)'.

Sometimes events with actions occur every time a state is entered or exited. For example, every time a phone enters the state where it is off the hook, but a number has not yet been dialled, it starts emitting a dialling tone which ends when the first number is dialled. These are known as entry and exit events and are shown in the label for the state with the associated action, as for example 'entry / start dialling tone' (see Figure 7.12). Behaviour that lasts for the duration of the state is called an activity and is modelled using the keyword 'do'. Unlike actions associated with events, activities can be interrupted.

Nested states. If a state diagram becomes too complex, it can be simplified by nesting related sets of substates. For example, the 'New bike' state in Figure 7.10 has three substates: 'Bike check', 'Assign Wheels number', 'Register bike on computer'. These are modelled as nested substates in Figure 7.13. If we showed the detail of the substates on the main diagram it would become too cluttered, but it is sometimes useful to be able to decompose states

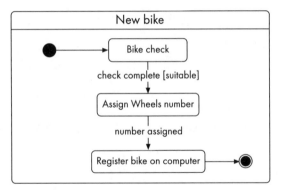

Figure 7.13   *New bike state showing internal nested substates*

to study the internal detail. Notice that the events and states within 'New bike' have their own start and stop states. The nested state diagram can be referenced in the higher level state using the keyword 'include'. For more details about nested substates, see Bennett *et al.*, (2002), Chapter 11.

Concurrent state diagrams. Sometimes the behaviour of an object depends on two independent sets of substates. For example, in a more complex version of the original Job Application state diagram (see Figure 7.6), there might be a set of substates dealing with setting up an interview, and a parallel set of substates to do with obtaining references. This can be shown by drawing a concurrent state diagram – see Figure 7.14. For more details about concurrent states see Fowler (2000), Chapter 8, and Bennett *et al.*, (2002), Chapter 11. It is important to remember, however, that too much detail in one diagram can make the diagram cluttered and difficult to read; it is often simpler and more effective to draw separate diagrams.

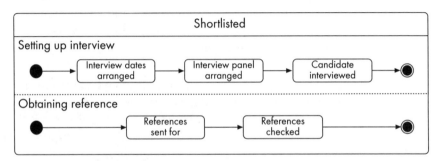

Figure 7.14   *Concurrent state diagram for the 'Shortlisted' state in the Job Application example*

Common problems

1   Can I draw a state diagram for the whole system?

No – a state diagram normally only models the behaviour of the objects of a single class. One of the most common mistakes that students make when learning the technique is to try to model the behaviour of the whole system in a single state diagram.

2   How do I know if I need to draw a state diagram for a particular class?

In order to decide whether or not to draw a state diagram, you need to look at how objects of the class behave in response to events; you can see this by studying the lifelines of the objects in all the relevant interaction diagrams, i.e. all the ones in which objects of this class feature. When you look at the lifeline of an object in a sequence diagram, you can see all the events that happen to it (i.e. the messages sent to it) and how many there are; you can also see whether or not the object always responds in the same way. This is even more apparent in collaboration diagrams as the way they are drawn emphasizes all the messages coming to an object. In fact examining interaction diagrams is one of the main starting points when drawing state diagrams. A good (i.e. representative) set of interaction diagrams will show all the events that can happen to an object during its lifetime (all the messages that can be sent to it) and all the different ways it can respond. From this a list of events can be drawn up like the ones we compiled for the Job Application and Bike state diagrams. State diagrams and interaction diagrams look at the same events but from a different viewpoint. An interaction diagram shows how the execution of a particular scenario affects all of the objects involved. A state diagram looks at a particular class of objects and shows how all of the scenarios affect them. So when your state diagram is complete you should be able to take each scenario in turn and trace through the state diagram following the sequence of events that affect that class.

Students often try to draw a state diagram for a class that is not complex enough to need one, such as the Customer class in the Wheels system. It is only useful to draw a state diagram in cases where the way an object of that class responds to an event depends on the state it is in. This is what textbooks mean when they refer to an object having dynamic behaviour. Only classes with dynamic behaviour are worth modelling with a state diagram.

3 How can I tell the difference between states and events?

Students often get confused about what is a state and what is an event, and it is sometimes difficult to make the distinction between them. The main difference is that an event is regarded as being almost instantaneous and uninterruptible, whereas a state lasts longer – it has duration. For example, in the Wheels system 'bike damaged' is regarded as an event that cannot be interrupted because it is in the past and has happened. On the other hand, 'Under repair' is a continuous state that a bike may be in for some time. It is helpful to label events and states with completely different names; for example, in Wheels we could have an event 'bike hired' leading to a state 'Hired', but it is much clearer to label the event 'customer hires bike' and the state 'On hire'.

4 What is the relationship between state diagrams and interaction diagrams?

The two types of diagram show related information (the behaviour of objects in use cases), but the emphasis is completely different. A state diagram shows how the different objects of a single class behave through all the use cases in which the class is involved. An interaction (sequence or collaboration) diagram concentrates on a single use case and shows how all the objects involved behave during the use case (see also the answer to Question 2, above).

5 How do I know whether to include all the fancy stuff, like concurrent states and different types of event?

There is no hard and fast rule for this, but you should remember that, as with all models, there is a risk of including too much detail and making the diagram so cluttered that it is unreadable. If the extra information is important to the overall understanding of how the system works, you should include it, otherwise leave it out. You may also find that the same information can be shown (possibly more effectively) in one of the other types of diagram and in that case it should not be duplicated.

Chapter summary

This chapter introduces state diagrams, which are used to model the ways in which the objects of a class respond to events that affect them. It describes when to use a state diagram, explains the notation used, and provides guidelines on how the diagrams are constructed. The basic steps that we describe for drawing a state diagram in this chapter are:

- Identify the events that affect an object of the class

- Identify the different states that objects of the class can be in, including the start state and (possibly) multiple stop states

- Check whether any events that are listed separately should be represented as the same event with different conditions (guards)

- Check whether there are any actions that the system must perform in response to an event or whilst in a given state; these should be represented as actions in the transition or state labels

- Begin to construct the diagram from the start state, the event that creates an object of the class, and the state that the object moves into

- Build up the diagram, working through the events and states on the list and adding them to the diagram

- Check that all guards and actions have been included on the relevant transition labels

- Check whether a superstate should be included to cater for events that may occur at any time during the life of an object

- Check the completed diagram against the information that has been gathered about the behaviour of the class.

Bibliography

Bennett, S., McRobb, S. and Farmer, R. (2002) *Object-Oriented Systems Analysis and Design Using UML* (2nd edition), McGraw-Hill, London.

Britton, C. and Doake, J. (2002) *Software System Development: A Gentle Introduction* (3rd edition), McGraw-Hill, London.

Fowler, M. (2000) *UML Distilled: A Brief Guide to the Standard Object Modeling Language* (2nd edition), Addison-Wesley, Reading, MA.

Quick check questions

You can find the answers to these in the chapter.

a   What aspect of a system is modelled by a state diagram?

b   What is meant by 'state' in this context?

c   What is meant by 'event' in this context?

d   What are the three parts of a transition label? Which parts have to be present?

e   What is a self-transition on a state?

f   Why must the guards relating to the same event coming out of a state be mutually exclusive?

g   When do you need to include a superstate on a state diagram?

h   For what types of system are state diagrams generally most useful?

Exercises

7.1   Burglar alarm.

a   When new, a burglar alarm is in a Resting state, and while it is in this state, the alarm may be set. This event moves the alarm into a Set state. While in the set state, the alarm may be turned off, and so returns to the Resting state. Draw a state diagram for the Burglar Alarm class.

b   While in the Set state, the alarm may be triggered; this moves it into the Ringing state. From here the alarm may be turned off, and so return to the Resting state. Amend the state diagram you drew in (a) to include this information.

c   The alarm may break at any time. Include this information on the diagram using a superstate.

7.2   Estate agent's property.
Figure 7.15 is a state diagram of a property in an estate agent's system. Study the diagram and then briefly describe in clear English what can happen to a property during its life in the system.

NB The superstate in this diagram is slightly different from those in the diagrams in the chapter in that it does not apply to all the states. You should be able to see from the diagram when the vendor can take the property off the market and when this is no longer possible.

7.3   Simple microwave oven.
When new, a microwave oven is initially off. From this state the cooking time may be set and the oven turned on. While the microwave is on, the time can be changed. When the time is up, the microwave turns itself off and gives three

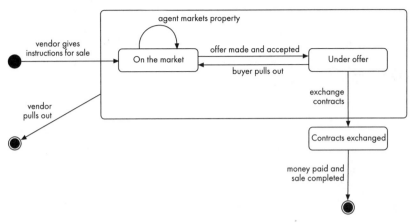

Figure 7.15 *State diagram for an estate agent's property*

short beeps. Draw a state diagram to represent the behaviour of the simple microwave oven.

7.4 Newsagent's customer.

A newsagent has customers who place regular orders for papers to be delivered and who are billed monthly. If the customer does not pay the bill within four weeks, the newsagent sends a reminder. If the bill is still unpaid after a further two weeks, the newsagent stops deliveries to the customer. Customers can change or cancel their orders, but only if they have paid all bills to date. Draw a state diagram to represent the behaviour of a customer in the newsagent's system.

7.5 Tea and coffee machine.

A tea and coffee machine in an office is initially idle, until a user inserts 50p. At this point the user can press the tea button to select tea, which the machine then dispenses, or the user can insert a further 20p. When 70p has been inserted, the user can press the coffee button to select coffee, which the machine dispenses, before returning to the idle state. The machine may break at any time. Draw a state diagram to represent the behaviour of the tea and coffee machine.

7.6 Internet book order.

Figure 7.16 is a state diagram of an order in an Internet book shop system. Study the diagram and then answer the questions below.

a How does the event 'user selects book' affect the state of an Internet Book Order object?

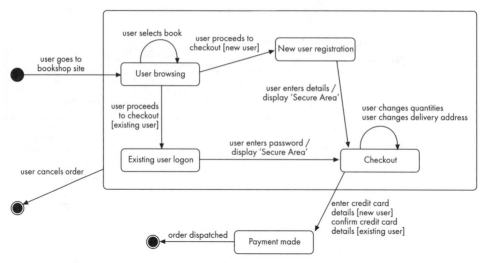

Figure 7.16   State diagram for an internet book order

b   What personal information does an existing user have to enter first?

c   At what point is the 'Secure Area' message displayed to a new user?

d   If the user wants to send a book to someone else, where can they arrange this?

e   Can a user change their mind and cancel once payment has been made?

f   In what ways can the life of an Internet Book Order object end?

8 Activity diagrams

Learning outcomes

The material and exercises in this chapter will enable you to:

- Explain the role and purpose of activity diagrams in object-oriented systems development

- Draw a simple activity diagram

- Use activity diagrams to analyse business workflows, use cases and operations on classes.

Key words that you will find in the glossary:

- activity
- guard
- object flow
- synchronization bar

- fork
- join
- swimlane

Introduction

As we have seen in Chapter 3, the functionality of the system is initially represented through use cases, which describe the main activities of the system from the perspective of the user. System functionality is also specified in the operations on each class in the class diagram (see Chapters 5 and 6); the interaction diagrams (Chapter 6) specify the inter-object message passing required to achieve a particular task, and state diagrams (Chapter 7) model all possible behaviours of the objects of a class.

In this chapter we look at activity diagrams, which are used to model the details of complex processes. Activity diagrams are similar to state diagrams in that they are concerned with states and

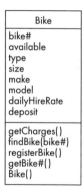

Bike
bike# available type size make model dailyHireRate deposit
getCharges( ) findBike(bike#) registerBike( ) getBike#( ) Bike( )

Figure 8.1   *The Bike class from the Wheels class diagram*

transitions between the states. However, in an activity diagram, all the states are activities (i.e. a state of doing something) and the transitions between them are triggered by the completion of the activity, rather than by an external event.

Activity diagrams show the internal flow of control in a process. They can be used to model processing at different levels, such as high-level workflows in an organization, the detail of what happens in a use case (as an alternative to a use case description), or they can specify in detail how an operation works (as an alternative to a process specification). Activity diagrams can be used to represent sequence, selection and iteration (structures that are found in nearly all programs) and they can also illustrate where different activities can be carried out in parallel.

Modelling a sequence of activities

The first example of an activity diagram is a simple model of the operation to calculate the amount to be paid when a bike is hired. Figure 8.1 shows the Bike class from the Wheels class diagram (for the complete diagram, see Figure 6.6 on page 155).

One of the operations on the Bike class is 'getCharges( )', but the class diagram only records the name of the operation. There are no details of what actually happens in the 'getCharges' operation. These can be specified in an operation specification (see Chapter 6) or an activity diagram.

Figure 8.2 shows an activity diagram illustrating the sequence of actions involved in the 'getCharges()' operation.

This is a very simple sequential diagram; most activity diagrams model more complex processing and use a fuller notation as shown in Figure 8.3.

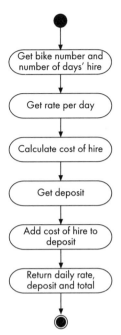

Figure 8.2   Simple activity diagram for the 'getCharges()' operation

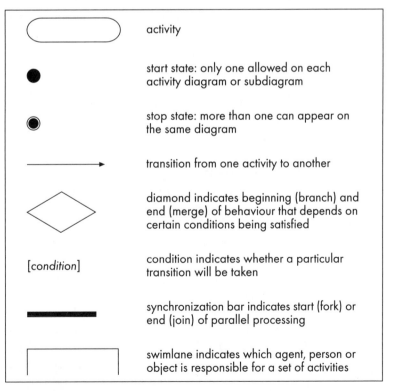

Figure 8.3   Activity diagram symbols

Figure 8.4   Initial activity diagram for the 'Issue bike' use case

Modelling alternative courses of action

One of the advantages of activity diagrams is that they can model different possible courses of action and the conditions which determine which course is taken.

Figure 8.4 shows an initial activity diagram for the 'Issue bike' use case.

Although this diagram illustrates the sequence of processing that occurs when a bike is issued, it only covers the situation where the customer is new to the Wheels system. In the case of an existing customer, it would be inefficient and confusing to input customer details each time the customer hires a bike; all the system needs to do is confirm that the customer details on record are correct.

Figure 8.5 shows an amended diagram for the 'Issue bike' use case that caters for both new and existing customers. The decision point is shown by the first diamond, and the conditions or guards for taking particular courses of action (whether the customer is new or existing) are indicated in square brackets.

As in state diagrams, it is essential that every guard evaluates to true or false, and that the guards on the alternative processing routes are mutually exclusive (for example, a customer cannot be both new and existing). This is to ensure that there is no ambiguity as to which route should be taken. The guard on one of the processing routes may be simply 'else', indicating that this is the default route in the case where all the other guards are false.

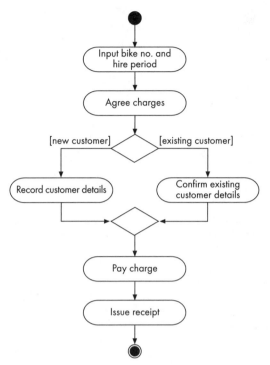

Figure 8.5   Activity diagram for the 'Issue bike' use case, showing alternative actions

Modelling iteration of activities

In addition to sequencing (see Figure 8.4) and selection (Figure 8.5) of activities, activity diagrams can also model iteration, where one or more activities need to be repeated. Figure 8.6 shows what happens when Naresh, the chief mechanic at Wheels, has to register a number of different bikes on the system. For each bike, Naresh has to enter the details and then assign a number; these activities are repeated until all the bikes have been registered. The diagram in Figure 8.6 shows the iteration loop, with the guard condition '[more bikes to add]' in square brackets.

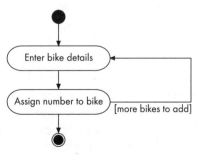

Figure 8.6   Activity diagram showing iteration of activities

Figure 8.7   *Initial activity diagram for the 'Handle bike return' use case*

Modelling activities that are carried out in parallel

A further advantage of activity diagrams is that they illustrate where activities can be performed in parallel. In fact, the process of drawing an activity diagram often uncovers the possibility of performing in parallel activities that have previously been carried out sequentially. Figure 8.7 shows an initial activity diagram for the use case 'Handle bike return'.

We know from earlier investigations (see Chapter 2) that the order in which these activities are performed is irrelevant; the return date can be processed before checking the bike or vice versa. This means that the activities 'Check bike' and 'Check return date' can be shown on the activity diagram in parallel, as can be seen in the amended diagram in Figure 8.8.

In Figure 8.8 the top synchronization bar indicates that once the activity ('Find hire details') that is the source of the single incoming transition has completed, the outgoing transitions ('Check return date' and 'Check bike for damage') are taken in any order. The bottom synchronization bar indicates that the single outgoing transition is only triggered once both these activities have completed. A synchronization bar that signals the start of parallel activities is known as a fork, and one that signals the end of the

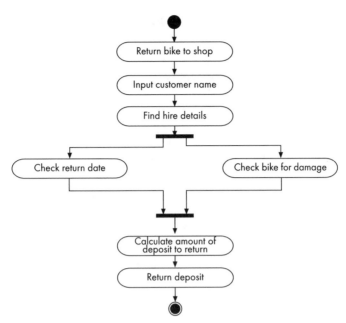

Figure 8.8   *Activity diagram for the 'Handle bike return' use case, showing parallel activities*

activities is known as a join. The transitions at the beginning and end of parallel activities must match; all outgoing transitions from the fork must eventually meet at the corresponding join.

Different types of activity structures, such as sequence, selection, iteration and parallel activities, can all occur in the same diagram, although this can sometimes make the diagram cluttered and difficult to read. Figure 8.9 shows a modified version of the activity diagram for the 'Handle bike return' use case, including selection and parallel activities. The diagram now shows what happens when a bike is overdue or returned damaged.

Swimlanes

None of the example activity diagrams shown so far in this chapter has given any indication of which person, agent or object carries out a given activity. Diagrams like these are actually very useful in the early stages of development when we want to think about what happens during processing without worrying about who or what has responsibility for a specific activity. Later on, however, it is useful in relation to each activity to be able to identify who, what, or which object in the system carries it out. We can add this information to an activity diagram by dividing the diagram into vertical zones, known as swimlanes. Swimlanes are separated from each other by lines and the top of each swimlane is labelled with

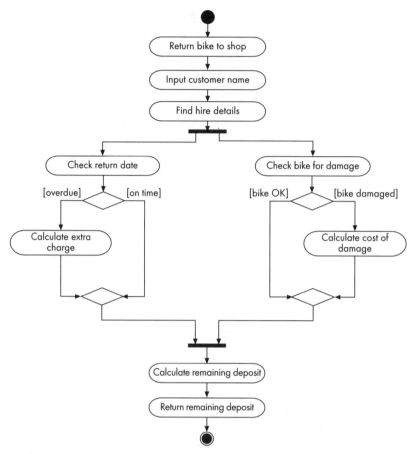

Figure 8.9   *Modified activity diagram for the 'Handle bike return' use case, showing parallel activities and selection*

the name of the person, organization or object responsible for carrying out the set of activities in the swimlane.

Figure 8.10 shows the activity diagram for the 'Handle bike return' use case (compare Figure 8.9). In Figure 8.10 swimlanes have been added to provide information about who carries out the various activities in the use case.

We can see from Figure 8.10 who or what carries out the different activities that make up the 'Handle bike return' use case. The customer is responsible for returning the bike to the shop. The receptionist inputs the customer name, and the computer carries out the activities of finding the hire details, checking the return date, calculating the extra charge if necessary, and calculating the remaining deposit. The mechanic is responsible for checking the bike for damage and calculating the cost of any damage discovered. Finally, the receptionist returns the remaining deposit to the customer.

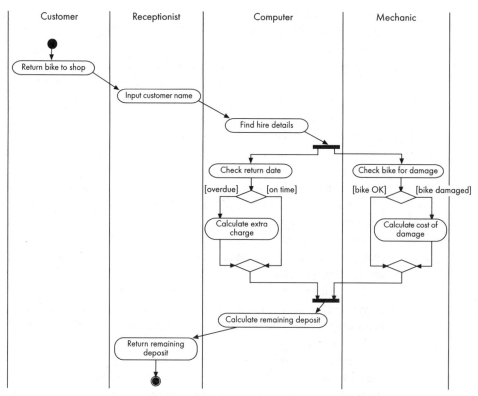

Figure 8.10   *Modified activity diagram for the 'Handle bike return' use case, showing responsibilities for different activities through the addition of swimlanes*

As we can see from the example, swimlanes are very useful for showing who does what in a workflow or use case, and how the processing in an operation is divided up between objects. However, the responsibilities of different objects can be seen more clearly in sequence and collaboration diagrams (see Chapter 6) and it is often better to omit extra details such as swimlanes from an activity diagram so that there is less risk of clutter. As with all diagrams, it is important to make sure that an activity diagram is easy to read.

Using activity diagrams in system development

Activity diagrams are a relatively recent addition to the UML, and many people dislike using them because they are process-based, rather than object-oriented. However, the diagrams are a useful and effective modelling tool that can be used throughout the system development process. They help to visualize the functionality of the system at different levels of detail, and aid communication between developers and clients. UML does provide text-based alternatives to activity diagrams, such as use case and process descriptions, but clients generally find diagrammatic techniques, such as activity diagrams, easier to understand.

Activity diagrams can be drawn in the initial stages of development to help both developers and clients to analyse business workflow processes and gain a shared understanding of what is going on in the system. At this stage they provide a useful vehicle for discussion, helping developers, clients and users to visualize the system functionality.

The ability of activity diagrams to represent activities that can be carried out in parallel is particularly useful in high-level business modelling, as drawing the diagrams can help to identify potential for parallel processing, even where activities are currently carried out sequentially. Representation of parallel processing is especially useful in certain types of system, such as real time, where synchronization of activities and tasks is central to the system functionality.

Once the system use cases have been identified (see Chapter 3), activity diagrams can be used to illustrate the steps involved in achieving a use case goal, showing the activities and the order in which they take place.

Finally, when development has reached a stage where classes have been identified together with their attributes and operations, activity diagrams are a useful means of describing how the operations work, particularly when these are based on complex algorithms.

Technical points

Modelling iteration. When we discussed iteration in activity diagrams earlier in this chapter, we showed how to model it using a loop between activities (see Figure 8.6). It is also possible to show iteration using a multiplicity symbol * on an activity, which is useful when there is a risk of a diagram becoming cluttered. Figure 8.11 shows a section of an activity diagram illustrating what happens when Annie Price, the shop manager for Wheels, checks that the insurance on each bike is up to date. The multiplicity symbol on the activity 'Check bike insurance details' indicates that this activity is repeated until the details on all the bikes have been checked.

Omitting the diamond decision symbol. It is not mandatory to include the diamond symbol to indicate a decision leading to alternative courses of action in an activity diagram, although the different paths through the diagram are often clearer when the diamond is included. Figure 8.12 shows two versions of a section from Figure 8.5 (Activity diagram for the 'Issue bike' use case) with and without the diamond decision symbol.

Figure 8.11 *Section of an activity diagram illustrating the use of the multiplicity symbol * to indicate repetition of an activity*

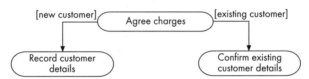

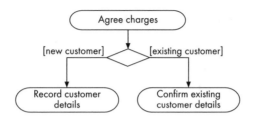

Figure 8.12 *Two versions of part of Figure 8.5, with and without the diamond decision symbol*

Partitioning the diagram. A subset of related activities on a diagram can be enclosed and labelled as shown in Figure 8.13, where the activities concerning the handling of customer details are represented as a subsection of the main diagram with its own start and stop states.

Partitioning an activity diagram in this way can help the readability of the overall diagram, and also supports reuse, since this subsection of the main diagram can be reused in any activity diagram which includes handling customer details.

Object flows. It is often useful to include in an activity diagram information about the input that an activity needs from a specific object, or how an object is affected by the output from an activity. In this way the processing represented in an activity diagram can be linked to its input and outputs.

Sometimes the name of an object is used as the name of an activity as in Figure 8.14.

Usually, however, the links between activities and objects are shown by including the relevant objects in the activity diagram, together with object flows to or from the associated activity. If an object provides input for an activity, an object flow (dashed arrow)

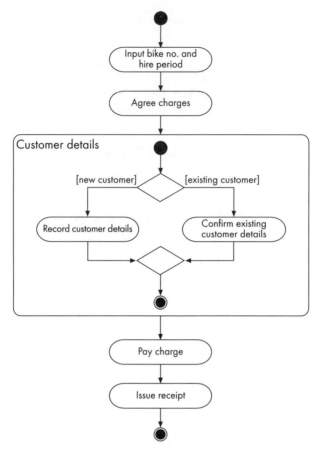

Figure 8.13   *Activity diagram of the 'Issue bike' use case, showing the subset of activities that relate to handling customer details*

Figure 8.14   *Activities may be given the name of an associated object*

is drawn from the object to the activity. If an activity creates or updates an object, an object flow is drawn from the activity to the object.

Figure 8.15 is the activity diagram of the 'Issue bike' use case (see also Figure 8.5) including the objects that are involved in the use case and the object flows that link them to specific activities.

In the case where the state of an object is altered by an activity, this can be shown as in the label on the object in Figure 8.16, which shows how the activity 'Update customer record' updates the relevant customer object.

Where the object flows imply a transition between objects, the transitions themselves can be omitted. This can be seen in Figure 8.17a and b, which shows part of the 'Issue bike' use case.

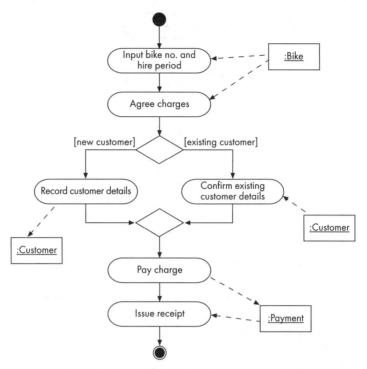

Figure 8.15   *Activity diagram for the 'Issue bike' use case, including associated objects and object flows*

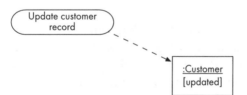

Figure 8.16   *Activity 'Update customer record' updates the relevant Customer object*

Figure 8.17a includes the transition between the activities 'Pay charge' and 'Issue receipt'; in Figure 8.17b these are replaced by the Payment object and the object flows linking the object to the activities.

Common problems

1   How do I know what makes a useful activity?

An activity is a situation in which something is happening. To identify useful activities, you need to mentally step through the process, use case or operation that you are describing and work out what has to be done and in what order.

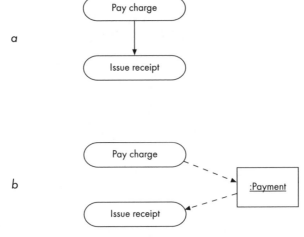

a

b

Figure 8.17   a *Part of the activity diagram for the 'Issue bike' use case, showing*
transition between two activities
b *Part of the activity diagram for the 'Issue bike' use case, replacing*
the transition with the Payment object and object flows between it
and the two activities

It is useful to remember to name all activities with an active
verb, such as 'Record customer details' or 'Calculate remaining
deposit'. It is important not to confuse an activity, for example
'Archive hire details', with the state, 'Archived', that a Hire
object can be in.

You need to be clear about the level of the activity diagram
that you are drawing and what exactly it aims to describe,
whether that is a high-level business workflow, a use case, or
the details of an operation. An activity such as 'Add cost of hire
to deposit' is appropriate as part of the activity diagram for the
'Get charges operation' (see Figure 8.2), but would be too
detailed for a diagram describing the 'Issue bike' use case.

2   How do I know whether to include swimlanes, object flows or
subsections in a diagram?

We have discussed all these techniques in the chapter because
each of them offers a way of adding useful information to the
basic activity diagram. The key word, however, is 'useful'. In
the initial stages of development, for example, nobody has
begun to think in detail about the objects in the system and
there is no point in worrying about objects or object flows. In
the same way, partitioning a diagram into subsets of activities
can come in handy when the diagram is large and complex, but
it should only be done to make the overall diagram easier to read
– not just to look clever. Techniques and diagrams are tools that

are there to help the developer, not to dictate what should or should not be included in a diagram.

3 How do I model activities that are a mixture of human actor action and computer action like calculating the remaining deposit?

It is quite straightforward to specify that some actions are manual (e.g. 'Check bike') and some are done using the system (e.g. 'Check return date'). This can be done with swimlanes, as in Figure 8.10 where the mechanic checks the bike and the computer checks the return date.

In the case where you want to show that one activity is a mixture of human and system actions, you would have to split the activity into two. In Figure 8.10 the activity of dealing with the return of a deposit is split into 'Calculate amount of deposit to return' (Computer) and 'Return deposit' (Receptionist).

Chapter summary

This chapter introduces activity diagrams, which are used at various stages of the development process to model the flow of actions and the decisions that cause them to take place. They can be used in the early stages of development to describe high level business workflows, then later to model use cases, and finally to clarify the details of individual operations on classes.

Activity diagrams can model sequencing, selection and repetition of activities. They can also show where activities may be carried out in parallel. It is possible to divide activity diagrams into swimlanes, indicating which person, organization or object has responsibility for which activities in the diagram. During detailed design it is also possible to indicate the input that an activity needs from a specific object, and how an object is affected by the output from an activity. However, activity diagrams are often most useful when used in their simplest form as a means for the developer and client to build a shared understanding of how the system works.

Bibliography

Bennett, S., McRobb, S. and Farmer, R. (2002) *Object-Oriented Systems Analysis and Design Using UML* (2nd edition), McGraw-Hill, London.

Fowler, M. (2000) *UML Distilled: A Brief Guide to the Standard Object Modeling Language* (2nd edition), Addison-Wesley, Reading, MA.

There are a large number of references on the World Wide Web, including:

http://www.modelingstyle.info/activityDiagram.html

http://sunset.usc.edu/classes/cs577a_2000/papers/
ActivitydiagramsforRoseArchitect.pdf

Quick check questions

You can find the answers to these in the chapter.

a   In what way do activities differ from states as found in state diagrams?

b   What types of process can activity diagrams model during the course of development?

c   What common features of most programming languages can be modelled by an activity diagram?

d   If an activity diagram shows two or more activities carried out in parallel does this mean that the activities must be carried out at the same time or that the order of processing does not matter?

e   What does the diamond symbol mean on an activity diagram?

f   What do two synchronization bars indicate in an activity diagram?

g   What do swimlanes show in an activity diagram?

Exercises

8.1   Figure 8.18 shows a simple sequential activity diagram for the purchase of tickets by telephone. Modify the diagram to show that the activities 'Calculate total cost' and 'Record customer details' can be carried out in any order.

8.2   The owners of a small retail company make regular orders to their supplier. First, they check their current stock, and then compile the order. When they receive the goods, they check them against the order, and update stock levels. They also pay the supplier's bill.

Draw an activity diagram to illustrate the ordering process. Your diagram should include an example of parallel processing.

8.3   Figure 8.19 shows a simple sequential activity diagram illustrating a car entering a car park. Add swimlanes to the diagram to show which of the activities are carried out by

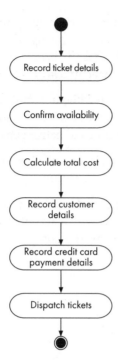

Figure 8.18   Simple activity diagram for the purchase of tickets by telephone

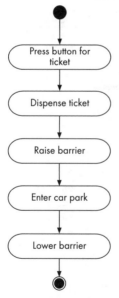

Figure 8.19   Simple activity diagram illustrating a car entering a car park

the driver of the car and which by the machine that controls entry to the car park.

8.4   When a driver wants to leave the car park, he or she drives to the exit barrier and puts the ticket into the machine, which calculates the amount owing. The driver inserts the money and if it is more than the amount owing, the machine gives change. The machine then raises the barrier, the driver drives out of the car park, and the machine lowers the barrier.

a   Draw an activity diagram without swimlanes to illustrate what happens when a driver leaves the car park. Your diagram should include an example of alternative behaviours.

b   Add swimlanes to your diagram to show who or what is responsible for the various activities.

8.5   Add swimlanes to Figure 8.5, the activity diagram for the 'Issue bike' use case, to show which activities are carried out by the receptionist, which by the computer and which by the customer.

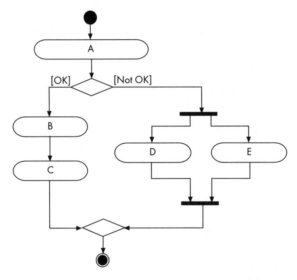

a   do A
    If OK then
        do B
        do C
    Else
        do D or E (*not both*)
    End

b   do A
    If OK then
        do B
        do C
    Else
        do D and E (*in any order*)
    End

c   do A
        do B
        do C
    If Not OK then
        do D and E
    End

d   do A
        If Ok then
            do B
            do C
        Else
            do D
            do E
        End

Figure 8.20   *Activity diagram and pseudocode for Exercise 8.6*

8.6 Figure 8.20 shows an activity diagram followed by four extracts of pseudocode. Which one of the extracts a–d corresponds to the diagram?

8.7 Figure 8.21 is an activity diagram illustrating the purchase of a book over the Internet. Study the diagram and the statements that follow it. Indicate whether each statement is true or false according to the diagram.

a Customer details must be recorded before the amount owing is calculated.

b If the title is not available, a new title is input.

c The transaction must always be confirmed immediately after the credit card details are recorded.

d The credit card details must be recorded before the transaction is confirmed.

e Customer details are only recorded if the title chosen is available.

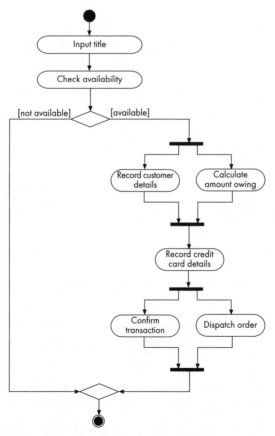

Figure 8.21   *Activity diagram for the purchase of a book over the Internet*

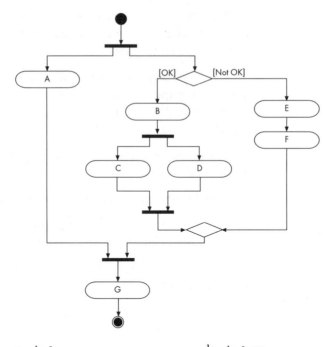

a   do A
       If OK then
             do B
             do C and D (*in any order*)
       do G
       Else do E
             do F
       do G
       End

b   do A or
       If OK then
             do B
             do C or D (*not both*)
       Else do E
             do F
       do G
       End

c   do A and
       If OK then
             do B
             do C
             do D
       Else do E
             do F
       do G
       End

d   do A and
       If OK then
             do B
             do C and D (*in any order*)
       Else do E
             do F
       do G
       End

Figure 8.22   Activity diagram and pseudocode for Exercise 8.8

8.8   Figure 8.22 shows an activity diagram followed by four extracts of pseudocode. Which one of the extracts a–d corresponds to the diagram?

8.9   Modify the 'Issue bike' diagram in Figure 8.5 to show what happens when a customer hires more than one bike.

8.10   Modify the 'Handle bike return' diagram in Figure 8.9 to show what happens when a customer returns more than one bike.

9 Design

Learning outcomes

The material and exercises in this chapter will enable you to:

- Recognize the difference between analysis and design
- Explain the role and purpose of a layered architecture in an object-oriented system
- Draw a simple component diagram
- Draw a simple deployment diagram
- Design a simple user interface
- Explain the difference between an object-oriented and a relational database
- Understand how to link an object-oriented program to a relational database
- Be able to convert a simple class diagram into a set of relational database tables
- Apply a simple design pattern.

Key words you will find in the glossary:

- architecture
- boundary class
- collection class
- component
- component diagram
- control class
- dependency
- deployment diagram
- design pattern
- domain class
- entity class
- foreign key
- hardware platform
- implementation-independent
- JDBC (Java database connectivity)
- layered architecture
- object-oriented database
- package
- presentation layer
- primary key
- relational database
- software platform
- subsystem
- user interface
- visibility

Introduction

The classic distinction between analysis and design is that analysis describes *what* a system must do and design describes *how* to do it; roughly speaking, analysis decisions are implementation-independent, design decisions tend to be implementation-dependent. During analysis we are concerned with understanding and modelling the users' requirements; analysis produces a specification of what the new system will do. During design we decide how to construct the system that will deliver the users' requirements; actually constructing the system is an implementation activity. The design is effectively an abstraction of the final code; it will omit much of the detail in the code but, nevertheless, will provide the essence of the structure and interactions of the programs. If we use a suitable CASE tool we can generate much of the code from the design models.

Design activities include those concerned with overall system design, and those concerned with detailed design. Overall system design activities include designing the overall architecture of the system, selecting a strategy for coping with persistent data and designing a user interface. Software and hardware platforms must be chosen and a test plan produced. Designing a test plan and choosing the software and hardware are beyond the scope of this book.

Detailed design activities include the detailed specifications of classes, their relationships and interactions. The models should contain sufficient information to allow them to be used as program specifications. Detailed design activities are discussed in Chapter 10.

The product of design activities will be a layered diagram of the system architecture, a set of component and deployment diagrams, a database definition, a test plan and screen and report layouts, a set of detailed class diagrams and supporting documentation such as data dictionary and operation specifications and a set of detailed interaction diagrams.

In this chapter we discuss the overall architecture in terms of a layered view of the system. We discuss packages and dependencies: how to use packages to manage large class diagrams and to arrange the system in layers. We introduce two new types of diagram, component diagrams and deployment diagrams, which can be used to specify the arrangement of the hardware components and the assignment of software components to hardware. The component diagram describes the physical software components of the system and their dependencies: such things as executable files, databases and libraries of classes. The deployment diagram shows the hardware components of the system, i.e.

computers and their peripherals. Deployment diagrams can also be used to show on which computers the various software components will be physically located. We include points to consider when designing a simple user interface. We discuss different strategies for dealing with persistent data. Guidelines are given for linking a Java application to a relational database.

Architecture

When we specify the architecture of the system we are describing the software and hardware components of the system, how they are structured and related. Software components can be described logically in terms of classes, packages, subsystems and their dependencies, or physically in terms of executable files, class libraries and databases. The logical software architecture is modelled using class diagrams and package diagrams; the physical software architecture is described using component diagrams (see below). Hardware architecture, from the system developer's perspective, is concerned with the computers, peripherals and networks on which the system will run. Hardware architecture is modelled using deployment diagrams.

Layered architecture

One approach to partitioning a system is to use a *layered architecture*. However, before we embark on a discussion of a layered architecture, we need to know about entity, boundary and control classes, about the visibility of classes, attributes and operations and about partitioning the system using packages.

Entity, boundary and control classes. The classes that we have considered during analysis have all been concerned with modelling the system requirements. These classes are variously referred to as *entity classes*, domain classes or application classes. All of the classes we have met so far have been entity classes. Entity classes model features of the problem domain, like bikes, customers and hires, and are usually classes which have data that needs persistent storage. They are capable of providing the functionality specified in the use cases. However, we have not considered *how* the entity classes will provide the functionality. During system design, we need to add classes to handle the human interface and to control the sequence of execution; these are called *boundary* (*or user interface*) and *control classes*.

Boundary classes model the system's interface with its actors, i.e. with the user or with other systems. These classes are used to capture user input and present results to the user. They take the form of menus, input screens, report screens, etc. Control classes control the sequencing of events, typically the sequences of events in the execution of a set of use case scenarios. In a system of any size you would expect to find a boundary object and a control object for each use case.

Visibility. When we talk about visibility in modelling, and in programming, we are essentially talking about the ability to limit the accessibility of certain features of the model or the program. The more features we can make inaccessible, the more control we have over isolating the effect of changes. However, we cannot make everything inaccessible. In an object-oriented system, objects must communicate with each other to carry out tasks; they can only do so by using operations they know about, i.e. operations that are part of some class's public interface. In the UML, any attribute or operation can be declared to be *public* (+), *private* (−) or *protected* (#). A class can have some operations that are public, which are there to provide services to other classes, and some that are private because they are only for the class's internal use. Programming languages interpret these visibility indicators slightly differently. The UML leaves the precise interpretation to be determined by the implementation language. However, a public operation is usually interpreted to be one that can be used by instances of any class. A private operation is usually interpreted to be one that can only be used by an instance of the owning class. A protected operation is usually interpreted to be one that can only be used by instances of the owning class or a subclass (or other descendent) of the owning class. As far as attributes are concerned, a public attribute can be accessed[1] by any object and it can be inherited; a private attribute cannot be accessed by any other object, it cannot be inherited; a protected attribute cannot be accessed by any other object, but it can be inherited.[2]

Packages and dependencies. As we move towards implementation, we are adding a great deal of extra detail to our models. The class diagram is bulging with new classes as we graft on boundary classes, control classes and collection classes.[3] Decisions need to be made about what software and hardware will be used − the software and hardware platforms. All this information has to be built into existing models and new models added to document our decisions. If the models are to be useful, they need to be organized and managed − we can't really deal (physically or intellectually)

1. *Viewed or modified.*
2. *In Java, protected visibility, for an operation or an attribute, gives public access to other classes in the same package, but is private to classes outside it.*
3. *Collection classes are described in Chapter 10.*

with any diagram that is bigger than an A4 sheet. This is especially true if we are using a CASE tool (it's hard to follow a diagram that we can't see on one screen). To control complexity and manage our models, we partition the system into packages.

A *package* is a UML mechanism for grouping modelling elements. A package itself does not represent anything in the system, but is used to group modelling elements that do represent things in the system. In Chapter 3 we discussed grouping use cases into a package. Packages can also be used to group classes, collaborations, subsystems or a complete view of the system such as a use case model. We can also use packages to nest models; we might have a high-level class diagram that contains a package which itself contains a class diagram, and so on. In fact we can have high-level class diagrams that show only packages and dependencies – these are sometimes referred to as package diagrams, although this is not a UML term. For example, we might divide the Wheels system into two subsystems Hire Bike (which deals with issuing bikes and handling bike returns) and Manage Data (which maintains the Wheels lists of customers and bikes). We could represent each subsystem with a package. Each package would contain a class diagram. Figure 9.1 shows, on level 1, a package diagram representing the two subsystems; on level 2 the class diagram for the Manage Data subsystem. In reality, the Wheels system is so small that we would be unlikely to split it into subsystems.

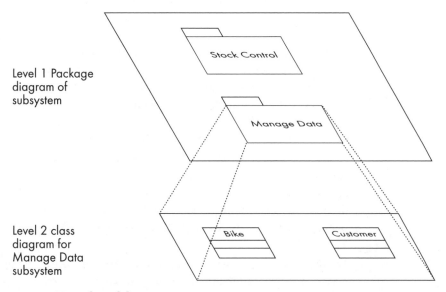

Level 1 Package
diagram of
subsystem

Level 2 class
diagram for
Manage Data
subsystem

Figure 9.1   *Nested models*

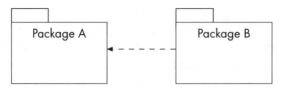

Figure 9.2   Packages and dependencies

When we group classes into packages we need some basis for doing so. We want to design packages that are cohesive and independent. One strategy is to group classes into functional subsystems, like the Wheels subsystems described above. Another strategy is to group classes by type, e.g. a group of the interface classes, a group of control classes, a group of domain classes, and a group of database classes. One advantage of this strategy is that the groups of classes can then be allocated to different programming teams who have skills in particular areas, e.g. interface programming, database programming, etc. Another advantage of grouping classes by type is reuse. For example, a package of interface classes may be suitable for reuse in a different application.

Dependencies. Package diagrams allow us also to specify dependencies between packages. A dependency exists between packages if a change in one can affect the other. If a change in package A can affect package B, then package B depends on package A. A dependency is modelled by a dashed arrow going from the dependent package to the one it depends on, see Figure 9.2.

A dependency exists between two packages, A and B, if a dependency exists between any class in package A and any class in package B. A dependency exists between two classes if, for example, they have a client–server relationship. In a client–server relationship, the client (i.e. the dependant) will be affected by a change to the server's interface. For example, let us suppose that the server changes an operation's signature from findBike(bike#) to findBicycle(bike#), if the client then sends a message that matched the old interface, e.g. bike[36].findBike(), it won't work.

In the example of the Wheels subsystems described above, several classes in the 'Hire Bike' package send messages to the Bike class, i.e. they use the services of the Bike class. The Bike class is defined in the 'Manage Data' package, therefore the 'Hire Bike' package depends on 'Manage Data', see Figure 9.3.

Localizing changes. In a well-designed system, only changes to a class's interface will affect its dependants. A package interface consists of the public operations of its public classes. The size of

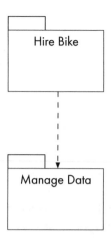

Figure 9.3   *Packages and dependencies*

the package interface can be controlled by judicious use of visibility. If a class is declared to be private, changes to it will only affect parts of the system that can see it, i.e. its own instances. Operations within a public class can be public, private or protected. In the interest of localizing the effect of changes, it is worth limiting the visibility of an operation to the parts of the system that really need to use it.

The importance of identifying dependencies is that it allows us to control the effect of introducing changes; to localize the consequences of changes to a package or a layer and so stop the effect of a change rippling through the system.

Localizing the effect of dependencies is made much easier if, as far as is possible, we can arrange our classes so that dependencies are one way only. In a client–server relationship, the dependency is one way – the client depends on the server. The client needs to know about the server's interface, but not vice versa. If two classes are mutually dependent, i.e. each class is both a client and a server, then both need to know about the other's interface. This makes a much tighter coupling between packages: a change in either class can affect the other.

In a layered architecture, packages are arranged into layers so that each layer only uses the services of the layer below it. In Figure 9.4 classes in layer 6 can only use the services of classes in layer 5, classes in layer 5 can only use the services of classes in layer 4 and so on. In this way the effects of changes are controlled. The only layers that can be directly affected by a change are the layer in which the change is made and the layer above it. If we make a change to layer 1, we know that we need to check to see if it affects itself and layer 2, but only layer 2. We only need worry about layer 3 if we change layer 2, and so on.

Layer 6
Layer 5
Layer 4
Layer 3
Layer 2
Layer 1

Figure 9.4   *A layered architecture*

Arranging packages in layers does not, in itself, limit dependencies, but it makes the developer aware of dependencies. It offers a logical structure to aim for. The layered approach only works if you have arranged your classes, packages and dependencies in a way that works as a layered architecture. If classes in layer 6 use classes in layer 3 or 1, or if classes in any layer use classes in the layers above them, the advantages of using a layered architecture are rapidly lost. The reason for structuring system models, and therefore ultimately the code elements generated by them, into a layered architecture is that it minimizes dependencies and the effects of dependencies. Being aware of, and carefully controlling, the dependencies between layers can make the difference between a robust system that is easy to maintain and one that is not.

Layers. Now that we understand how the layers work together, we need to think about what to put in each layer. If the layers are to be arranged in such a way that each layer only uses the services of the layer below, we are quite limited in where we place our packages. The normal arrangement is to put what is called the presentation layer near the top and the data storage layer towards the bottom, with the application layers in the middle. A simple four layer architecture might look like Figure 9.5. The presentation layer contains a package of boundary or interface classes, the application logic layer contains the control classes, the application layer contains the domain classes (entity and related classes) and the storage layer contains the database and related classes. This is a standard sort of arrangement because, generally, interface classes depend on control classes which in turn depend on application classes which depend on database classes. In a large and complex system there will be more layers and more packages in each layer.

Having decided on the layers, we have a basis for grouping our classes into packages. Figure 9.6 shows a possible arrangement which includes some implementation decisions.

We have grouped all of the interface classes into a package, 'Application UI classes', and put them in the presentation layer. If we decide to implement in Java we might use the Java Swing

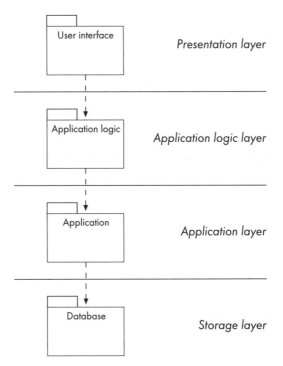

Figure 9.5   A simple four layer architecture showing dependencies

package, a Java GUI (Graphical User Interface) toolkit. The Java Swing package also goes in the presentation layer (see Figure 9.6). The application logic layer contains the control classes. The application layer contains the application or entity classes (Bike, Customer, Hire, etc.). On the assumption that we are using Java and a relational database, the storage layer has the database itself, a JDBC (Java Database Connectivity) package, a Java SQL (Structured Query Language) package and a package of relational classes. The JDBC package is a package of classes that allows a Java application to establish a connection with a relational database. The Java SQL package is needed to manipulate the database. The relational classes package contains a set of classes that structure the application classes into a form that can be handled by a relational database (see below). In a large and complex system each layer may be partitioned into subsystems, so that, for example, the presentation layer might contain the Java Swing package and several packages of interface classes – one for each subsystem.

Implementation diagrams

Component diagrams. The UML has two kinds of implementation diagrams: component diagrams and deployment diagrams. A component diagram represents the actual physical software

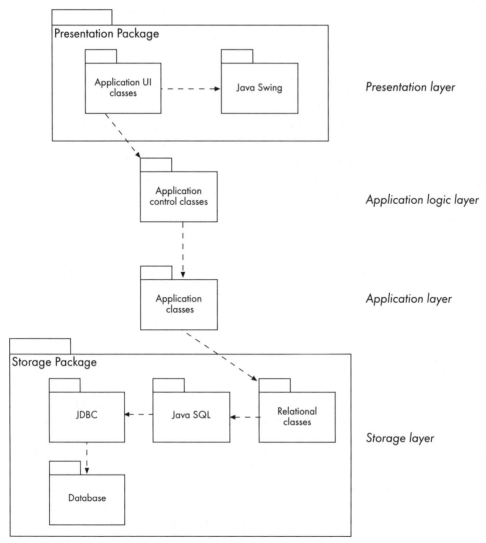

Figure 9.6   Four layer architecture showing packages and dependencies

components and their dependencies. The *components* of a system often correspond to packages, but this is not necessarily the case, as components represent physical software files and the packages identified in design are logical units. For a small system such as Wheels, the code for the whole system might be put in a single source file, or we might divide it into two subsystem files and a database file (see Figure 9.7). A component can represent a source, binary or executable file. Equally, it can represent a database file, a library file or a web page, etc.

Component diagrams also model the dependencies between components. A dependency between two components represents a usage relationship. In Figure 9.7 the component Hiring.java

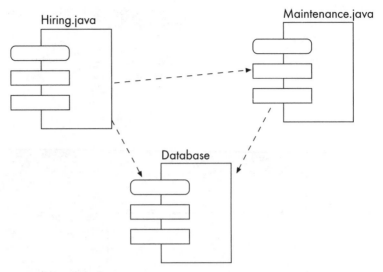

Figure 9.7   *Software components*

depends on Maintenance.java because objects in Hiring.java use the services of objects in Maintenance.java. Both of these components use the database.

Deployment diagrams. Deployment diagrams show the physical arrangement of the hardware elements of a computer system. Each item in a deployment diagram represents a piece of hardware, such as a PC, a workstation or a printer. Figure 9.8 shows one possible hardware arrangement for the Wheels system. It shows a database server linked to two PCs. One PC is located in the reception area, where it will be used to process bike hires and bike returns. The other PC is located in the shop, but at a different desk. This will be used by the Administrator to enter details of new bikes when they are delivered to the shop, and generally to keep the bike list and the customer list up to date. Both PCs will be linked to the database server which will hold the database storing the system's persistent data.

The user interface

One of the most important aspects of any computer system is the interface with its users. An interface that is difficult to cope with, intrusive or irritating, can ruin a system, no matter how efficiently it runs, how reliable it is, or how easy it is to maintain. The interface is what users see and interact with, and if they don't like it they won't use the system. Nobody today can avoid contact with computers, even if this is only receiving a computerized bill or letter. Increasingly, people expect to organize their work, holidays and

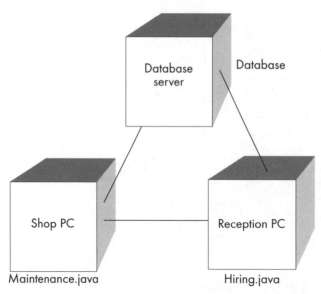

Figure 9.8   *Deployment diagram showing a hardware configuration for the Wheels system*

leisure time by means of the computer, and their decisions about which holiday to choose, or which on-line store to shop at, are strongly influenced by the 'look and feel' of the interface and the ease with which they can access the information they need. In this book, we only have room for a brief discussion about designing the user interface, so this section simply gives pointers to the principal issues that have to be considered. You can find more information about this subject in books such as Shneiderman (2004).

Designing the interface means putting yourself in the position of the user and trying to see the system from that point of view. The nearest we have come to this so far is in Chapter 3, where we talked about seeing the system from the users' point of view in order to identify the use cases. When designing the interface we have to consider the type of person who is most likely to use the system How experienced are they with computers? How familiar are they with the system? How often will they be using it? What sort of tasks will they want to carry out? In the case of Wheels, for example, the main user is Annie, the Shop Manager. Wheels already have a computer, so we can assume that Annie is fairly familiar with it. She will not initially be familiar with the new system that is being developed, but she will have some training and she will be a frequent user, so we can assume that she will soon become proficient at using the system. Annie will generally be carrying out routine tasks, such as issuing and returning bikes, printing receipts and keeping details about bikes and customers up to date. She will need to be able to enter data into the system, issue commands to manipulate the data, understand the system responses and outputs, and deal with errors.

Once we have a profile of a typical user, we have to consider how the system can best respond to their needs. Is it a priority that the system is quick and easy to learn? Or that there are a number of different ways of carrying out a task? Or that a lot of support is provided to help the user cope with errors? Is the most efficient method of data entry going to be keyboard, touch screen or speech recognition? Each user-computer relationship is different and what is ideal for one user will be hopeless for another. However, there are some general guidelines that are useful to bear in mind when designing any user interface; some of these are listed below.

- The system should be consistent, for example screen layouts should follow the same general pattern, similar tasks should be performed in similar ways, and messages from the system to the user should always be in the same format.

- User tasks that are boring and prone to error should be minimized; this means that the system should provide shortcuts for experienced users and, where possible, data should be entered by selecting from a menu rather than typing.

- Screens should be free of clutter, containing all the relevant information and no more. An overcrowded screen is tiring to look at and irritating to work with. Dramatic colour combinations and flashing signals should be avoided and highlighting should only be used to pick out important information, not to add decoration to the screen. Screens should be self-sufficient and self-explanatory. It should not be necessary to refer constantly to on-line help or the user manual to find out what to do next or how to escape out of the screen. As an example, Figure 9.9 shows a screen for entering customer details from the Wheels system.

- The dialogue with the system should be easy to follow and it should be obvious to users how to navigate their way through the various screens. A simple menu hierarchy that is easy to grasp and use is much more effective than a sophisticated navigation system that may be impressive, but is difficult for users to find their way around. Figure 9.10 shows the main menu screen from the Wheels system with the option 'Maintain customer list' selected. This takes the user to the customer menu screen shown in Figure 9.11 with the 'Add customer' option highlighted, which takes the user to the customer details entry screen shown in Figure 9.9.

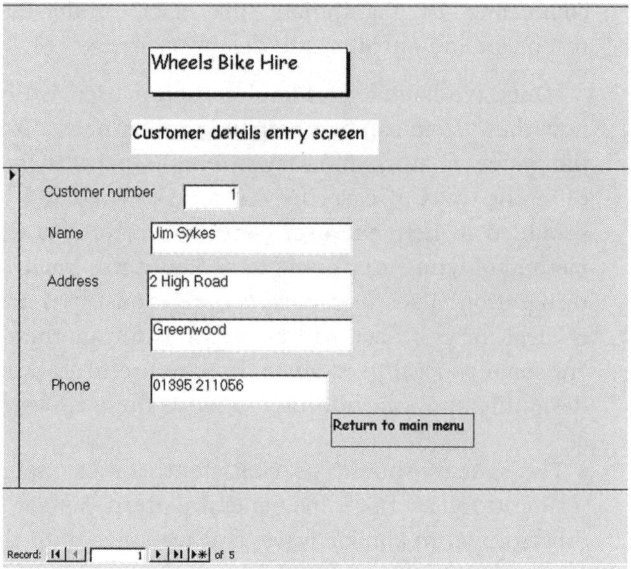

Figure 9.9   Customer details entry screen from the Wheels system

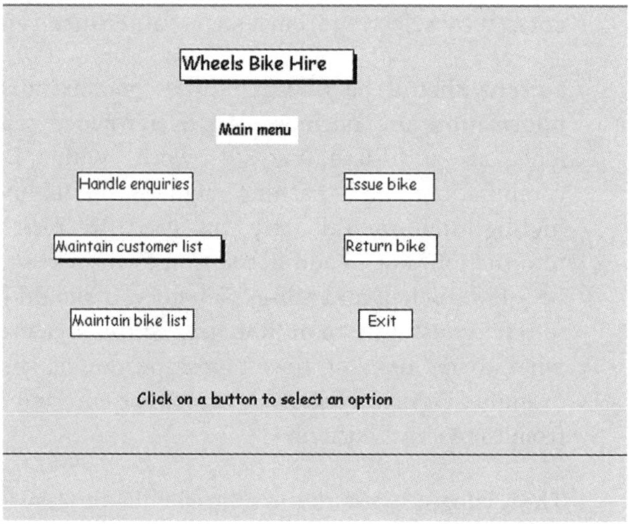

Figure 9.10   Main menu screen from the Wheels system with the option 'Maintain customer list' selected

- Feedback should be informative, but not intrusive, so the user always knows what is happening, but is not overwhelmed with details of what the system is doing. For example, when adding new bikes to the Wheels bike list, the system should confirm that each bike's details have been successfully recorded.

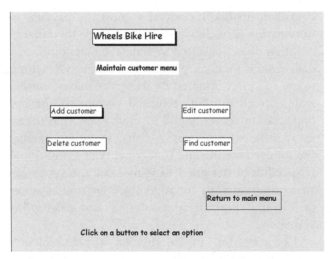

Figure 9.11 *Customer menu screen from the Wheels system with the option 'Add customer' selected*

- The language used in instructions and messages to the user should be clear, concise and free of jargon. Error messages should state the cause of the error, if possible show how it can be rectified, and indicate where more help can be found. For example, if Annie enters £4000 as a deposit instead of £40, the message 'Invalid input' is a lot less helpful to her than 'You have not entered a valid amount. Deposits must be between £20 and £100. Select Help for more information'.

- There must be adequate user support with clear instructions, messages and comprehensive on-line help.

The user interface is an area where the users really do know best. They are the people who are going to use the system and it is essential that they are closely involved with the design of the interface. An interface that the users find attractive and easy to work with and that matches their view of the tasks in hand means not only a happier user but also fewer errors and a more efficient and effective performance.

Dealing with persistent data

Object-oriented and relational databases

Each time a program executes it receives, manipulates and outputs data. Almost all systems depend not only on data that is entered by the user, but on data that is stored and remains accessible during the life of the system. The Wheels system, for example, has to store data about its bikes, customers, hires and payments so that all this information is readily available each time the program runs.

In an object-oriented system, the most obvious way of storing data in such a way as to maintain a seamless development process is to use an object-oriented database. A database stores, organizes and maintains all the data required to support the operations of an organization centrally and in such a way that it can be shared by many different programs. An object-oriented database provides all the storage facilities and functionality of a traditional database, but is specifically designed to implement the types of complex data structure frequently found in object-oriented systems, particularly multimedia, computer-aided design, and geographical information systems.

However, for an information system, such as Wheels, a developer would be much more likely to choose a relational rather than an object-oriented database. Relational database technology has dominated the market for many years; object-oriented databases, on the other hand, are relatively recent. Relational databases are established, flexible and have proved themselves extremely efficient for the sort of data that they were designed to handle. This is precisely the sort of data that information systems deal with. Many business organizations have invested money, time and effort into creating, populating and maintaining their relational database systems, and they would be very reluctant to throw all that away in order to change to an object-oriented database. For the majority of clients, developers have to find some way of allowing new object-oriented programs to share an existing relational database.

Linking an object-oriented program to a relational database poses two problems for developers. First, some means must be provided to allow the program to access the database, and second, the object-oriented analysis and design models have to be modified in some way so that they can be implemented within the relational database framework.

Linking an object-oriented program to a relational database

If an object-oriented program is to access and manipulate data in a relational database, there has to be supplementary code that can establish a connection with the database, relay the program instructions to it, and process the results. JDBC (Java Database Connectivity) is an application program interface (API) that performs these tasks for a program written in the object-oriented language Java. The application program is the Java code and JDBC is the interface that interacts with both the code and the database. The details of the way JDBC works are too complex to include here,

Customer

CustID	Name	FirstName	Street	Town	PhoneNo
1	Sykes	Jim	2 High Road	Greenwood	01395 211056
2	Perle	Lee	14 Duke Street	Greenwood	01395 237851
3	Hargreaves	Les	11 Forest Road	Prestwich	01462 501339
4	James	Sheena	4 Duke Street	Greenwood	01395 237663
5	Robins	Charlie	11 Juniper Road	Greenwood	01395 267843

Figure 9.12   Example of a table of customers in a relational database

but you can find more information in books on Java, such as Deitel and Deitel (2003).

Implementing a class diagram in a relational database

If a system is to be implemented in an object-oriented programming language using data stored in a relational database, the developer needs to think about the transition between the object-oriented models and the constraints of the database. Although there is no standard way of adapting the models, there are guidelines, and these are discussed briefly in this section. First, we look at how data is stored in a relational database.

Tables. The foundation of a relational database is its tables. Each table represents an entity that is important in the system and about which it needs to store information. A table is similar to a class in an object-oriented system in that it provides a template or pattern for all instances of the entity it represents.[4] The table is made up of rows and columns, where each column stores a field, or attribute of the entity, and each row stores a single record, typically the complete set of values for a single instance of the entity. Figure 9.12 shows a simple table to store details about customers in the Wheels bike hire system. Operations in the Wheels system that involve customers will all use data from this table.

Single classes. The basic rule, when implementing a class diagram in a relational database, is that one class maps onto one table. Figure 9.13 shows the Bike class from the Wheels class diagram. This figure does not include the Bike class operations, as our interest here is not the functionality of the system, but how the data is stored.

It is straightforward to implement this class as a table, with bike# as the primary key (the attribute in a relational table that

---

4. *Although tables have some similarity to classes, they do not in themselves have any functionality, unlike classes, which have operations.*

Figure 9.13   *The Bike class from the Wheels class diagram*

Bike

Bike No.	Available	Type	Size	Make	Model	Daily hire rate	Deposit
249	On hire	mountain	woman's	Scott	Atlantic Trail	£8.00	£50.00
250	Available	tourer	man's	Raleigh	Pioneer	£9.00	£60.00
251	On hire	mountain	woman's	Scott	Atlantic Trail	£8.00	£50.00
252	On hire	tourer	man's	Dawes	Galaxy	£8.00	£50.00
253	Available	mountain	child's	Raleigh	Chopper	£5.00	£25.00

Figure 9.14   The Bike class implemented as a table

uniquely identifies each individual bike). An extract from the table is shown in Figure 9.14.

One to many associations. Figure 9.15 shows an association between the Customer and the Payment class from the Wheels class diagram. This is a one to many association indicating that one customer can make one or any number of payments, but a specific payment is only made by one customer.

There are two ways in which one to many associations can be implemented. The first of these is to create a table for each of the two linked classes, and a third table to implement the association. We will also need to assign an identifier to the Payment table to

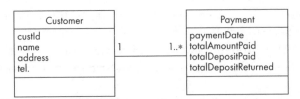

Figure 9.15   *One to many association between the Customer and Payment classes*

uniquely identify individual payments. The table representing the association (the Customer-Payment table) contains fields that in combination uniquely identify each instance of a customer and a payment. Each row in the Customer-Payment table represents a link between a customer and a payment, for example we can see that customer number 3, Les Hargreaves, is associated with payment number 404. We can also see that customer number 2, Lee Perle, is associated with two separate payments (we know that this is possible because of the one to many relationship shown in Figure 9.15). Extracts from the three tables, Customer, Payment and Customer-Payment are shown in Figure 9.16.

Customer

CustID	Name	FirstName	Street	Town	PhoneNo
1	Sykes	Jim	2 High Road	Greenwood	01395 211056
2	Perle	Lee	14 Duke Street	Greenwood	01395 237851
3	Hargreaves	Les	11 Forest Road	Prestwich	01462 501339
4	James	Sheena	4 Duke Street	Greenwood	01395 237663
5	Robins	Charlie	11Juniper Road	Greenwood	01395 267843

Payment

Payment No	Date	Total amount paid	Total deposit paid	Total deposit returned
401	19/03/04	£56.00	£50.00	£50.00
402	19/03/04	£20.00	£25.00	£25.00
403	19/03/04	£145.00	£80.00	£80.00
404	20/03/04	£186.00	£100.00	£84.00
405	20/03/04	£44.00	£40.00	£40.00

Customer–Payment

CustID	Payment No.
1	409
2	513
2	405
3	404
11	501

Figure 9.16   One to many association between the Customer and Payment classes implemented as three separate tables

Customer

CustID	Name	FirstName	Street	Town	PhoneNo
1	Sykes	Jim	2 High Road	Greenwood	01395 211056
2	Perle	Lee	14 Duke Street	Greenwood	01395 237851
3	Hargreaves	Les	11 Forest Road	Prestwich	01462 501339
4	James	Sheena	4 Duke Street	Greenwood	01395 237663
5	Robins	Charlie	11Juniper Road	Greenwood	01395 267843

Payment

Payment No	CustID	Date	Total amount paid	Total deposit paid	Total deposit returned
401	4	19/03/04	£56.00	£50.00	£50.00
402	20	19/03/04	£20.00	£25.00	£25.00
403	4	19/03/04	£145.00	£80.00	£80.00
404	3	20/03/04	£186.00	£100.00	£84.00
405	2	20/03/04	£44.00	£40.00	£40.00

Figure 9.17   *One to many association between the Customer and Payment classes implemented as two tables with a foreign key*

The second way of implementing a one to many association is to include a foreign key[5] in the table for the many class. This method of implementation has the advantage that it results in fewer tables, which means that navigation around the database is simplified. The two tables implementing the association between Customer and Payment are shown in Figure 9.17. Note the extra field, CustID, in the Payment table – this is the foreign key. In this example it is customer number 4 who is associated with more than one payment.

When converting relationships in a class diagram to tables in a relational database, aggregation is treated in the same way as a one to many association.

Many to many associations. Many to many associations are always implemented as in the first method shown for one to many associations. Separate tables are created for each class and for the association.

---

5. *If one table contains the primary key of another, this is called a foreign key. A foreign key permits a link between the two tables.*

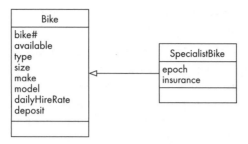

Figure 9.18   Inheritance relationship between the Bike and SpecialistBike classes

Inheritance.   Figure 9.18 shows the inheritance relationship between the Bike and SpecialistBike classes in the Wheels system.

There are three different ways of implementing an inheritance relationship, and each situation has to be considered carefully in order to select the most suitable approach. This example from the Wheels system is a very simple relationship; there is only one subclass and it only adds two new attributes, so in this case we would implement the relationship in a single table as shown in Figure 9.19. The bottom record in the table is for a specialist bike and so fills all the fields in the table. The disadvantage of implementing an inheritance relationship in this way is that it may result in a lot of null values, particularly if there are many fields that are only relevant to the subclass, or (as here) when there are comparatively few instances of the subclass.

The decision as to how to implement an inheritance relationship is more complicated in the case where there are two or more subclasses. It is possible to create tables for the subclasses only; this option is suitable in the case where the superclass is abstract (i.e. there are no actual instances of it) or where very few of the attributes are shared and appear in the superclass. The disadvantage is that the

Bike

Bike No.	Available	Type	Size	Make	Model	Epoch	Insur- ance	Daily hire rate	Deposit
249	On hire	mountain	woman's	Scott	Atlantic Trail			£80.00	£50.00
250	Available	tourer	man's	Raleigh	Pioneer			£9.00	£60.00
251	On hire	mountain	woman's	Scott	Atlantic Trail			£8.00	£50.00
252	On hire	tourer	man's	Dawes	Galaxy			£8.00	£50.00
253	Available	mountain	child's	Raleigh	Chopper			£5.00	£25.00
254	Available	tandem	man's	Sunbeam	Voyager	1930s	£15.00	£20.00	£100.00

Figure 9.19   Inheritance relationship between the Bike and SpecialistBike classes implemented as a single table

shared superclass attributes have to be replicated in each of the subclass tables.

The third option when implementing an inheritance relationship is to create separate tables for the superclass and each of the subclasses. This has the advantage of being a straightforward approach, but will produce a very large number of tables in a complex system with many inheritance relationships, and may result in problems with navigability. There may also be problems with maintenance if the superclass is modified.

Although object-oriented databases do exist, it seems unlikely at present that they will replace relational databases for systems with reasonably straightforward data storage requirements. For the moment the most widely used approach to dealing with persistent data in an object-oriented system is to adapt the object-oriented models to fit a relational database, and to incorporate supplementary code, such as JDBC, to act as an interface between the database and the main program.

Technical points

Design patterns

Design patterns are tried and tested solutions to commonly occurring problems. For example, if you need to create a class that will only ever have one instance, you do not need to worry about how to do this – you can use the Singleton pattern. If you want to write code to access all the elements of a collection one by one without revealing the underlying structure of the collection, the Iterator pattern will provide the functionality to do this for you.

One of the aims of the object-oriented approach to developing systems is to promote genuine, effective reuse, and patterns are one of the main ways of achieving this. Using design patterns means that developers do not have to reinvent the wheel for each problem they encounter when they are designing and coding a system. Since patterns have been built up from the cumulative experience of many developers, they exhibit sound object-oriented principles, such as abstraction, cohesion and autonomy.[6]

A design pattern belongs in one of three categories, creational, structural or behavioural. Table 9.1 explains these categories and gives an example of each.

6. *For a discussion of these, see Chapter 4.*

Table 9.1:   *Categories of design patterns*

Category	*Description*	*Example*
Creational	Deals with creating objects	Singleton – creates a class with only one instance
Structural	Deals with how classes and objects are combined	Façade – provides a higher-level interface for a set of interfaces in a subsystem
Behavioural	Deals with how classes and objects interact	Iterator – accesses all the elements of a collection one by one without revealing the underlying structure

Patterns are not hard-and-fast rules, but descriptions of how particular types of problem may be solved. It is still down to the expertise of the developer to see that a specific pattern will provide the right answer to a specific problem. Patterns are documented using standard templates; there is no general agreement as to the format of the templates, but most of them provide some or all of the following information:

• Pattern name

• Brief description of what the pattern does

• The problem that the pattern addresses

• Constraints on the use of the pattern

• The design of the solution in UML class or sequence diagrams

• The participants in the pattern (the classes or objects involved)

• An example of where the pattern has been used successfully

• Frequency of use of the pattern

• Sample code and details of implementation

• Rationale for the pattern, why it has developed in this way.

We show in Figure 9.20 a simple example of the Façade pattern, including the name of the pattern, what it does, the problem addressed, the participants, an example and a UML diagram.

We do not have room in this book to cover the topic of design patterns in detail. If you want to read more about this subject, the classic book is by Gamma *et al.*, (1995).

Name: Façade

What it does: Provides a higher-level interface for a set of interfaces in a subsystem

Problem: A simple interface is needed to a complex set of classes

Participants: Façade. In a system, the Façade object relays requests from other objects in the system to the appropriate subsystem object

               Subsystem classes. In a system these objects are assigned tasks by the Façade object and carry out the required functionality

Example: Example Façade class: HousePurchase
               Example subsystem classes: Purchaser, Vendor, Property, Mortgage

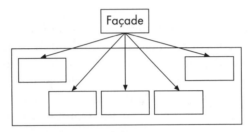

Figure 9.20   *A simple example of the Façade pattern*

Chapter summary

This chapter looks at the principal activities that take place during the overall design of the system. The models produced during design activities show how the different elements of the system will work together. This chapter is concerned with aspects of design that affect the whole system. The layered model shows the overall structure of the software architecture logically and the dependencies between the layers. The component diagram shows the physical software files and their dependencies. Deployment diagrams model the hardware units and their links. Deployment diagrams can also be used to show where the software files are physically located on the hardware, i.e. map the component diagram to the deployment diagram. A user interface must be designed so that it is appropriate for the type of users involved. For an information system, such as the Wheels system, system designers must decide how to deal with persistent data. If a relational database is selected the designer must understand how to link it to the object-oriented application, and how to convert the class diagram to a set of relational tables. Finally, the chapter looks briefly at how design patterns can be used as solutions to commonly recurring problems.

Bibliography

Bennett, S., McRobb, S. and Farmer, R. (2002) *Object-Oriented Systems Analysis and Design Using UML* (2nd edition), McGraw-Hill, London.

Deitel, H.M. and Deitel, P.J. (2003) *Java: How to Program* (5th edition), Prentice Hall, Upper Saddle River, NJ.

Fowler, M. (2000) *UML Distilled: A Brief Guide to the Standard Object Modeling Language* (2nd edition), Addison-Wesley, Reading, MA.

Gamma, E., Helm, R., Johnson, R. and Vlissides, J. (1995) *Design Patterns: Elements of Reusable Object-Oriented Software*, Addison-Wesley, Reading, MA.

Lunn, K. (2003) *Software Development with UML*, Palgrave Macmillan, Basingstoke.

Priestley, M. (2000) *Practical Object-Oriented Design with UML*, McGraw-Hill, London.

Quatrani, T. (1998) *Visual Modeling with Rational Rose and UML*, Addison-Wesley, Reading, MA.

Shneiderman, B. (2004) *Designing the User Interface: Strategies for Effective Human-Computer Interaction* (4th edition), Addison-Wesley, Reading, MA.

Stevens, P., with Pooley, R. (2000) *Using UML. Software Engineering with Objects and Components* (updated edition), Addison-Wesley, Harlow.

Quick check questions

You can find the answers to these in the chapter.

a   Briefly describe and give an example of: an entity class, a boundary class and a control class.

b   What does visibility mean in relation to operations and attributes? What values can visibility have?

c   Why is visibility important?

d   What do we use packages for?

e   What do we mean when we say there is a dependency between two packages?

f   What is a layered architecture? What would you expect the layers to be in a four-layered architecture, and in what order would you expect them to be?

g   What do component diagrams model?

h   What do deployment diagrams model?

i   List six guidelines that a developer should bear in mind when designing the user interface.

j   What is JDBC used for?

k   How is data stored in a relational database?

l   What is a design pattern?

m   Name the three pattern categories.

n   Give an example of each pattern category.

Exercises

9.1   We have grouped classes into a Stock package and an Ordering package as follows:

Stock package	Ordering package
Product	Customer
Supplier	Order
	OrderLine

Each :Product knows its price. Each :OrderLine has a numberOfItems attribute and is linked to a :Product. Each :OrderLine must work out its line cost by asking for the price from the appropriate :Product and multiplying this by the numberOfItems. What is the dependency between the two packages?

9.2   When a customer returns a bike to Wheels, Annie has to find the details of the relevant hire transaction. Design a screen that displays the customer name, bike number, bike

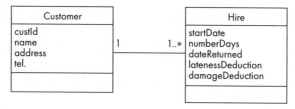

Figure 9.21   *One to many association between the Customer and Hire classes*

make, model and size, the start date of the hire, the number of days' hire, the deposit and the hire fee paid.

9.3   Using fictitious data, show how the Hire class from the Wheels system can be implemented in a relational database. Hint: remember to add a field to uniquely identify individual hires.

9.4   Figure 9.21 shows a one to many relationship between the Customer and the Hire class. List two ways in which this could be implemented in a relational database.

10 Designing objects and classes

Learning outcomes

The material and exercises in this chapter will enable you to:

- Explain the role of boundary, control and entity classes

- Understand the need for collection classes

- Specify the implementation of relationships between classes

- Specify the visibility of attributes and operations

- Specify attribute and operation signatures in full

- Add detailed design information to interaction diagrams.

Key words you will find in the glossary:

- asynchronous message
- concurrent processing
- constraint
- multiobject
- navigability
- package
- private
- protected
- public
- single-threaded
- synchronous message
- transient object

Introduction

Detailed design activities include the detailed specifications of classes, their relationships and interactions. The models should contain sufficient information to allow them to be used as a program specification.

In this chapter we revisit many of the topics described earlier in the book and discuss them from the design perspective. We revisit class diagrams to discuss extra classes that we might consider adding at this stage; for example, classes to manage the interface and control the sequence of execution. Issues that were less important during analysis such as the technical details of associations between classes and the visibility of classes, attributes and operations are now specified in detail. We revisit interaction diagrams to discuss how to model the creation and deletion of objects and how to specify condition and control.

The class diagram

One of the differences between an analysis class diagram and a design class diagram is the amount of detail shown in the models. During analysis, models are deliberately kept simple and free of implementation decisions; this makes the diagrams uncluttered and therefore easier to read and discuss with the client. It also avoids premature implementation decisions. As we move towards coding, we need to make and document decisions about the implementation. Detailed design activities include:

- Adding classes, such as interface, control and collection classes[1] to help deliver the solution

- Specifying in detail the links between objects

- Specifying the visibility of attributes and operations

- Specifying attributes in detail

- Specifying operations in detail.

During analysis, the focus is on what the organization does and what it wants the new system to do. In an analysis class diagram, most of the classes are entity classes, i.e. they model features of the problem domain. Identifying boundary and control classes can be started during analysis but detailed consideration of these classes is primarily a design and an implementation activity. One of the main reasons for separating the control and interface functions from the information and behaviour of the entity classes, is to isolate the effect of changes. For example, any changes to how the interface works should not affect the entity classes.

Boundary and control classes

As we mentioned above, boundary classes handle the system's interface with the user; they are used, for example, to translate the

---

1. *The selection of classes from the implementation language library, such as classes to implement windows, buttons, mouse-listeners, etc., should be left to the programmer.*

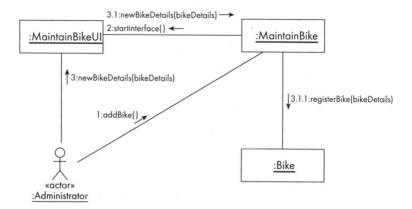

Figure 10.1   *Collaboration diagram for the 'Maintain bike list/Add bike scenario'*

user's menu selection into a message to an object. Normally every use case will have an interface object and a control object. The control object handles the sequencing of events in the execution of the use case.

Figure 10.1 shows a collaboration diagram for the 'Add bike' scenario of the 'Maintain bike list' use case.[2]

We have added a control object, :MaintainBike, and an interface object, :MaintainBikeUI, to the 'Maintain bike list' collaboration. The sequence of events during the execution of the scenario is initiated by a message from the user to the control object (via a higher-level MainMenuUI object, see footnote) and then completely controlled by the control object.

The interaction between the actor and the objects is as follows:

- The Administrator selects the Add bike option from a welcome screen

- This choice goes (via a MainMenuUI object) to the control object :MaintainBike

- The :MaintainBike creates a new interface object :MaintainBikeUI

- The Administrator enters details of the bike he wants to add on the interface object's screen

- The interface object passes these details to the control object

- The control object passes the bike details to the Bike object.

2. *Strictly speaking, the addBike() call would be to a MainMenuUI object, as an actor wouldn't be able to call directly into the controller class. For simplicity the MainMenuUI object is omitted.*

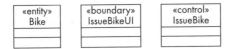

Figure 10.2 *Entity, boundary and control classes*

The same interaction is shown as a sequence diagram in Figure 10.7.

Entity, boundary and control classes are modelled as stereotypes. We have already come across stereotypes in Chapter 3 when discussing use case modelling: an actor is stereotyped class, «include» and «extend» are stereotyped associations. A stereotype is a specialized use of a modelling element which allows us to extend the basic UML set of modelling elements. Guillemets «» are used to indicate stereotypes, see Figure 10.2. Notice that it is not always useful to display the stereotype of a class on a diagram – we have managed quite well up to now without knowing that Bike, Customer, Hire, etc. were entity classes. As with many of the advanced modelling features, it is only worth showing the stereotype when it adds meaning to the diagram.

In reality, the Wheels system is so small that, when we implemented it, we combined the functions of a control and boundary class in a single class, see Figure 10.11. For the purposes of discussing the use of boundary and control classes, however, we have modelled them separately.

Designing associations

When we are designing, we need to make decisions about how the relationships between classes will be implemented. On early analysis class diagrams, associations between the classes Customer, Payment, Hire and Bike simply reflected the fact that in real life customers make payments and hire transactions, and hire transactions are for bikes, etc. Identification of class responsibilities and collaborators using CRC cards gave us more idea of what the associations should be. By the time we get to design, we know, from doing the interaction diagrams, exactly which objects need to communicate and the nature and direction of the messages. Associations between classes specify a requirement to implement navigable paths between objects of those classes. How we implement an association depends on the multiplicity of the association and whether communication is one way or two way.

One to one associations. There are no 1:1 associations in the Wheels system. Figure 10.3 shows a 1:1 association between a School class and a SchoolLibrary class. School objects need to be able to send

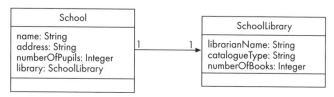

Figure 10.3   *Unidirectional one to one association*

messages to SchoolLibrary objects, but not vice-versa. The direction in which messages are sent is called the *navigability* of the association. One-way associations are referred to as *unidirectional*. The direction of the navigability is indicated by the arrowhead. Two-way navigability can be shown either by an arrowhead on both ends of the association, or by having no arrows. However, no arrowheads can also mean that the navigability has not been specified, as is the case on the analysis model. It is clearer to show the arrowheads.

To implement the one to one association, School has an attribute, library, which is used to hold the object identifier (otherwise referred to as a pointer or reference) of the SchoolLibrary object with which it needs to communicate. In a two-way association each class needs to hold a reference to the other. If the association between School and SchoolLibrary were two way, School would need to hold a reference to SchoolLibrary and SchoolLibrary would need to hold a reference to School.

One to many associations. Figure 10.4 shows a unidirectional, one to many association between the interface class MaintainBikeUI and the Bike class. A MaintainBikeUI object has to communicate with objects of the Bike class but not vice versa.

A MaintainBikeUI object has to be able to send messages to more than one :Bike, sometimes it will send a message to a specific :Bike identified by bike#, sometimes to a selection with the same make,

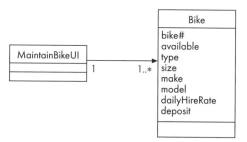

Figure 10.4   *Unidirectional one to many association*

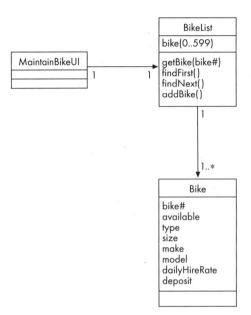

Figure 10.5   *A collection class used to implement a one to many association*

sometimes to all of the :Bikes. To do this :MaintainBikeUI has to know the identifiers of all the Bike objects. It could hold these in a simple array; however, it would also need operations to manage the array: to facilitate adding, deleting and finding bike identifiers. The problem with this is partly that this is not the job of a UI class and partly that other classes (for example the IssueBikeUI class) will need the same functionality: they too will need a set of :Bike identifiers and code to manipulate it. It would be more efficient to create a class specially to hold and manipulate the identifiers, a *collection class*.

Figure 10.5 shows BikeList, a collection class which can find a specific bike by bike#, add and delete bikes, etc. MaintainBikeUI has a 1:1 relationship with BikeList. This association therefore can be implemented as explained above, by keeping a reference to BikeList in MaintainBikeUI. A :BikeList will contain a list of :Bike references – bike[0..599] (in arrays we count from zero).

Accessing a particular :Bike will be done as follows. :MaintainBikeUI will send a getBike(bike#) message to :BikeList asking it to find a bike with a particular bike#. :BikeList will iterate through the list of :Bikes looking for one whose bike# matches. The identifier of this :Bike will then be returned to :MaintainBikeUI which can then send a message directly to that :Bike. This interaction is modelled in the sequence diagram in Figure 10.6.

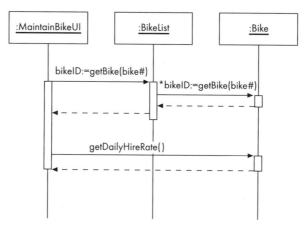

Figure 10.6   *Sequence diagram showing how the collection class works*

In other words, if an object needs to send a message, it must know how to get the message to the recipient. This means it must know the recipient object's identifier. It can do this is various ways.

- Via a direct link as in an association, e.g. in Figure 10.3 the School attribute, library, holds the object identifier for a SchoolLibrary object; this provides a direct link between a School object and a SchoolLibrary object.

- The calling object can be sent the target object's identifier by another object that has a link to the target object. In Figure 10.6 the attribute bikeID is set to the object identifier of the required bike, i.e. :BikeList finds the identifier of the :Bike and returns it to :MaintainBikeUI.

- An object identifier can be passed in as a parameter by a constructor to the object it creates. For example, in Figure 10.11 the interface object :IssueBikeUI creates a new Payment object and passes it the identifier of the relevant Customer object as a parameter. :IssueBikeUI also creates a new Hire object and passes it Bike and Customer object references.

For other ways of creating navigable paths between objects see Deitel and Deitel (2003).

Designing attributes and operations

Attribute signatures. During design we need to specify the details of each attribute's signature. The UML format of an attribute signature is:

visibility name : type-expression = initial-value

For example, the signature of the attribute, deposit, in the Bike class is:

#deposit : Integer = 0

- # indicates the visibility of the attribute; in this case it is protected, i.e. it cannot be viewed or modified by any other object but it can be inherited. It is normal practice to make attributes private or protected. The attribute deposit must be protected rather than private because it is inherited by SpecialistBike.

- deposit is the *name* of the attribute; this is the only compulsory part of an attribute's signature.

- Integer is its *type*.[3]

- 0 – when a Bike object is created by its constructor, deposit is set to zero. An attribute should always be set to a default value rather than be unspecified. If unspecified it might pick up a value left over from a previous use of its memory location.

Operation signatures. We also need to specify operation signatures. Operations can take parameters and return values. The UML format of an operation signature is:

visibility name (parameter list) : return-type

For example:

+findBike(bike# : Integer) : Bike

- + indicates the visibility of the operation. This is a public operation, i.e. it can be used by any object.

- findBike is the name of the operation.

- bike# : Integer is the parameter for this operation; there can be more than one parameter in which case parameters are separated by commas. Each parameter is specified in terms of its name and type, in this case the parameter name is bike# and its type is Integer.

- The type returned by this operation is Bike, i.e. the object identifier of an object of the Bike class.

3. *The data types we mention in this chapter are not language specific. Common primitive data types include Integer, Floating Point, Character, Boolean. Most languages also provide String, Date, Money.*

Designing operations. During detailed design, we look more closely at operations or more precisely at the methods that implement the operations. We design the algorithms that will be used. Our decisions can be documented using an activity diagram (see Chapter 8), or one of the techniques for describing processes described in Chapter 6, structured English, decision tables, decision trees or specification by contract.

In general, when designing (and when programming), it is best to keep algorithms as simple as possible. If you are tempted to use clever and intellectually satisfying or performance enhancing techniques, think of the poor maintenance programmer who will be forced to follow your tortuous thought patterns.

Interaction diagrams

During analysis we are using interaction diagrams primarily to work out how groups of objects will collaborate in a process, usually in the form of a use case scenario. At this stage we are still ironing out the wrinkles in the allocation of responsibilities to classes and the implications of this in terms of operations on classes and messaging between objects. During design we focus on the code; we use the interaction diagrams, essentially, to give an abstract view of what is happening when the program is running. To achieve this we need to add more detail to the models: we discuss how to specify the creation and deletion of objects, how to specify conditional behaviour and repeated behaviour, how to use interaction diagrams at different levels of detail using multiple objects and packages.

In the following section we introduce you to a lot of extra notation which will allow you to build more information into your sequence diagrams. However, it is important to remember that the greatest appeal of sequence diagrams is their simplicity, so use the extra notation with care. If you try to show too much detail on a sequence diagram it loses its chief attraction.

Object creation and deletion. During the execution of a use case scenario, the group of objects is not necessarily fixed; new objects can be created, existing objects can be deleted. Objects that are created or deleted in an interaction are called *transient* objects.

We have already met the UML notation for object creation in Chapter 6; instead of appearing at the top of the page the object icon appears further down the page, at the point where it is created. The notation for object destruction is a large X at the bottom of the object's lifeline, see Figure 10.7. Objects can either self-destruct or be destroyed by receiving a message from another

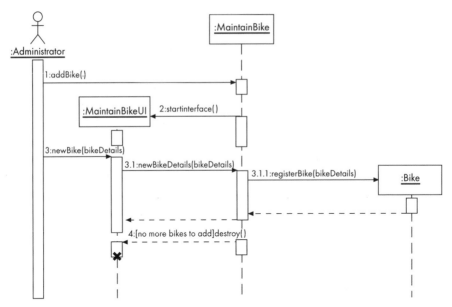

Figure 10.7   *Object creation and deletion*

object. For example, a PhoneCall object may self-destruct, when the caller hangs up, or may be cut off (destroyed) by the exchange.

Figure 10.7 shows, as a sequence diagram, the same interaction as the collaboration diagram in Figure 10.1. We have added the destruction of the interface object. When there are no more bikes to add, the control object, :MaintainBike, sends a destroy() message to the interface object :MaintainBikeUI.

The destroy() message will only be sent if the condition [no more bikes to add] evaluates to true.

Iteration. In Chapter 6 we explained message iteration: we can use an asterisk to indicate a message that is sent repeatedly. We can specify how many times the message is sent with an iteration clause. We can also indicate that the message is sent to many objects by using a multiobject icon. If we want to specify that a series of messages is repeated, we can do so by outlining the block of messages and adding an iteration clause. In Figure 10.8 everything inside the rectangle is repeated while there are more bikes to add.

Conditional behaviour and branching. We have already seen examples of messages guarded by conditions; in Figure 10.8 the destroy() message is guarded by the condition [no more bikes to add]. Putting a guard on a message means that the message will only be sent if the Boolean expression in the square brackets

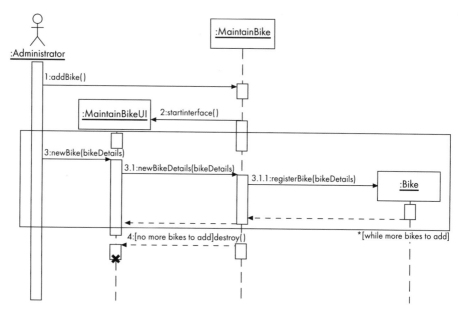

Figure 10.8   Repeated block of code

evaluates to true. The UML does not dictate a format for writing conditions – natural language, structured English, pseudo-code, OCL (Object Constraint Language)[4] or a programming language expression are all acceptable.

Sequence diagrams allow us to model conditional branching, i.e. sending different messages depending on the value of a condition. Figure 10.9 shows a fragment of a sequence diagram from the Wheels system – for simplicity we have omitted interface and control objects. If a customer has not hired a bike before, the Receptionist must enter their details into the system. The Receptionist inputs the customer's name; if the system finds a :Customer with a matching name it displays the address. Otherwise a new :Customer is created. Only one of these messages should be sent, so it is important that the conditions should be mutually exclusive.

Showing conditional behaviour has the effect of modelling more than one possible sequence of events on one diagram. This means you can get away with drawing fewer sequence diagrams, but the disadvantage is that the diagrams become more complicated. If your diagram starts to get too complicated, show the different sequences of events on different diagrams.

4. *The UML's formal language for specifying constraints.*

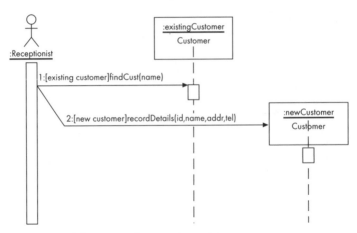

Figure 10.9   *Fragment of diagram showing branching*

Concurrency. Sequence diagrams can also be used to model synchronous and asynchronous messages. All of the messages we have met so far have been synchronous. When an object sends a *synchronous* message, it must wait for a response from the object it calls. The sending object, therefore, cannot continue with its own processing until it gets a response. This is often because it is waiting for data. Up till now, at any given time, we have only modelled situations where a single object is processing. This is not particularly surprising as many information systems are *single-threaded* and designed to run on single processor computers. However, in a multi-threaded system, i.e. one designed to have several processes executing in parallel, it is useful to be able to model asynchronous messages. When an object sends an *asynchronous* message it can invoke an operation on another object without interrupting its own processing; the two objects can process in parallel. This is also known as *concurrent* processing. In Figure 10.10 we model the home-coming of a teenager, chris, after a hard day at school. He is very hungry and makes a bee-line for the fridge. Without pausing in his stride, or rather his hunt for food, he tells his little brother to put the television on so that he can watch the football, asks his baby sister to give him a smile and drops his games kit on the ground telling his mum that he needs it washed by tomorrow. All of these are asynchronous messages, he starts three processes in motion without interrupting his own job which is the search for food. An asynchronous message is indicated by a half arrowhead.

Notice another new notation in the diagram in Figure 10.10; there is a {by tomorrow} constraint on the message washKit(kit). A *constraint* is simply an assertion about the modelling element it

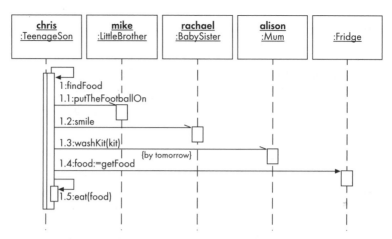

Figure 10.10   Asynchronous messages

describes; it can be added to most modelling elements. Constraints are often attached to classes, e.g. we might add a constraint {hire limit three weeks} to the Hire class if we wanted to impose a time limit on the length of a hire.

The ability to distinguish synchronous from asynchronous messages means that sequence diagrams can be used to model concurrent processing.

We might, more realistically, use asynchronous messages in an automated greenhouse which uses multiprocessing. The greenhouse could have three machines (a fan, heater and sprinkler) controlled by a computer system. We could have a separate process to control each machine. One controlling object could monitor thermostats and send asynchronous messages to objects running the three processes. Because the messages are asynchronous, the three processes could run concurrently.

Suppressing detail. Sometimes it is useful to be able to look at sequence diagrams at different levels of detail. The UML has no specific notation to indicate that some detail is hidden in a sequence diagram. However, as we saw in Chapter 6, when an interaction diagram gets too complicated, we can use a package to group cohesive sets of objects. The package is then treated as though it were a single object. A message sent from an object outside the package to any object inside the package is simply sent to the package. The details of inter-object messaging inside the package are suppressed. Another acceptable way of suppressing detail is simply to add a note to a diagram indicating that detail suppressed in this diagram can be found in another diagram.

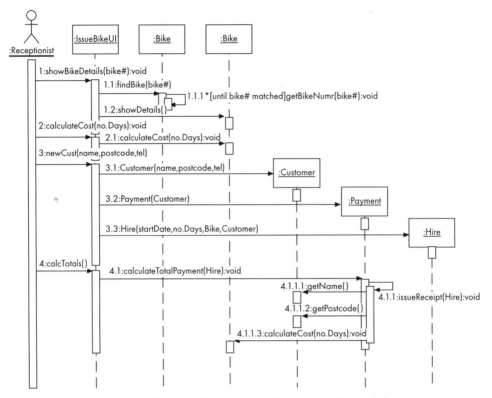

Figure 10.11   *Sequence diagram for the Wheels system – 'Issue bike' use case,*
successful hire scenario

Wheels sequence diagram at design. The sequence diagram in
Figure 10.11 shows how the process of issuing a bike has evolved
from the analysis model. Because Wheels is a very small system,
rather than introduce three new objects (an interface object, a
control object and a collection object), we have added a single
object (:IssueBikeUI) which combines the functions of interface and
control objects. It controls the interaction between the actor and
the system and it controls the main sequence of inter-object
messaging. We have altered the Bike class so that it combines the
functions of a collection and an entity class. The Bike class contains
an array of bikes. It knows the identifier of each of the :Bikes.

The sequence of execution is as follows:

1   Presumably, at a higher level than this sequence diagram, the
    Receptionist has made a menu choice to issue a bike. This
    results in a message being sent to :IssueBikeUI indicating the
    bike# of the bike the customer has chosen.

2   :IssueBikeUI passes the bike# to Bike (the collection class)
    which iterates through the list of bike identifiers, sending a
    message to each :Bike in turn until it finds the one with a

matching bike#. :IssueBikeUI then sends a message to that :Bike which displays its details (to check that the correct bike has been found).

3 :IssueBikeUI asks the actor how long the hire is for, collects the actor response and sends a message to the :Bike asking it for the costs, the :Bike displays the deposit, daily hire rate and cost of the hire for the specified number of days.

4 :IssueBikeUI waits for a response from the actor to know whether or not to proceed with the hire. The actor responds with a request to create a new :Customer. :IssueBikeUI creates a new Customer object and populates its attributes with the values passed in by the actor.

5 :IssueBikeUI automatically creates a new Payment object when it creates the Customer object.

6 :IssueBikeUI automatically creates a new Hire object and sets the start date to today's date and the number of days to the number specified in step 3.

7 :IssueBikeUI then asks :Payment to calculate the total cost, including the deposit.

8 :Payment issues a receipt. To do this it asks its :Customer for the name and postcode so that this can be printed on the receipt. :Payment then asks the :Bike for the total cost so that this too can be printed on the receipt.

Notice that the sequence diagram in Figure 10.11 has two Bike object icons. On a sequence diagram it is permissible to represent more than one object of the same class. In this case we use the first Bike icon to represent Bike in its capacity as a collection class and the second to represent the individual Bike object with the matching bike#.

Chapter summary

Analysis is concerned with specifying what a system has to do; design is concerned with specifying how to deliver that functionality. Design activities concerning the overall system design specify the overall system architecture logically, using a layered model, and physically using component and deployment diagrams. This is discussed in Chapter 9. Detailed design activities in an object-oriented system require us to specify the class diagram in more detail. Boundary, control and collection classes must be added. Attribute and operation signatures must be completely specified. Decisions must also be made about how relationships between classes will be implemented. Interaction diagrams are revisited to incorporate the behaviour of new classes to add more detail concerning iteration, branching and other conditional behaviour.

Bibliography

Bennett, S., McRobb, S. and Farmer, R. (2002) *Object-Oriented Systems Analysis and Design Using UML* (2nd edition), McGraw-Hill, London.

Deitel, H.M. and Deitel, P.J. (2003) *Java: How to Program* (5th edition), Prentice Hall, Upper Saddle River, NJ.

Quick check questions

You can find the answers to these in the chapter.

a   Name four detailed design activities.

b   What is a navigable path?

c   What is meant by unidirectional navigability?

d   How might we implement a 1:1 unidirectional navigable path?

e   What is the format of an attribute's signature?

f   What is the format of an operation's signature?

g   How would you indicate the creation and the deletion of an object on a sequence diagram?

Exercises

10.1   An association relationship on a class diagram should be interpreted differently at analysis and design. Explain the difference.

10.2   Using the class diagram in Figure 10.12, draw a sequence diagram to capture the following behaviour.

:OrderUI sends a priceOrder() message to :Order; :Order sends a getLineCost() message to each :OrderLine; each :OrderLine sends a getPrice() message to the appropriate :Product, it then returns the lineCost which is the price*numberOfItems. Your answer should use an iteration clause.

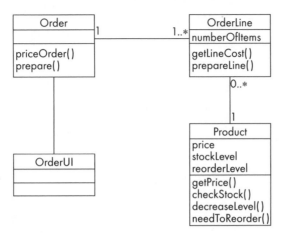

Figure 10.12   Class diagram for order processing

10.3   This question is based on Figure 10.12.

a   Draw a sequence diagram to model the following order processing behaviour:

An :OrderUI sends a prepare() message to an :Order; the :Order sends a prepareLine() message to each :OrderLine; the :OrderLine must check if there is sufficient stock of its :Product and adjust the stock level as appropriate.

b   Each time the stock level is decreased, the :Product checks whether it needs to reorder. It does this by comparing the stockLevel with reorderLevel. If it needs to reorder, the :Product sends a message to the :Supplier. How would you adjust the class diagram in Figure 10.12 and your sequence diagram to include this information?

10.4   For all the message passing specified in the description of the sequence diagram in Figure 10.11, work out how the sending object knows the object identifier of the recipient object.

11 The code

Learning outcomes

The material and exercises in this chapter will enable you to:

- Understand a simple Java program
- Understand how a class diagram maps onto a Java implementation
- Understand how a sequence diagram maps onto a Java implementation
- Follow the sequence of execution in a simple Java program.

Key words that you will find in the glossary:

- class declaration
- compiler
- constructor
- front end
- get method

- member variable
- method call
- reverse engineer
- self-referencing
- set method

Introduction

In this chapter we discuss the code written to implement the Wheels system. The object of this chapter is not to give you a crash course in programming, but to demonstrate how some of the models we have developed throughout the book map onto the code. We do not attempt to explain every instruction in the code – that is beyond the scope of the book. The code is discussed in terms of how it relates to the class diagram and how it relates to the sequence diagram. For the class diagram we indicate which lines of code implement the classes, attributes, methods and relationships. We use the sequence diagram as a road map to guide us through the sequence in which the programming instructions are executed. Otherwise the discussion of the code is limited to an explanation of significant features that were not present in earlier models.

The system is implemented in the object-oriented programming language Java. The main reason for this choice was simply that it is a popular programming language taught on many programming courses. It is also supported by Together, the CASE tool we have used to produce many of the UML models in this book.

For simplicity, the code reproduced in this chapter is only a partial implementation of the Wheels system: one scenario of the 'Issue bike' use case. The code is limited to handling one customer hiring one bike. This means that some of the methods, e.g. the Payment method, calculateTotalPayment(), seem pointless as they were designed to handle multiple bike hires. As the code we require for this chapter is for illustrative purposes only, it was more important to have simple code than fully functional code.

Many details, such as references to other classes, have been added to the classes. We have, therefore, omitted some attributes and methods that were present on the analysis model. This allows us to keep the diagrams within manageable proportions.

Throughout this chapter we refer to methods rather than operations[1]; this is appropriate at this stage because programmers are concerned with the body of code that implements a process. In earlier chapters we talked about operations rather than methods because analysis and design activities are more concerned with the interface of a process than its implementation.

The implementation class diagram

The implementation class diagram in Figure 11.1 was originally generated from the code by the CASE tool Together. It shows full implementation detail as described in Chapter 10, i.e. visibility, types and initial values of attributes, method parameters (with types and return types) and method return types. For the purpose of producing the diagram, Together ignores *gets* and *sets*, i.e. methods that simply set or return the value of an attribute. For example, Customer has three get methods, getCustomerNumber(), getName() and getPostcode(), which are not shown on the class diagram.

StartUp Class. StartUp is a new class. Applications in Java must always contain the method main(); it is always the first method to be executed when a Java application is run. In Java every method, including main(), must be inside a class; we invented the StartUp class partly to house main().

The other purpose of StartUp is to simulate what would happen if this code were part of a fully implemented system with a front

---

1. *For a discussion on the difference between operation and method see Chapter 4.*

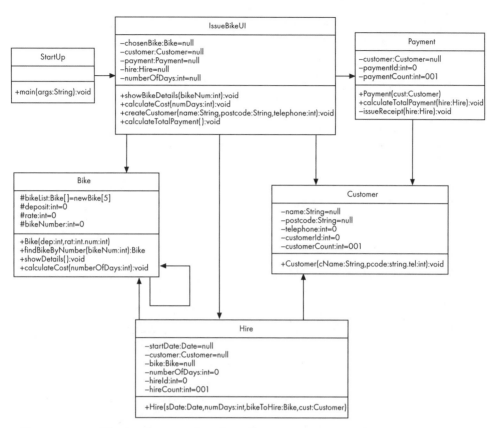

Figure 11.1   The implementation class diagram

end consisting of a welcome menu and other layers of interface screens. The class effectively simulates the function of Receptionist as modelled in the sequence diagram in Figure 10.11, reproduced here as Figure 11.2. The four method calls, showBikeDetails(), calculateCost(), newCust() and calcTotals(), sent by the Receptionist to :IssueBikeUI, are now made from StartUp.

IssueBikeUI class. This class has already been introduced in Chapter 9. It combines the functions of controller and interface class. Its first four attributes, chosenBike, customer, payment and hire are all used to hold the object identifiers of (or references to) objects with which the IssueBikeUI needs to interact. These attributes are used to implement the unidirectional navigable paths shown on the class diagram issuing from IssueBikeUI. The last attribute, numberOfDays, holds the length of a hire. It is set when calculateCost(numDays) is called and subsequently used as a parameter when the Hire object is created.

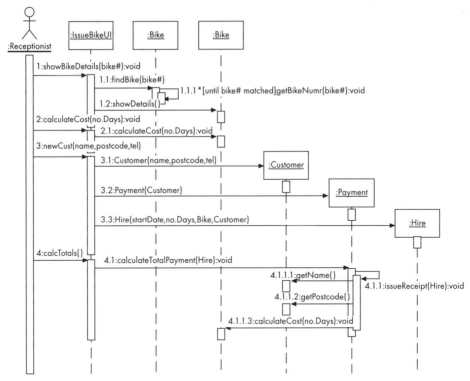

Figure 11.2   *The design sequence diagram for the 'Issue bike' use case, successful hire scenario*

Payment class. The Payment class is the same entity class that featured in the analysis model. For simplicity some attributes have been omitted.

Attributes:

- customer is used to hold a reference to a Customer object; this allows each Payment object to be linked to the right Customer object. It implements the unidirectional navigable path to the Customer class shown on the class diagram.

- paymentId is used to hold a number that uniquely identifies each :Payment. This number is an integer that can be read and understood by humans, unlike a reference (or object identifier) that is only used by a computer.

- paymentCount is a class variable[2] which allows the application to assign a number that uniquely identifies each :Payment (paymentId). It is updated each time a new Payment object is created.

2. *A class variable belongs to the class unlike a member variable which belongs to the instances of a class.*

Methods:

- Payment(cust:Customer) is a *constructor*.[3] When invoked, it creates a new Payment object and links it to the :Customer reference which is passed in as a parameter.

- calculateTotalPayment(hire:Hire) is designed to work out the total payments for a customer who has hired several bikes. As, in this implementation, there is only one customer hiring one bike, this method is only partially implemented. calculateTotalPayment() calls the private method issueReceipt().

- issueReceipt(hire:Hire) prints a receipt. Notice that on the diagram this method has a minus sign in front of it, indicating that it is a private method. This means that it can only be used by instances of the Payment class.

Bike class The Bike class combines the functions of the entity class, Bike, and a collection class that has a list of all the :Bike identifiers. For simplicity we have limited the Bike attributes to deposit, rate and bikeNumber.

Methods:

- Bike(dep:int, rat:int, num:int) is a constructor. When invoked, it creates a new Bike object and sets its attributes to the values passed in as parameters.

- findBikeByNumber(bikeNum:int) is part of the collection class functionality; it iterates through a list of :Bikes until it finds one with a matching bike number.

- showDetail() is used to display the bike details that have been found by findBikeByNumber().

- calculateCost(numberOfDays:int) works out the cost of hiring the bike for the specified period.[4]

Customer class. The Customer class is the same entity class that featured in the analysis model. As with the Payment objects, each :Customer has a unique customerId which is generated by the class variable customerCount. For simplicity, we use a postcode attribute instead of a full address. Although, in the code, it has three get methods, the only method shown on the model is a constructor.

3. *A constructor is readily identifiable as its name is always the same as the class name.*
4. *This method replaces the getCharges(no.Days) method shown on the analysis class diagram.*

Hire class. The Hire class is the same entity class that featured in the analysis model. As with Payment and Customer objects, each :Hire has a unique hireId which is generated by the class variable hireCount. The attributes customer and bike are used to hold references to Customer and Bike objects. Although it has four get methods, the only method shown on the diagram is a constructor.

The code

Don't be dismayed if you cannot follow all of the code. This book is not about programming. The purpose of this section is to demonstrate how the class diagram maps onto the code. For the moment, just ignore the parts you do not understand and accept that there is some reason why they have to be there. In this section, for three of the classes only, we compare the class diagram model of the class with the section of code that implements it.

StartUp class

The class diagram for the StartUp class is shown in Figure 11.3, the code for the StartUp class is shown in Figure 11.4.

- Line 01 of the code declares that StartUp is in a package called bikeshop (as are all of the classes in the code).

- The StartUp class declaration is in line 05. Everything in the class must be contained within two curly brackets {}, these brackets tell the compiler where the class begins and ends. The opening bracket is on line 05, the closing one on line 27.

- The method, main(), is declared in line 07. All of the program instructions for this method are inside a second pair of curly brackets, the opening bracket is on line 07, the closing bracket is on line 26.

- The first instruction in main() creates an IssueBikeUI object, ui (line 13), the next four instructions are calls to the IssueBikeUI object. These four instructions implement the main steps in the 'Issue bike' use case scenario.

- Lines beginning with a double forward slash, //, are comments and are ignored by the compiler.[5] Comments can also be contained within /* */; the compiler ignores everything after an opening /* until it finds the closing */.

---

5. *A compiler is a program that translates source code (e.g. a Java program) into machine code, i.e. code which can be executed by a computer.*

Figure 11.3   Class diagram for the StartUp class

```
1   package bikeshop;
2
3   /* Generated by Together */
4
5   public class StartUp {
6
7       public static void main(String[] args){
8
9           /* This little program will run through the methods on IssueBikeUI
10           * calling each in turn, like a user with a front end would do. */
11
12          // First, create the UI
13          IssueBikeUI ui = new IssueBikeUI();
14
15          //1. Show details for chosen bike
16          ui.showBikeDetails(100);
17
18          // 2. Calculate cost of hiring this bike for 5 days
19          ui.calculateCost(5);
20
21          // 3. Create new customer, payment and hire
22          ui.createCustomer("Les Hargreaves", "PW2 6TR", 01462501339);
23
24          // 4. Calculate the total cost
25          ui.calculateTotalPayment();
26      }
27 }
```

Figure 11.4   Code for the StartUp class

IssueBikeUI class

The class diagram for the IssueBikeUI class is shown in Figure 11.5, the code for the IssueBikeUI class shown in Figure 11.6.

- The IssueBikeUI class is declared in line 34.

- The attributes (also known as member variables) are declared in lines 37–41.

- The showBikeDetails(bikeNum:int):void method is declared on line 42. This method calls findBikeByNumber(bikeNum) in the Bike class.

```
┌─────────────────────────────────────────────────────────────┐
│                        IssueBikeUI                          │
├─────────────────────────────────────────────────────────────┤
│ −chosenBike:Bike=null                                        │
│ −customer:Customer=null                                      │
│ −payment:Payment=null                                        │
│ −hire:Hire=null                                              │
│ −numberOfDays:int=0                                          │
├─────────────────────────────────────────────────────────────┤
│ +showBikeDetails(bikeNum:int):void                           │
│ +calculateCost(numDays:int):void                             │
│ +createCustomer(name:String,postcode:String,telephone:int):void │
│ +calculateTotalPayment():void                                │
└─────────────────────────────────────────────────────────────┘
```

Figure 11.5   *Class diagram for the IssueBikeUI class*

- findBikeByNumber(bikeNum) iterates through its array of bike objects until it finds one with a matching bike number (one that matches the value of the parameter bikeNum). The reference (object identifier) of the matching bike is returned and assigned to the attribute chosenBike. This reference is then used to send the message, showDetails(), to the matching bike.

The remaining method declarations are:

- +calculateCost(numDays:int):void on line 50

- +createCustomer(name:String,postcode:String,tel:int):void on line 57

- +calculateTotalPayment():void on line 64.

Notice that all of these methods are public, i.e. they can be called by any object. The method, createCustomer(), actually creates a Customer object, a Payment object and a Hire object.

Bike class

The class diagram for the Bike class is shown in Figure 11.7, the code for the Bike class is shown in Figure 11.8.

- The Bike class is declared in line 71.

- An array of 5 Bike objects, bikeList, is declared in line 74.

- The attributes (also known as member variables) are declared in lines 76–78.

- The Bike constructor is declared on line 91; in lines 93-95 the member variables are set to the values passed in as parameters to the constructor.

There are three get methods:

- getDeposit() declared on line 98

- getRate() declared on line 102

- getBikeNumber() declared on line 106.

The method findBikeByNumber() is declared on line 110. This method, as we mentioned above, iterates over the array of

```
28  /* Generated by Together */
29
30      package bikeshop;
31
32      import java.util.Date;
33
34      public class IssueBikeUI {
35
36      // Set up the member variables
37      private Bike chosenBike = null;
38      private Customer customer = null;
39      private Payment payment = null;
40      private Hire hire = null;
41      private int numberOfDays = 0;

42      public void showBikeDetails(int bikeNum){
43          // Find the bike by its number
44          chosenBike = Bike.findBikeByNumber(bikeNum);
45          if(chosenBike !=null){
46              // then ask it for its details
47              chosenBike.showDetails( );
48          }
49      }
50      public void calculateCost(int numDays){
51          // set the member variable so it can be used later
52          numberOfDays = numDays;
53          // then ask the bike for the cost
54          chosenBike.calculateCost(numDays);
55      }
56
57      public void createCustomer(String name, String postcode, int telephone){
58          // Create a customer and associated hire and payment
59          customer = new Customer(name, postcode, telephone);
60          payment = new Payment(customer);
61          hire = new Hire(new Date( ), numberOfDays, chosenBike, customer);
62      }
63
64      public void calculateTotalPayment( ){
65          // get the total payment from the payment object
66          payment.calculateTotalPayment(hire);
67      }
68      }
```

Figure 11.6   Code for the IssueBikeUI class

Bike
#bikeList:Bike[]=newBike[5] #deposit:int=0 #rate:int=0 #bikeNumber:int=0
+Bike(dep:int,rat:int.num:int) +findBikeByNumber(bikeNum:int):Bike +showDetails( ):void +calculateCost(numberOfDays:int):void

Figure 11.7   Class diagram for the Bike class

```
69  package bikeshop;
70
71     public class Bike {
72
73     // create the BikeList
74     protected static Bike[] bikeList = new Bike[5];ᵃ
75     //    set up member variables
76     protected int deposit = 0;
77     protected int rate = 0;
78     protected int bikeNumber = 0;
79
80     /* This block is run when the class is loaded and sets up our bike store.
81      * It arbitrarily populates the attributes: deposit, rate and bikeNumber */
82     static{
83         int j = 0;
84         for(int i=10;i<15;i++){
85             Bike b = new Bike(i, i, (j*100));
86             bikeList[j] = b;
87             j++;
88         }
89     }
90
91     public Bike(int dep, int rat, int num){
92         // set the member variables
93         deposit = dep;
94         rate = rat;
95         bikeNumber = num;
96     }
97
98     public int getDeposit( ){
99         return deposit;
100    }
101
102    public int getRate( ){
103        return rate;
104    }
105
106    public int getBikeNumber( ){
107        return bikeNumber;
108    }
109
110    public static Bike findBikeByNumber(int bikeNum){
111        int numberOfBikes = bikeList.length;
112
113        // iterate over the list of bikes
114        for(int i=0;i<numberOfBikes;i++){
115            // if we find the bike with the correct number...
116            if(bikeList[i].getBikeNumber( ) == bikeNum){
117                // tell user that we've found it
118                System.out.println("Bike with number '" + bikeNum + "' found" + "\n");
119                // and return it to the UI
120                return bikeList[i];
```

Figure 11.8   Code for the Bike class

```
121                    }
122                }
123            // if we don't find the bike, tell the user and return nothing
124            System.out.println("Bike with number '" + bikeNum + "' not found" + "\n");
125            return null;
126        }
127
128        public void showDetails( ){
129            // print out all the details
130            System.out.println("Details for bike number '" + bikeNumber + "'");
131            System.out.println("DEPOSIT: " + deposit);
132            System.out.println("RATE: " + rate + "\n");
133        }
134
135        public void calculateCost(int numberOfDays){
136            // work out the cost
137            int cost = deposit + (rate*numberOfDays);
138            System.out.println("COST would be £" + cost + "\n");
139
140 }
```

Figure 11.8   *Code for the Bike class (continued)*

a. *For purposes of computational efficiency, bikeList is implemented as a static array of :Bikes and findBike() as a static method in the Bike class. For more information on the Java keyword static, see Deitel and Deitel (2003).*

:Bikes until it finds one with a bike number that matches the value of bikeNum, which is passed in as a parameter. When a match is found the reference to the :Bike is returned to the calling method. Notice that the signature for this method, +findBikeByNumber(bikeNum:int):Bike, specifies that a Bike reference must be returned. All of the other methods we have met so far have specified a void return, meaning nothing is returned by the method.

The method showDetails() is declared on line 128. This method displays the bike number, deposit and rate of the :Bike to which it is sent. The method calculateCost() is declared on line 135. This method calculates the total cost of hiring the :Bike to which it was sent.

Sequence diagram

For students new to the topic, trying to follow the sequence of execution in an object-oriented program can be very confusing. The architecture of the code is dictated by the classes, but the sequence of execution is dictated by the use cases. The effect of this is that the sequence of execution jumps about all over a code listing. In this section we compare the sequence diagram for one of the 'Issuebike' use case scenarios, with the code that implements it. We map each message in the sequence diagram to the line of code

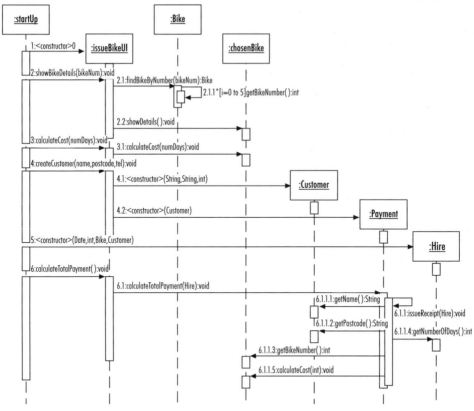

Figure 11.9   *The implementation sequence diagram for a successful scenario in the 'Issue bike' use cas*

that implements it. In so doing, we follow the sequence in which the code is executed by the computer. This demonstrates the usefulness of the sequence diagram as a map to guide us through the code.

The sequence diagram we will be using is shown in Figure 11.9. The full code listing is in Figure 11.10. Table 11.1 maps each sequence code message to the number of the line of code that implements it.

Table 11.1 shows:

- In column 1, the message in the sequence diagram

- In column 2, the number of the line of code that implements the message

- In column 3 the object or class that sends the message

- In column 4 the object or class that receives the message.

A Java application always starts by executing the main() method. The main() method is in the StartUp class, on line 07 of the code. Our sequence diagram starts with the first message sent by the main() method, on line 13, i.e. IssueBikeUI ui = new IssueBikeUI(). This creates a new :IssueBikeUI.

- The next message, showBikeDetails(bikeNum), on line 16, is sent by StartUp to the new :IssueBikeUI.

- To find out what happens next we need to find the method showBikeDetails(bikeNum) in the IssueBikeUI class (on line 42) and follow through the lines of code that implement this method until we find the next message (or method call).

- The next message is findBikeByNumber(bikeNum), in the instruction chosenBike = Bike.findBikeByNumber(bikeNum) on line 44. This is a call from :IssueBikeUI to the Bike class.

- We then go to the Bike class, find the method findBikeByNumber(bikeNum) and follow through the lines of code that implement it until we come across the next method call. The method findBikeByNumber(bikeNum) is on line 110.

- The next method call is in line 116 where the getBikeNumber() message is sent to each of the :Bikes in the bikeList array. As the array of :Bikes is in the Bike class, this is a reflexive or self-referencing message. The number of each :Bike in turn is compared to the value of bikeNum. When a matching :Bike is found, the reference to that :Bike is returned to :IssueBikeUI.

- With a return statement, control is returned to the calling method at the point immediately after the method call. This means that the next line to be executed will be line 45. Line 45 is an 'if' statement that checks that a matching bike has been found (if no bike is found a null is returned). If a bike is found, its reference is returned and assigned to the variable chosenBike. A showDetails() message (line 47) is then sent to the appropriate :Bike.

- showDetails() displays details of the :Bike and returns control to :IssueBikeUI at line 48.

- Line 48 contains the curly bracket that indicates the end of the 'if' statement. Line 49 contains the curly bracket that indicates the end of the showBikeDetails() method, so control is returned to StartUp at line 19.

We hope that this explanation will allow you to follow the rest of the sequence of execution on your own, using Table 11.1.

Table 11.1: *Table showing mapping of sequence diagram messages to lines of code*

Sequence diagram message	Code line	Sending object/ class	Receiving object/class
1 constructor()	13	StartUp	IssueBikeUI
2 showBikeDetails(bikeNum)	16	StartUp	IssueBikeUI
2.1 findBikeByNumber(bikeNum)	44	IssueBikeUI	Bike
2.1.1 getBikeNumber()	116	Bike	Bike
2.2 showDetails()	47	IssueBikeUI	Bike
3 calculateCost(numDays)	19	StartUp	IssueBikeUI
3.1 calculateCost(numDays)	54	IssueBikeUI	Bike
4 createCustomer(name,postcode,tel)	22	StartUp	IssueBikeUI
4.1 constructor(String,String,int)	59	IssueBikeUI	Customer
4.2 constructor(Customer)	60	IssueBikeUI	Payment
5 constructor(Date,int,Bike,Customer)	61	IssueBikeUI	Hire
6 calculateTotalPayment()	25	StartUp	IssueBikeUI
6.1 calculateTotalPayment(Hire)	66	IssueBikeUI	Payment
6.1.1. issueReceipt(Hire)	237	Payment	Payment
6.1.1.1 getName()	242	Payment	Customer
6.1.1.2 getPostcode()	243	Payment	Customer
6.1.1.3 getBikeNumber()	247	Payment	Bike
6.1.1.4 getNumberOfDays()	248	Payment	Hire
6.1.1.5 calculateCost(int)	250	Payment	Bike

StartUp class

```
1       package bikeshop;
2
3       /* Generated by Together */
4
5       public class StartUp {
6
7           public static void main(String[] args){
8
```

Figure 11.10   The code listing for the Wheels system

```
9                       /* This little program will run through the methods on IssueBikeUI
10                       * calling each in turn, like a user with a front end would do. */
11
12                      // First, create the UI
13                      IssueBikeUI ui = new IssueBikeUI( );
14
15                      // 1. Show details for chosen bike
16                      ui.showBikeDetails(100);
17
18                      // 2. Calculate cost of hiring this bike for 5 days
19                      ui.calculateCost(5);
20
21                      // 3. Create new customer, payment and hire
22                      ui.createCustomer("Les Hargreaves", "PW2 6TR", 01462501339);
23
24                      // 4. Calculate the total cost
25                      ui.calculateTotalPayment( );
26              }
27       }
```

IssueBikeUI class

```
28       /*IssueBikeUI Class*/
29
30       package bikeshop;
31
32       import java.util.Date;
33
34       public class IssueBikeUI {
35
36           // Set up the member (or class-level variables)
37           private Bike chosenBike = null;
38           private Customer customer = null;
39           private Payment payment = null;
40           private Hire hire = null;
41           private int numberOfDays = 0;
42           public void showBikeDetails(int bikeNum){
43               // Find the bike by its number
44               chosenBike = Bike.findBikeByNumber(bikeNum);
45               if(chosenBike !=null){
46                   // then ask it for its details
47                   chosenBike.showDetails( );
48               }
49           }
50           public void calculateCost(int numDays){
51               // set the member variable so it can be used later
52               numberOfDays = numDays;
53               // then ask the bike for the cost
54               chosenBike.calculateCost(numDays);
55           }
56
57           public void createCustomer(String name, String postcode, int telephone){
```

Figure 11.10   *The code listing for the Wheels system (continued)*

```
58                      // Create a customer and associated hire and payment
59                      customer = new Customer(name, postcode, telephone);
60                      payment = new Payment(customer);
61                      hire = new Hire(new Date( ), numberOfDays, chosenBike, customer);
62              }
63
64          public void calculateTotalPayment( ){
65                      // get the total payment from the payment object
66                      payment.calculateTotalPayment(hire);
67              }
68      }
```

Bike class

```
69      package bikeshop;
70
71      public class Bike {
72
73      // create the BikeList
74      protected static Bike[] bikeList = new Bike[5];
75      //    set up member variables
76      protected int deposit = 0;
77      protected int rate = 0;
78      protected int bikeNumber = 0;
79
80      /* This block is run when the class is loaded and sets up our bike store.
81       * It arbitrarily populates the attributes: deposit, rate and bikeNumber */
82      static{
83          int j = 0;
84          for(int i=10;i<15;i++){
85              Bike b = new Bike(i, i, (j*100));
86              bikeList[j] = b;
87              j++;
88          }
89      }
90
91      public Bike(int dep, int rat, int num){
92          // set the member variables
93          deposit = dep;
94          rate = rat;
95          bikeNumber = num;
96      }
97
98      public int getDeposit( ){
99          return deposit;
100     }
101
102     public int getRate( ){
103         return rate;
104     }
105
106     public int getBikeNumber( ){
107         return bikeNumber;
```

Figure 11.10   The code listing for the Wheels system (continued)

```
108      }
109
110      public static Bike findBikeByNumber(int bikeNum){
111          int numberOfBikes = bikeList.length;
112
113          // iterate over the list of bikes
114          for(int i=0;i<numberOfBikes;i++){
115              // if we find the bike with the correct number...
116              if(bikeList[i].getBikeNumber( ) == bikeNum){
117                  // tell user that we've found it
118                  System.out.println("Bike with number '" + bikeNum + "' found" + "\n");
119                  // and return it to the UI
120                  return bikeList[i];
121              }
122          }
123          // if we don't find the bike, tell the user and return nothing
124          System.out.println("Bike with number '" + bikeNum + "' not found" + "\n");
125          return null;
126      }
127
128      public void showDetails( ){
129          // print out all the details
130          System.out.println("Details for bike number '" + bikeNumber + "'");
131          System.out.println("DEPOSIT: " + deposit);
132          System.out.println("RATE: " + rate + "\n");
133      }
134
135      public void calculateCost(int numberOfDays){
136          // work out the cost
137          int cost = deposit + (rate*numberOfDays);
138          System.out.println("COST would be £" + cost + "\n");
139
140 }
```

Customer class

```
141      /* Generated by Together */
142
143      package bikeshop;
144
145      public class Customer {
146
147          //     set up member variables
148          private String name = null;
149          private String postcode = null;
150          private int telephone = 0;
151          private int customerId = 0;
152
153          private static int customerCount = 001;
154
155          public Customer(String cName, String pcode, int tel){
156              // set the member variables
```

Figure 11.10   The code listing for the Wheels system (continued)

```
157                 name = cName;
158                 postcode = pcode;
159                 telephone = tel;
160                 customerId = customerCount++;
161         }
162
163         public int getCustomerNumber( ){
164                 return customerId;
165         }
166
167         public String getName( ) {
168                 return name;
169         }
170
171         public String getPostcode( ) {
172                 return postcode;
173         }
174
175     }
```

Hire class

```
176     /* Generated by Together */
177
178     package bikeshop;
179
180     import java.util.Date;
181
182     public class Hire {
183
184         private Date startDate = null;
185         private Customer customer = null;
186         private Bike bike = null;
187         private int numberOfDays = 0;
188         private int hireId = 0;
189
190         private static int hireCount = 001;
191
192         public Hire(Date sDate, int numDays, Bike bikeToHire, Customer cust) {
193             startDate = sDate;
194             numberOfDays = numDays;
195             customer = cust;
196             bike = bikeToHire;
197             hireId = hireCount++;
198         }
199
200         public Customer getCustomer( ){
201             return customer;
202     }
203
204         public Bike getBike( ) {
205             return bike;
```

Figure 11.10   The code listing for the Wheels system (continued)

```
206                }
207
208            public int getNumberOfDays( ) {
209                    return numberOfDays;
210            }
211
212            public Date getStartDate( ) {
213                    return startDate;
214            }
215
216        }
```

Payment class

```
217        /* Generated by Together */
218        package bikeshop;
219
220        public class Payment {
221
222            // Set up the member variables
223            private Customer customer = null;
224            private int paymentId = 0;
225
226            private static int paymentCount = 001;
227
228            public Payment(Customer cust){
229            // set the member variables
230
231                customer = cust;
232                paymentId = paymentCount++;
233            }
234
235            public void calculateTotalPayment(Hire hire){
236            // call the private method
237                issueReceipt(hire);
238            }
239
240            private void issueReceipt(Hire hire){
241            // print out all the relevant details
242                String cust = hire.getCustomer( ).getName( );
243                String pCode = hire.getCustomer( ).getPostcode( );
244                System.out.println("Printing out receipt for '" + cust + "'.....");
245                System.out.println("In postcode: " + pCode + "\n");
246
247                System.out.println("Hiring bike number '" + hire.getBike( ).getBikeNumber( )
248                            + "' for " + hire.getNumberOfDays( ) + " days" + "\n");
249
250                hire.getBike( ).calculateCost(hire.getNumberOfDays( ));
251            }
252        }
253
```

Figure 11.10   *The code listing for the Wheels system (continued)*

Chapter summary

This chapter demonstrates that there is a close relationship between the class diagram and the code. The classes, attributes and operations of the class diagram form the framework of the code. The relationship is so close that in a CASE tool like Together the skeleton of the code is automatically generated from the class diagram. All the programmer has to do is flesh out the methods. Conversely, a CASE tool can automatically reverse engineer the class diagram from the code. This chapter also demonstrates the usefulness of the sequence diagram. The sequence of execution in an object-oriented program is complicated; it is hard to follow the flow of control as it is passed backwards and forwards between objects. Sequence diagrams provide an overview of the inter-object messaging sequence; this is useful for software designers and for programmers, both when they are writing the code and when they are maintaining it.

It is interesting, looking back at the process of developing the software for the Wheels system, to see that the entities Bike, Customer, Hire and Payment existed initially in the real world of the Wheels bike shop, were then classes in the analysis and design models, and are still present in the code. Towards implementation, we picked up a few extra classes and the original classes picked up a few extra features, but basically there was a seamless transition from requirements elicitation through to code.

Bibliography

Britton, C. and Doake, J. (2000) *Object-Oriented Systems Development: A Gentle Introduction*, McGraw-Hill, London.

Charatan, Q. and Kans, A. (2002) *Java in Two Semesters*, McGraw-Hill, London.

Deitel, H.M. and Deitel, P.J. (2003) *Java: How to Program* (5th edition), Prentice Hall, Upper Saddle River, NJ.

Quick check questions

You can find the answers to these in the chapter.

a   Which method must be present in all Java applications?

b   Which two types of method are usually omitted on a class diagram?

c   What is a constructor? How can you identify it?

d   How does the Java compiler know where a class starts and ends?

e   How are comments identified in Java?

f   What are member variables?

g   What is a self-referencing message?

Exercises

11.1   In Chapter 4 we discussed the European class hierarchy. The Java code for this hierarchy is listed in Figure 11.11.

a   Identify the constructors for each class.

b   Indicate the Java keyword that implements the inheritance relationship between the classes European and Briton.

c   If we run the program, what would the output be?

European class

```
1      public class European {
2          private String language;
3
4          public European( ) {
5              language = "";
6          }
7
8          public void greet( ) {
9          }
10     }
```

Briton class

```
11     public class Briton extends European {
12     // 'private String language' does not need to be declared as it is inherited
13
14         public Briton( ) {
15             language = "English";
16         }
17
18         public void greet( ) {
19             System.out.println ("Good morning");
20         }
21     }
```

Frenchman class

```
22     public class Frenchman extends European {
23     //'private String language' does not need to be declared as it is inherited
24
25         public Frenchman( ) {
26             language = "French";
27         }
```

Figure 11.11   Java code for the European hierarchy

```
28
29          public void greet( ) {
30          System.out.println ("Bonjour");
31          }
32      }
```

German class

```
33      public class German extends European {
34      //'private String language' does not need to be declared as it is inherited
35
36          public German( ) {
37              language = "German";
38          }
39
40          public void greet( ) {
41              System.out.println ("Guten Tag");
42          }
43      }
```

Italian class

```
44      public class Italian extends European {
45      // 'private String language' does not need to be declared as it is inherited
46
47          public Italian( ) {
48              language = "Italian";
49          }
50
51          public void greet( ) {
52              System.out.println ("Buongiorno");
53          }
54      }
```

Salutation class

```
55      public class Salutation {
56
57          public static void main(String[] args) {
58              European euMember[];
59                  int i;
60                  euMember = new European[4];
61                  euMember[0] = new Briton( );
62                  euMember[1] = new Frenchman( );
63                  euMember[2] = new German( );
64                  euMember[3] = new Italian( );
65
66                  for (i = 0;i<4;i++) {
67                      euMember[i].greet( );
68                  }
69          }
70      }
```

Figure 11.11   Java code for the European hierarchy (continued)

11.2 Figure 11.12 contains the Java code for the scoring of points in a league. The league consists of three teams: teamA, teamB and teamC. A game involves two teams. There are three games in total; each team plays both of the others. A team scores 2 points if they win, 1 point if they draw and 0 if they lose.

a Draw a class diagram to model the classes and relationships in the code; your model should show attributes, methods and relationships.

b Draw a sequence diagram to model the sequence of messages in the execution of main(). Your answer should include constructors.

c What will be the output from main()?

Team class

```
class Team
{
        private String teamName; //team name
        private int score;       //score in a game
        private int points;      //cumulative points

        public Team(String tmName)        //constructor
        {
                teamName = new String(tmName); // populate attributes
                score = 0;
                points = 0;
        };

        public String getName()     //returns team's name
        {
                return teamName;
        };

        public void setScore(int inscore) //allocate score to team
        {
                score = inscore;
        };

        public int getScore() //returns score
        {
                return score;
        };

        public void addPoints(int inpoints) //adds points
        {
                points +=inpoints;
        };
```

Figure 11.12   Java code for Exercise 11.2

```
        int getPoints()   //returns current points
        {
                return points;
        };
}
```

Game class

```
class Game
{
        private Team team1;              // references to teams
        private Team team2;

        public Game(Team first, Team second)   //game constructor
        {
          team1=  first;
          team2 = second;
    };

        public void winLose()    // identify winner and allocate points
        {
                if (team1.getScore() > team2.getScore())
                  team1.addPoints(2);
                else
                  if (team1.getScore() < team2.getScore())
                     team2.addPoints(2);
                  else
                  {
                          team1.addPoints(1);
                          team2.addPoints(1);
                  }
        };

        public void scorer(int firstScore, int secScore)   // sets scores of a game
        {
          team1.setScore(firstScore);
          team2.setScore(secScore);
        };
}
```

League class

```
public class League
{
        public static void main(String[] args)
        {
                //set up the teams
                Team teamA = new Team("Alan    ");
                Team teamB = new Team("Ian     ");
                Team teamC = new Team("Martin ");

                // set up the games
                Game gameAB = new Game(teamA,teamB);
```

Figure 11.12   Java code for Exercise 11.2 (continued)

```
            Game gameBC = new Game(teamB,teamC);
            Game gameAC = new Game(teamA,teamC);

            // play the games
            gameAB.scorer(20,10);      // allocate scores of teamA vs teamB
            gameAB.winLose();          // allocate points (2 for A, 0 for B)

            gameBC.scorer(15,15);      // ditto for B & C
            gameBC.winLose();

            gameAC.scorer(5,9);
            gameAC.winLose();

            // output league results
            System.out.println("Team    Points");
            System.out.println(teamA.getName() +"  "+ teamA.getPoints());
            System.out.println(teamB.getName() +"  "+ teamB.getPoints());
            System.out.println(teamC.getName() +"  "+ teamC.getPoints());
        }
}
```

Figure 11.12   Java code for Exercise 11.2 (continued)

A Material for the Wheels bike hire case study

Introduction

The case study which is used as the basis for examples and exercises in this book is a typical bicycle hire shop. If you have ever hired a bicycle, you will already be familiar with some of the details; in fact, if you have ever hired anything, such as a car or even a video, you will see that the basic processes are very similar.

The bike hire shop is called Wheels, and was started by Mike Watson, the current owner, about ten years ago. Mike has always been a keen cyclist, and still competes regularly in local races and rides for charity. He has an encyclopaedic knowledge of all types of bike, and is very proud of the range and quality of his stock. The business has done well, and now occupies large premises near the centre of town with a big storage and workshop area in the basement. Wheels attracts a lot of passing custom because of the position of the shop, and also gets many returning customers who know that they will be given a good quality bike that will suit their needs.

As well as Mike, who is very much involved in the day-to-day running of the business, there is a full-time shop manager, Annie Price, the head mechanic, Naresh Patel, and three other mechanics who work part-time. There is a computer in the reception area, and all the Wheels bikes are recorded on file, with details such as the bike number, type, size, make, model, daily charge rate and deposit. Unfortunately, however, that's all there is on the computer, and the actual hire and return procedures are carried out in much the same, slightly disorganized way that they always have been.

Mike has recently come to realize that, although he has a successful business, he will not be able to expand as he would like to unless he gets his business processes up to date, and that to do this he will have to make much more effective use of the computer. He decides to hire a small local firm to investigate the way things are done at the moment, suggest possible improvements, and develop a computer system that will bring the Wheels business into the twenty-first century.

Interview plan

Interview Plan			
System: **Wheels**		Project reference: **Wheels/04**	
Participants:	**Annie Price (Shop manager for Wheels)** **Simon Davis (Developer)**		
Date **10 February 2004**	Time **14.30**	Duration **45 minutes**	Place **Manager's office**
Purpose of interview **Preliminary meeting to discuss procedures and problems with the current system**			
Agenda • **current procedures for hiring bikes** • **problems with the current system** • **initial ideas on how these could be addressed** • **follow-up actions**			
Documents to be brought to interview • **bike card** • **any other documents relating to current procedures**			

Figure A.1   (see also Figure 2.1 on Page 24) Interview plan for interview with Annie Price, shop manager at Wheels

Interview

SD: …so could you tell me what happens typically when someone wants to hire a bike? Just talk me through it bit by bit.

Annie: OK, well say someone comes in and says they want to hire a bike for that afternoon, so I ask them if they know what sort they want – it's always easier in that case. Then, when I've got an idea of what they're looking for, I get Naresh or one of the other mechanics to come and suggest a couple of bikes that might suit.

SD: And is the customer always happy with that?

Annie: Yes, usually they go with whatever Naresh says. He's the head mechanic and he's pretty clued up about bikes. We hardly ever get any of them coming back and complaining after the ride.

SD: So what's next?

Annie: I get the bike's number – that's stencilled onto the bike – and then I use that to look up the bike card. There's a card for each bike and we keep them under the counter in this box.

SD: Ok, and what order do you keep them in?

Annie: We keep them in the order of the bike numbers – it's the only way really – though it does cause problems with queries. For example, the other day I had a man on the phone wanting to know if we had two bikes, a Raleigh Pioneer for him and a Dawes Galaxy for his partner, and how much it would cost for three day's hire. First of all I had to look on the shop floor to see if we'd got the right bikes, then I had to search through all the cards and then I had to work out how much it was going to cost him. He was very patient, but that sort of thing takes ages. Anyway, I'll show you one of the cards.[1]

SD: Thanks. Can you tell me – are the hire charge and the deposit the same for all the bikes?

---

1. *The bike card is shown in (see also Figure A.2 on Page 296) (see also Figure 2.2 on Page 25) Example bike card from the current Wheels system.*

| Bike Number: 1591 | Make: Scott | Model: Atlantic Trail | Type: mountain |
| Clour: black | Daily rate: £8 | Deposit: £50 | Size: womans |

Customer	Start date	Return date	Paid	Extras
Mrs V. Patel 16 St Johns Road	31/08/03	2/9/03	£74	
Ms C. Wilson 112 Regent Street	9/9/03	12/9/03	£82	£8
Dr F. Green 67 Grange Road	4/10/03	4/10/03	$58	
Ms C. Wilson 112 Regent Street	19/1/04	19/1/04	£58	

Figure A.2   *(see also Figure 2.2 on Page 25) Example bike card from the current Wheels system*

Annie: No, they vary a lot. Well, you couldn't charge the same for a child's bike as for an 18-gear racer, could you? Anyway, then I fill in all the details on the bike card, the customer gives me the money to cover the hire and deposit and off they go.

SD: Don't they get a receipt?

Annie: Oh yes, sorry, I forgot. I write one out from the receipt book. It would be nice if we could use the computer system for that, but all we've actually got on it is a list of the bikes that we own and all their details like make, model, size, cost and all that. Even that can be a bit of a problem – for Naresh that is – he's the one who has to enter all the details about the bikes that the boss buys in and that can be really tedious.

SD: Well, I'm sure we can improve on that. So tell me, if a customer hires more than one bike, how do you record that?

Annie: Well, you can see this card only has details for this particular bike, so if a customer is hiring three bikes I have to put the details on three separate cards, including writing out their name and address three times. We have to do it like that because sometimes people hire more than one bike, but for different times. For example, we get families on holiday who hire bikes for the children for the whole week, but maybe just a couple of days for the parents. When people do want a number of bikes it's a bit of a pain looking out all the cards and filling in the same customer details on each one, not to mention working out what it all costs. We once had a customer who hired 20 bikes for his daughter's birthday party, which took me ages. That was a bit of a one-off though; we do get requests for parties and events, but it's generally the special stuff that they want.

SD: Special stuff?

Annie: Sorry, I should have told you about that. We have some novelty items that Mike (he's the boss) has picked up at auctions, like a couple of genuine working penny farthing cycles. Those are very popular for period style photos and charity events. People tend to notice them, so they're a really good advertisement for us as well. Last year we had a local couple who hired one of our old tandems for their wedding and we got loads of publicity from that.

SD: Presumably hiring those out is rather more complicated.

Annie: Oh yes, we have to write on the card extra details about our special bikes, such as their age, value and restrictions on what they can be hired for.

SD: OK, so just to get back to the actual hire procedures. You fill in the details on the card, the customer pays and you give them a receipt.

Annie: Yes that's it really.

SD: Thanks, that's very helpful. So what happens when the customer comes back with the bike?

Annie: Well they come in, usually all hot and sweaty, but never mind that. I get the bike number and I check that the bike they're returning is the one on the card. And I have to check the return date as well, because if they're late they have to pay extra.

SD: And you return the customer's deposit if they bring back the bike on time?

Annie: Usually, but not if the bike's been damaged of course. One of the mechanics gives every bike a quick check to make sure it's in reasonable condition. If there's a problem we keep some of the deposit and if it's really bad then we keep all of it. We once had one that was a write-off; goodness knows what the customer had been doing with it. The bikes are insured of course, but keeping deposits helps keep down the claims.

SD: Can you tell me about your customers in general, do you think they're happy with the hire system as it is, or do you get a lot of complaints?

Annie: I don't think it's too bad, though we do get complaints occasionally. I don't think the system's very efficient; for example, it can be really slow if I'm trying to work out the cost of hiring more than one bike. If it's my day off and one of the others is in charge it's even slower because they're not used to it. Sometimes I think the customers are just too nice to complain. They can see that I'm doing my best and they don't want to get me into trouble. I think if you asked them they might say that there are quite a few things that could be improved.

SD: Well I'm thinking of doing just that. Would it be all right to leave a short questionnaire on the counter for customers to fill in and return to you? I think it would give us a good idea of how your customers view the hire system and where they think the problems are.

Annie: That's a great idea. You can leave them on the counter and I'll make sure that every customer gets one...

Interview summary

Interview Summary			
System: Wheels	**Project reference:** Wheels/04		
Participants: Annie Price (Shop manager for Wheels) Simon Davis (Developer)			
Date 10 February 2004	**Time** 14.30	**Duration** 45 minutes	**Place** Manager's office
Purpose of interview Preliminary meeting to discuss procedures and problems with the current system			

No.	Item	Action
1	Difficult to deal with queries.	Bike details and availability should be easily accessible.
2	No records of customer details or hires, so there is a problem when a customer wants the same bike as previously.	A record of previous bikes hired could be stored with customer details.
3	A customer hiring more than one bike is very complicated and makes a lot of extra work.	Investigate ways of simplifying hire procedures for more than one bike.
4	Receipts written out by hand.	New system must produce a computerized receipt.
5	Need to write extra details about specialist bikes on card.	Redesign card to cater for specialist as well as standard bikes.
6	Feeling that customers may not be happy with the current system.	Produce questionnaire about current procedures and ask customers to complete.
		Arrange interviews with Mike, Naresh and other staff.

Figure A.3   (see also Figure 2.8 on Page 35) Summary from interview with Annie Price

Questionnaire

Wheels customer survey

Our aim is always to give you the best service possible. We are investigating our current hiring procedures to identify any problems and improve the present system. It would be very helpful if you could give us your opinion on what you like or dislike about how we do things now and how we could improve.

Please spare a few minutes to answer the questions below and return the form to Annie in reception.

Please answer questions 1 and 2 by ticking one of the boxes:

1. Roughly how many times have you hired a bike from us in the past year?

   no hire ☐   once only ☐   2–5 times ☐   6–10 times ☐   more than 10 times ☐

2. Roughly how many times have you hired a specialist bike from us in the past year?

   no hire ☐   once only ☐   2–5 times ☐   6–10 times ☐   more than 10 times ☐

3. For each of the statements (a)–(e) below, circle the number that is closest to your own view. 1 means that you strongly agree with the statement, and 5 means that you strongly disagree.

		strongly agree				strongly disagree
a	The hire service is easy to understand	1	2	3	4	5
b	The hire service is fast and efficient	1	2	3	4	5
c	I always get a bike that suits me	1	2	3	4	5
d	It is easy to work out how much it's going to cost	1	2	3	4	5
e	The bike checking is quick and fair	1	2	3	4	5

4.

Overall are you happy with our curent bike hire system? YES/NO	Please give details of any concerns:
Do you have any suggestions for improving the bike hire system?	Any further comments or observations?

If you would like more information about our bikes please give your details:

Your name: _____

Your address: _____

_____

Thank you for completing this questionnaire.

Figure A.4   (see also Figure 2.3 on Page 29) Questionnaire for Wheels customer survey

Sample scenarios

- Stephanie arrives at the shop at 9.00am one Saturday and chooses a mountain bike
- Annie sees that its number is 468
- Annie enters this number into the system
- The system confirms that this is a woman's mountain bike and displays the daily rate (£2) and the deposit (£60)
- Stephanie says she wants to hire the bike for a week
- Annie enters this and the system displays the total cost £14 + £60 = £74
- Stephanie agrees this
- Annie enters Stephanie's name, address and telephone number into the system
- Stephanie pays the £74
- Annie records this on the system and the system prints out a receipt
- Stephanie agrees to bring the bike back by 9.00am on the following Saturday.

Figure A.5   *(see also Figure 3.3 on Page 43) Successful scenario for the use case 'Issue bike'*

- Michael arrives at the shop at 12.00 on Friday
- He selects a man's racer
- Annie see the number is 658
- She enters this number into the system
- The system confirms that it is a man's racer and displays the daily rate (£2) and the deposit (£55)
- Michael says this is too much and leaves the shop without hiring the bike.

Figure A.6   *(see also Figure 3.4 on Page 43) Scenario for 'Issue bike' where the use case goal is not achieved*

> - A customer, Steve Chen, arrives at the shop with a bike to return
> - Annie contacts the mechanics to ask for someone to come and check the bike
> - Annie gets the bike number, looks out the relevant bike card and checks Steve's name and address
> - Annie makes sure that the bike being returned is the one on the card
> - She confirms that the bike is being returned on time by checking the return date against the current date
> - One of the mechanics checks the bike and confirms that it has been returned in good condition
> - Annie returns Steve's deposit.

Figure A.7   (see also Figure 2.4 on Page 30) Simple scenario for the return of a bike in the current Wheels system

> - Two customers, Paul and Debbie White, arrive at the shop with bikes to return
> - Annie contacts the mechanics to ask for someone to come and check the bikes
> - Annie gets the bike numbers, looks out the relevant bike cards and checks Paul and Debbie's names and addresses
> - Annie makes sure that the bikes being returned are the ones on the cards
> - She checks to see if the bikes are being returned on time by verifying the return date against the current date
> - Annie finds that the bikes are one day overdue
> - She tells the customers that there is a charge for the extra day's hire
> - One of the mechanics checks the bikes and confirms that they have been returned in good condition
> - Annie returns the customers' deposit, minus the extra day's hire charge
> - Annie writes out a receipt for the extra charge.

Figure A.8   (see also Figure 2.5 on Page 31) A more complicated scenario for the return of a bike in the current Wheels system

Problem definition

Problem Definition

Client Wheels

Problems with current system
- It is difficult to answer queries
- The hire and return processes are slow
- Having one card for each bike means that Annie has to look out a number of cards and write the same name and address on each one if a customer hires more than one bike
- Producing one receipt for a hire of more than one bike is very complicated and can lead to miscalculations
- Staff have a feeling that customers are not particularly happy with the current hire system.

Objectives of new system
- To provide an efficient and speedy hire process
- To simplify the situation where a customer hires more than one bike
- To record details of customers and previous hires for marketing purposes, and to simplify dealing with requests for the same bike as hired previously
- To improve overall customer satisfaction.

Scope of new system
- The project will encompass the following areas of the business:
- Hire procedures
- Return procedures
- Recording bike details
- Some marketing to regular customers.
- The project will not cover payroll, personnel or general accounting.

Preliminary ideas
- Carry out a customer survey about current procedures
- Design a user-friendly, computerized bike card
- Provide facilities for the system to handle hiring of multiple bikes more efficiently.

Recommended action
- Design and agree questionnaire for customer survey
- Investigate information to be stored about customers
- Review design of the bike card using the computer.

Figure A.9   (see also Figure 2.6 on Page 32) Initial problem definition for Wheels

No.	Source	Date	Description	Priority	Related Reqs.	Related Docs.	Change Details
5.1	Meeting with Annie Price at Wheels	10 Feb. 2004	Keep track of how many bikes a customer is hiring, so that he gets one unified receipt	Essential	1.3 2.3 6.1	Bike cards	

No.	Source	Date	Description	Priority	Related Reqs.	Related Docs.	Change Details
2.2	Customer survey	March 2004	Keep record of previous bikes hired by customers	Desirable	2.1 2.4	Bike cards	

Figure A.10   *(see also Figure 2.7 on Page 33) Two examples from the problems and requirements list for the Wheels system*

Requirements for the Wheels system

The new Wheels system must:

R1   keep a complete list of all bikes and their details including bike number, type, size, make, model, daily charge rate, deposit (this is already on the Wheels system)

R2   keep a record of all customers and their past hire transactions

R3   work out automatically how much it will cost to hire a given bike for a given number of days

R4   record the details of a hire transaction including the start date, estimated duration, customer and bike, in such a way that it is easy to find the relevant transaction details when a bike is returned

R5   keep track of how many bikes a customer is hiring so that the customer gets one unified receipt not a separate one for each bike

R6   cope with a customer who hires more than one bike, each for different amounts of time

R7   work out automatically, on the return of a bike, how long it was hired for, how many days were originally paid for, how much extra is due

R8   record the total amount due and how much has been paid

R9   print a receipt for each customer

R10   keep track of the state of each bike, e.g. whether it is in stock, hired out or being repaired

R11   provide the means to record extra details about specialist bikes.

Use cases

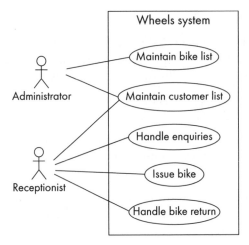

Figure A.11   *(see also Figure 3.2 on Page 41) Use case diagram for Wheels*

Use case: Issue bike
Actors: Receptionist
Goal: To hire out a bike

Description:
When a customer comes into the shop they choose a bike to hire. The
Receptionist looks up the bike on the system and tells the customer how
much it will cost to hire the bike for a specified period. The customer pays,
is issued with a receipt, then leaves with the bike.

Figure A.12   *(see also Figure 3.5 on Page 45) High-level description of the 'Issue bike' use case*

Use case: Issue bike
Preconditions: 'Maintain bike list' must have been executed
Actors: Receptionist
Goal: To hire out a bike

Overview:
When a customer comes into the shop they choose a bike to hire. The Receptionist looks up the bike on the system and tells the customer how much it will cost to hire the bike for a specified period. The customer pays, is issued with a receipt, then leaves with the bike.

Cross-reference:
R3, R4, R5, R6, R7, R8, R9, R10

Typical course of events:

Actor action	System response
1 The customer chooses a bike	
2 The Receptionist keys in the bike number	3 Displays the bike details including the daily hire rate and deposit
4 Customer specifies length of hire	
5 Receptionist keys this in	6 Displays total hire cost
7 Customer agrees the price	
8 Receptionist keys in the customer details	9 Displays customer details
10 Customer pays the total cost	
11 Receptionist records amount paid	12 Prints a receipt

Alternative courses:

Steps 8 and 9   The customer details are already in the system so the Receptionist needs only to key in an identifier and the system will display the customer details.

Steps 7–12   The customer may not be happy with the price and may terminate the transaction

Figure A.13   *(see also Figure 3.8 on Page 48) Expanded description of the 'Issue bike' use case with preconditions*

CRC cards

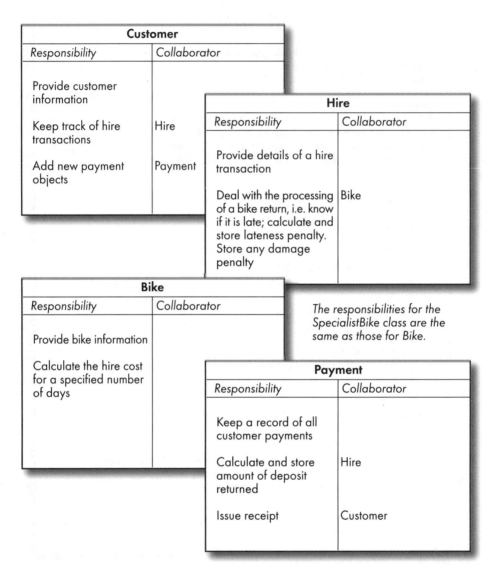

Figure A.14 (see also Figure 6.4 on Page 152) CRC cards for the Wheels system

The analysis class diagram

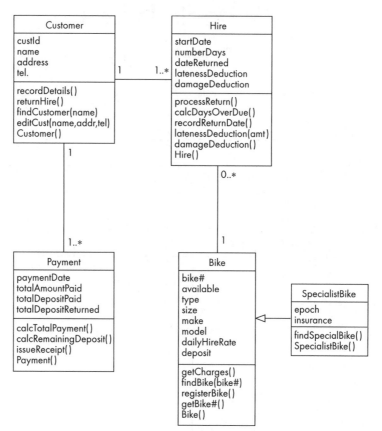

Figure A.15   *(see also Figure 6.6 on Page 155) Completed class diagram with attributes and operations*

Data dictionary

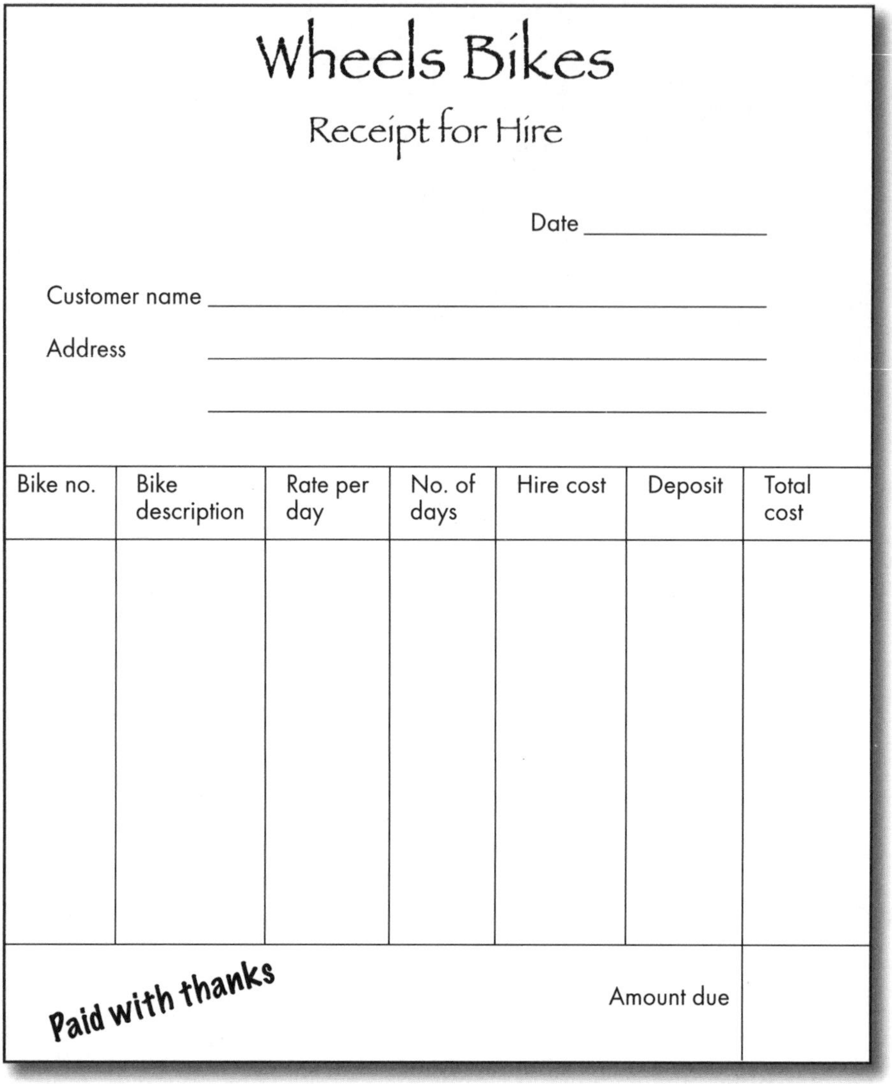

| Wheels Bikes |
| Receipt for Hire |

Date _____

Customer name _____

Address _____

_____

Bike no.	Bike description	Rate per day	No. of days	Hire cost	Deposit	Total cost

Paid with thanks   Amount due

Figure A.16 (see also Figure 5.16 on Page 135) Receipt form used in the current Wheels system

Receipt = title + customerDetails + {hireDetails} *a customer may
    hire more than one bike at a time* + total
title = "Wheels Bikes Receipt for Hire" + receiptDate
customerDetails = customerName + customerAddress
hireDetails = bike# + bikeDescription + ratePerDay + no.OfDays
    + hireCost + deposit + totalCost
total = amountDue + "Paid with thanks"

Examples of operation specifications

From the Bike class:

findBike(bike#)

This operation finds the Bike object whose number corresponds to the bike number input (bike#) and returns details about the bike (bike# + available + type + make + model + size + dailyHireRate + deposit)

From the Payment class:

calcTotalPayment(amt, deposit)

This operation calculates and records the sum of amounts paid as hire fees and the sum of deposits paid. This operation must find all current customer hire objects and for each one calculate the hire fee (Bike.dailyHireRate² * Hire.numberOfDays). The hire fees for all of the customer's hires are summed and recorded in Payment.totalAmountPaid. It also finds the deposit for each bike hired, sums them and records the result in Payment.totalDepositPaid.

From the Bike class:
getCharges(no.Days)

- getCharges(no.Days) : (deposit, dailyHireRate, total)

- This operation works out the cost of hiring a particular bike for a given number of days

- The bike details must have been found and the requested number of days of hire known

- The Bike object attribute dailyHireRate is multiplied by the number of days (no.Days). The result is added to the deposit to give the total. The operation returns the deposit, the dailyHireRate and the total

- This operation does not call any others

- This operation does not change the values of any attributes.

---

2. *This notation means the attribute dailyHireRate in the class Bike.*

Interaction diagrams

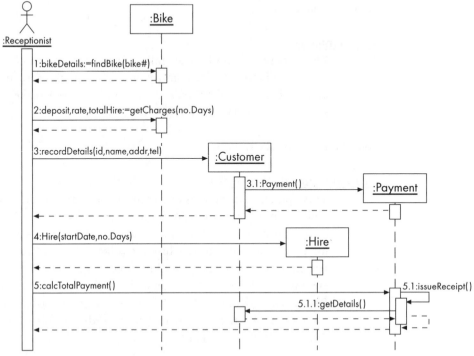

Figure A.17   (see also Figure 6.12 on Page 161) Complete sequence diagram for the 'Issue bike' scenario

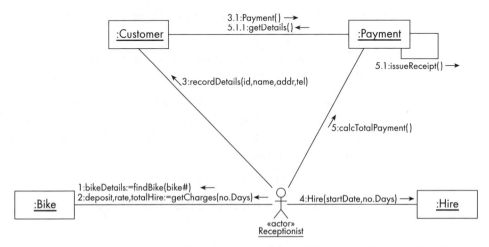

Figure A.18   (see also Figure 6.14 on Page 163) Collaboration diagram for the 'Issue bike' scenario

State diagram

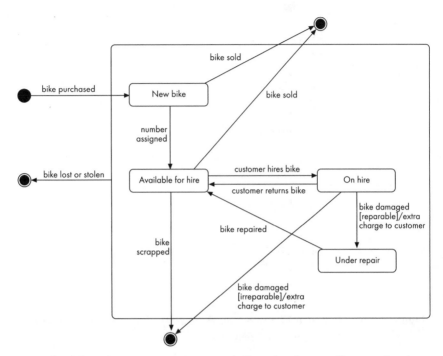

Figure A.19   *(see also Figure 7.10 on Page 191) Completed state diagram for the Bike class*

Activity diagrams

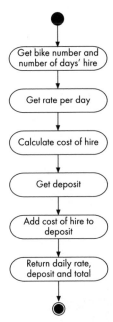

Figure A.20   *(see also Figure 8.2 on Page 203) Simple activity diagram for the 'getCharges()' operation*

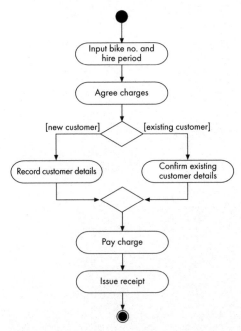

Figure A.21   *(see also Figure 8.5 on Page 205) Activity diagram for the 'Issue bike' use case, showing alternative actions*

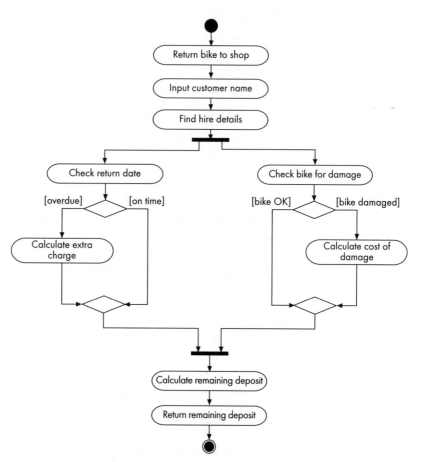

Figure A.22   *(see also Figure 8.9 on Page 208) Activity diagram for the 'Handle bike return' use case*

Screen design

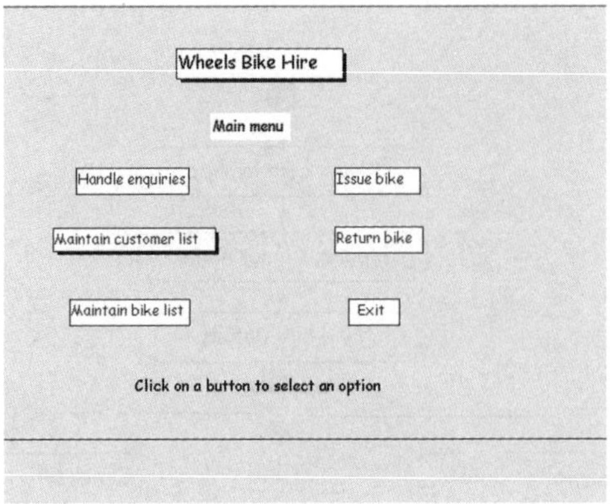

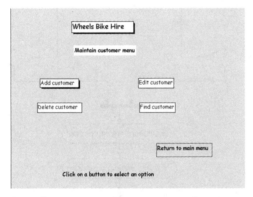

Figure A.23   *(see also Figure 9.10 on Page 234) Main menu screen from the Wheels system with the option 'Maintain customer list' selected*

Figure A.24   *(see also Figure 9.11 on Page 235) Customer menu screen from the Wheels system with the option 'Add customer' selected*

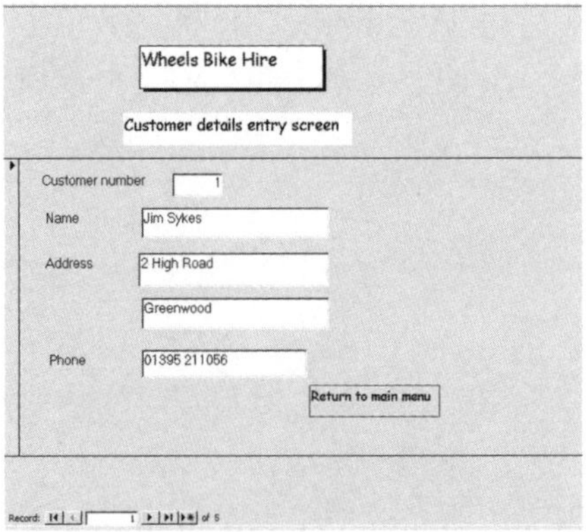

Figure A.25   *(see also Figure 9.9 on Page 234) Customer details entry screen from the Wheels system*

Database tables

Customer

CustID	Name	FirstName	Street	Town	PhoneNo
1	Sykes	Jim	2 High Road	Greenwood	01395 211056
2	Perle	Lee	14 Duke Street	Greenwood	01395 237851
3	Hargreaves	Les	11 Forest Road	Prestwich Albans	01462 501339
4	James	Sheena	4 Duke Street	Greenwood	01395 237663
5	Robins	Charlie	11Juniper Road	Greenwood	01395 267843

Figure A.26   *(see also Figure 9.12 on Page 237) Example of a table of customers in a relational database*

Bike

Bike No.	Available	Type	Size	Make	Model	Daily hire rate	Deposit
249	On hire	mountain	woman's	Scott	Atlantic Trail	£8.00	£50.00
250	Available	tourer	man's	Raleigh	Pioneer	£9.00	£60.00
251	On hire	mountain	woman's	Scott	Atlantic Trail	£8.00	£50.00
252	On hire	tourer	man's	Dawes	Galaxy	£8.00	£50.00
253	Available	mountain	child's	Raleigh	Chopper	£5.00	£25.00

Figure A.27   *(see also Figure 9.14 on Page 238) The Bike class implemented as a table*

Customer

CustID	Name	FirstName	Street	Town	PhoneNo
1	Sykes	Jim	2 High Road	Greenwood	01395 211056
2	Perle	Lee	14 Duke Street	Greenwood	01395 237851
3	Hargreaves	Les	11 Forest Road	Prestwich	01462 501339
4	James	Sheena	4 Duke Street	Greenwood	01395 237663
5	Robins	Charlie	11Juniper Road	Greenwood	01395 267843

Payment

Payment No	CustID	Date	Total amount paid	Total deposit paid	Total deposit returned
401	4	19/03/04	£56.00	£50.00	£50.00
402	20	19/03/04	£20.00	£25.00	£25.00
403	4	19/03/04	£145.00	£80.00	£80.00
404	3	20/03/04	£186.00	£100.00	£84.00
405	2	20/03/04	£44.00	£40.00	£40.00

Figure A.28   *(see also Figure 9.17 on Page 240) One to many association between the Customer and Payment classes implemented as two tables with a foreign key*

Design diagrams

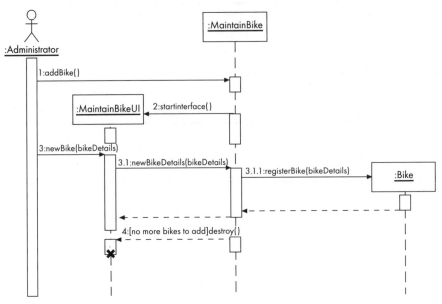

Figure A.29 (see also Figure 10.7 on Page 258) Sequence diagram showing object creation and deletion

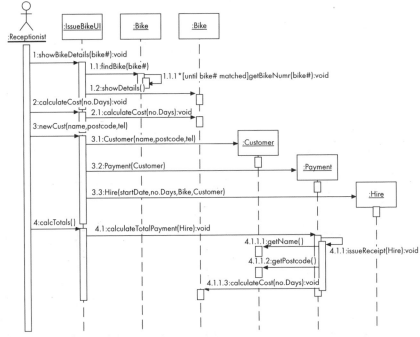

Figure A.30 (see also Figure 10.11 on Page 262) Sequence diagram for the Wheels system – 'Issue bike' use case, successful hire scenario

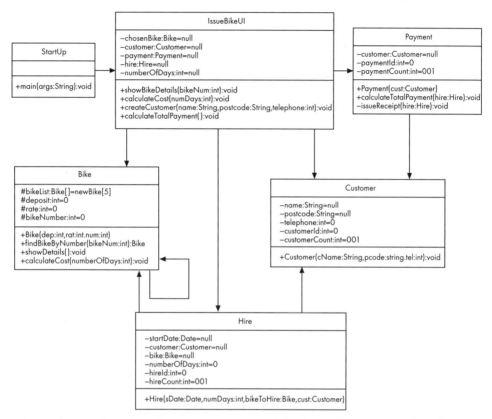

Figure A.31   *(see also Figure 11.1 on Page 269) The implementation class diagram*

The code for a simplified version of the Wheels system can be found in Chapter 11 starting on page p. 280.

B Introductory material for a new case study

This material can be used to practise the techniques introduced in the book; lecturers can find some example solutions on the book website, http://books.elsevier.com/manualsprotected/0750661232.

Introduction to the case study

Just the Job is a company that provides house cleaning services on a one-off basis, for example when people move house.

At the moment, when a potential customer contacts the Just the Job office, the receptionist books an appointment for the office manager to visit the property to be cleaned and give the customer a date and price for the job. Once these have been agreed, a booking form is filled out (see below); one copy of the form is given to the customer and two copies are filed at the Just the Job office.

On the date arranged, a team of two or three cleaners arrive at the property and carry out the cleaning as specified. The customer then signs a copy of the original booking form to confirm the job has been carried out satisfactorily. When the signed booking form arrives back at the Just the Job office, the receptionist sends an invoice to the customer for the payment. A receipted copy of the invoice is sent to the customer when full payment is received.

Just the Job also deals with customers who require cleaning services on a regular basis. This cleaning is carried out on the same day each week, and is charged at an hourly rate, negotiated with the customer. The office manager tries to send the same cleaner each week, as this helps customer relations.

Just the Job allocates customer numbers and keeps details on file of all its customers for marketing purposes. The office also keeps records of all the cleaners, including name, address, contact number and the number of hours worked each week.

The office manager has decided that she needs a new computer system to handle most of the paperwork involved in Just the Job's daily routines.

JUST THE JOB

Booking form for Single Cleaning

Job Details

Job Number _____

Address of property _____

to be cleaned _____

_____

Date _____

Start time _____

Length of job _____

Price of job _____

Amount of deposit paid _____

Balance to pay _____

Customer Details

Customer number _____

Name _____

Address _____

(if different from above) _____

_____

Telephone number _____

Email _____

The above job has been carried out to my satisfaction.

Cutomer signature: _____

Figure B.3   *Just the Job booking form for a single cleaning*

The new system

The new system must keep a record of customers, cleaners and jobs. The office manager, Eileen, wants to be able to use the system to produce printed monthly invoices for regular customers and one-off invoices for single jobs. She would also like the system to produce a weekly schedule for each cleaner showing where and when they are working. This will be given to the cleaners at the start of the week along with a copy of the Booking Form for the customer to complete. The system will also be used to produce a weekly list showing how many hours each cleaner has worked.

Invoices for one-off jobs are to be printed and sent out as soon as the signed booking form is returned to the office. Invoices for regular jobs are to be printed and sent out once a month. Customers who have regular cleaning jobs on several properties should receive a single invoice.

Eileen would also like the system to be able to keep track of her appointments and produce a printed schedule for her.

C Bibliography

Bennett, S., McRobb, S. and Farmer, R. (2002) *Object-Oriented Systems Analysis and Design Using UML* (2nd edition), McGraw-Hill, London.

Booch, G., Rumbaugh, J. and Jacobson, I. (1999) *The Unified Modeling Language User Guide*, Addison-Wesley, Reading, MA.

Britton, C. and Doake, J. (2000) *Object-Oriented Systems Development: A Gentle Introduction,* McGraw-Hill, London.

Britton, C. and Doake, J. (2002) *Software System Development: A Gentle Introduction* (3rd edition), McGraw-Hill, London.

Brown, D. (1997) *Object-Oriented Analysis: objects in plain English*, John Wiley, NY.

Charatan, Q. and Kans, A. (2002) *Java in Two Semesters*, McGraw-Hill, London.

Deitel, H.M. and Deitel, P.J. (2003) *Java: How to Program* (5th edition), Prentice Hall, Upper Saddle River, NJ.

Fowler, M. (2000) *UML Distilled: A Brief Guide to the Standard Object Modeling Language* (2nd edition), Addison-Wesley, Reading, MA.

Gamma, E., Helm, R., Johnson, R. and Vlissides, J. (1995) *Design Patterns: Elements of Reusable Object-Oriented Software*, Addison-Wesley, Reading, MA.

Graham, I., Henderson-Sellers, B. and Younessi, H. (1998) *The OPEN Process Specification,* Addison-Wesley, Harlow, UK.

Howe, D. (2001) *Data Analysis for Database Design* (3rd edition), Butterworth-Heinemann, Oxford.

Jacobson, I. (1992) *Object-Oriented Software Engineering: A Use Case Driven Approach*, Addison-Wesley, Wokingham, England.

Jacobson, I., Booch, G. and Rumbaugh, J. (1999) *The Unified Software Development Process*, Addison-Wesley, Reading, MA.

Kotonya, G. and Sommerville, I. (1997) *Requirements Engineering. Processes and Techniques*, John Wiley and Sons, Chichester.

Larman, C. (1998) *Applying UML and Patterns: An Introduction to Object-Oriented Analysis and Design*, Prentice Hall, NJ.

Lunn, K. (2003) *Software Development with UML*, Palgrave Macmillan, Basingstoke.

Macaulay, L. (1996) *Requirements Engineering*, Springer-Verlag, London.

Pfleeger, S.L. (1998) *Software Engineering, Theory and Practice*, Prentice Hall, Upper Saddle River, NJ.

Priestley, M. (2000) *Practical Object-Oriented Design with UML*, McGraw-Hill, London.

Quatrani, T. (1998) *Visual Modeling with Rational Rose and UML*, Addison-Wesley, Reading, MA.

Rumbaugh, J., Blaha, M., Premerlani, W., Eddy, F. and Lorensen, W. (1991) *Object-Oriented Modeling and Design*, Prentice-Hall, Englewood Cliffs, NJ.

Shneiderman, B. (2004) *Designing the User Interface: Strategies for Effective Human-Computer Interaction* (4th edition), Addison-Wesley, Reading, MA.

Sommerville, I. (2000) *Software Engineering* (6th edition), Addison-Wesley, Wokingham.

Sommerville, I. and Sawyer, P. (1997) *Requirements Engineering: A Good Practice Guide*, John Wiley and Sons, Chichester.

Stevens, P., with Pooley, R. (2000) *Using UML. Software Engineering with Objects and Components* (updated edition), Addison-Wesley, Harlow.

Wirfs-Brock, R., Wilkerson, B. and Wiener, L. (1990) *Designing Object-Oriented Software,* Prentice Hall, Englewood Cliffs, NJ.

There are a large number of references on the world wide web, including:

http://www.modelingstyle.info/activityDiagram.html

http://sunset.usc.edu/classes/cs577a_2000/papers/
ActivitydiagramsforRoseArchitect.pdf

D Glossary

Abstract class a class that is never instantiatied, because one or more of its operations has no method to implement it.

Abstraction the process of ignoring currently irrelevant details of a problem in order to concentrate on the most important parts.

Action behaviour that occurs when a transition takes place, as shown in a state diagram.

Activity behaviour that is related to a state; it is ongoing and can be interrupted by an event.

Activity diagram a UML diagram used to model the details of complex processes.

Actor person, organization or physical device that interacts with the system in some way. An actor inputs and receives information from the system and is associated with at least one use case (major functional activity).

Actor description documentation about an actor's job title and role in relation to the system.

Aggregation the relationship that occurs when one class is made up of several others, or when one class is made up of many occurrences of another class; sometimes referred to as the 'part-of' or 'consists-of' relationship.

Algorithm	description of a process, decomposing it into a series of smaller steps.
Analysis	involves investigation into and modelling of both the problem and the developing system. Analysis is one of the stages of the traditional development life cycle; it is classed as a workflow in object-oriented development.
Application domain	see *Problem domain*.
Architecture	the underlying structure of the system.
Association	a link between two classes indicating a possible relationship between objects of the classes.
Asynchronous message	a message sent from one object to another, where the sending object does not wait for a response from the receiving object.
Attribute	data item defined as part of a class or object. Also known as member variable.
Behaviour	the effects of a system that are visible to an external observer.
Boundary	defines what is to be considered inside the system. Outside the boundary is the system environment.
Boundary class	also known as interface class. Boundary classes handle the system's interface with its users.
Cardinality	see *Multiplicity*.

CASE	Computer Aided Software Engineering. Software tools that automate the system development process.
Child class	a subclass, specialization of another class.
Class	the description or pattern for a group of objects that have the same attributes, operations, relationships and meaning. Template or factory for creating objects.
Class declaration	statement in the code that introduces a new class.
Class diagram	a diagram showing the classes in a system and their relationships to each other. Optionally, attributes and operations may be included.
Class library	a collection of fully coded and tested classes that may be reused in other software applications.
Class-responsibility-collaboration cards	see *CRC cards*.
Client	the person or organization who requests and pays for the new system. The client will often also be a user of the system, but this is not always the case.
Client and server	in an object-oriented system a client is a class that uses the services of another and a server is a class that provides services to another.
Cohesion	a module is cohesive if it has a clearly defined role, a single, obvious purpose in the application. This makes the module easier for a maintaining programmer to read and understand.

Collaboration	the situation where a class needs the help of another class to fulfil one of its responsibilities.
Collaboration diagram	illustrates the behaviour specified in a scenario, with the interactions organized around the objects and the links between them, rather than shown in a time sequence.
Collection class	a class designed to access collections of objects.
Communication association	describes a link between an actor and a use case.
Compiler	program that translates source code (e.g. a Java program) into machine readable code.
Component	used in component diagrams to represent a physical software file, e.g. a source or executable file.
Component diagram	a UML implementation diagram representing software components and their dependencies.
Composition	a rigorous form of aggregation in which the parts live and die with the whole.
Concurrent processing	two or more processes running at the same time.
Constraint	extra information relating to an element of a model; expressed within curly brackets.
Constructor	an operation that creates a new object of a class.
Control class	a class that controls the sequence of events, for example in the execution of a use case.

CRC cards	a technique, using small index cards, to identify the responsibilities of classes in the system and the classes with which they have to collaborate to fulfil these responsibilities.
Database	all the data required to support the operations of an organization, collected, organized and maintained centrally in such a way that it can be used by many different applications.
Data decomposition	breaking down a system into smaller parts in terms of its data.
Data dictionary	a modelling technique that uses English and a small set of symbols to define the data in the system.
Data hiding	the technique of hiding implementation details behind a public interface.
Decision table	a tabular technique that can be used to specify the details of an operation; it is particularly useful when an outcome depends on a complicated combination of conditions.
Decision tree	a graphical technique used in the same way as a decision table.
Decomposition	the process of breaking down a problem into successively smaller parts in order to understand it better.
Deliverable	output that is produced during the development of a system, for example a specification of requirements, design models or program code.

Dependency　　　　　　　a relationship between two elements of a model such that a change in one may require a change in the other.

Deployment diagram　　　a UML implementation diagram showing the physical arrangement of the hardware elements of a computer system, e.g. PCs and printers, and their links. This diagram can also show how the software and hardware elements are related.

Design　　　　　　　　　whereas analysis is concerned with what the system has to do, design is concerned with how to build the system.

Design pattern　　　　　a tried and tested solution to a commonly occurring problem.

Development method　　　see *Methodology/method*.

Domain class　　　　　　also known as entity class. A domain class represents something in the real world of the system that is being developed, such as a customer, a bike or a hire.

Domain model　　　　　　a class diagram that models all of the classes in the problem domain together (as opposed to a diagram that models only the classes relating to a specific use case).

Dynamic binding　　　　the binding at run time of a message to a particular implementation of an operation.

Elicitation　　　　　　　see *Requirements elicitation*.

Encapsulation　　　　　　packaging data and operations into objects.

Entity class　　　　　　　see *Domain class*.

Environment	the system environment refers to anything outside the system that affects it in some way – e.g. people or organizations generating or responding to system data.
Essential use case	an essential use case is one that is completely free of implementation or detailed design decisions. See also *Real use case*.
Event	an instantaneous occurrence that is of significance to the system. An occurrence that triggers a state transition.
Expanded use case description	detailed structured description of a use case.
Fagan inspection	a systematic and structured method of checking the documented output from any stage of the system development process in order to identify omissions and errors.
Feasibility study	part of the traditional system life cycle which attempts to determine whether there is a practical solution to the problem under consideration.
Feature	a collective term for the attributes and operations of a class.
Fire	when a state transition occurs, it is said to fire.
Foreign key	if one table in a database contains an attribute which is the primary key of another table, this attribute is called a foreign key. A foreign key permits a link between the two tables.
Fork	a symbol in an activity diagram indicating the start of parallel processing.

Framework	a high-level structure within which to develop a system.
Front end	the set of programs that implement the user interface.
Functional decomposition	breaking down a system into smaller parts in terms of its processes.
Functionality	what a system does in terms of the behaviour that it supports.
Get method	a method that retrieves or displays the value of an attribute.
Granularity	level of detail.
Guard	a condition that must be satisfied if a transition is to fire.
Happy day scenario	a scenario which records the normal sequence of events in a use case.
Hardware platform	the hardware (computers, networks, processors, etc.) on which a system runs.
High-level use case description	overview of a use case, incorporated in an expanded use case description.
Human–computer interface	see *User interface*.
Implementation	the translation of a system design into code.

Implementation independent	system models (such as the analysis models) that are not tied to a particular software or hardware platform and can be implemented in a variety of different ways.
Incremental development	a life cycle model in which the system is partitioned according to areas of functionality. Each major functional area is developed and delivered independently to the client.
Information hiding	making the internal details of a module inaccessible to other modules.
Inheritance	a relationship between two classes where one is a refinement of the other; sometimes referred to as the 'is-a' relationship. A mechanism that allows a class to reuse features already defined in another class.
Initiating actor	the actor who starts off the sequence of events in a use case.
Input	data which is entered into the system by the user.
Instance	an object that belongs to a particular class.
Instantiation	the creation of a new instance of a class (i.e. an object).
Interaction	a set of messages exchanged between objects to achieve a specific goal.
Interaction diagram	diagram showing a set of messages that take place between objects to achieve a specific goal.

Interface	the system interface is its connection to the outside world. The interface of a module, class or package is the information that it presents to its environment.
Interface class	see *Boundary class*.
Iteration	doing something repeatedly.
Iterative development	a way of developing systems, often using prototyping, that involves several releases of the complete system, each one showing an improvement on the one before.
JDBC (Java database connectivity)	a package of classes that allows a Java application to establish a connection with a relational database.
Join	a symbol in an activity diagram indicating the end of parallel processing.
Layered architecture	a way of structuring logical software units in order to minimize dependencies.
Life cycle	also known as system life cycle. A recognizable pattern of steps taken to develop a software system. Traditionally, these include the key stages of analysis, design, implementation, testing and maintenance.
Lifeline	a dotted line connected to an object in a sequence diagram that indicates the existence of the object over a period of time.
Maintenance	the stage in the life of a system, after it has been handed over to the user, where errors are corrected and modifications carried out.

Member variable	see *Attribute*. Member variable is the term commonly used by programmers.
Message	request from one object to another to invoke one of its operations.
Methodology/method	recipe for developing a system. The detailed description of the steps and stages in system development, together with a specified list of inputs and outputs for each step.
Method	the implementation of an operation.
Method call	see *Message*.
Milestone	indicates the completion of a stage in the development process.
Modelling	the process of building a representation of all or part of a problem or the system that is designed to solve it.
Module	section of a program designed to execute a logically identifiable unit.
Multiobject	an icon in an interaction diagram representing several objects of the same class.
Multiplicity	the multiplicity of an association indicates the number of objects of each class that are allowed to participate in the association.
Multi-threaded	a multi-threaded system is one designed to have several processes executing in parallel.

Navigability	the direction of the link between two objects. This can be unidirectional or two way.
Notation	written language that may include text, symbols and diagrams.
Noun analysis	the technique of identifying objects and classes by picking them out from a written description of the problem.
Object	In the early stages of development an object is something that exists independently in the problem domain. Later in the development process, the term refers to an instance of a class in the system. At implementation, an object is a software unit packaging together data and methods to manipulate that data.
Object activation	this term refers to the state of an object in a sequence diagram. An object becomes active as soon as it receives a message. This is indicated on the sequence diagram by a thin rectangle on the object's lifeline.
Object flow	this term relates to activity diagrams. An object flow provides information about the input that an activity needs from a specific object, or how an object is affected by the output from an activity.
Object Management Group (OMG)	group of people who control issues of standardization relating to object-oriented system development.
Object-orientation	an approach to developing software systems that is based on data items and the attributes and operations that define them.
Object-oriented database	an object-oriented database provides all the storage facilities and functionality of a traditional database, but is

specifically designed to implement the types of complex data frequently found in object-oriented systems.

Operation procedure or function defined as part of a class or object; using this term refers to the procedure's public interface with the rest of the software.

Operation specification detailed description of what an operation does. This can be done using, for example, specification by contract, structured English, a decision table or a decision tree.

Output information produced by the system for the user.

Override a feature in a subclass which uses the same name as the feature in the superclass, but redefines and replaces it.

Package a UML notation for grouping elements of a model. Packages do not represent anything in the system, but are used to group elements that do represent things in the system.

Parent class superclass, generalization of other classes.

Participating actor an actor who is involved in a use case.

Pattern see *Design pattern*.

Persistent data refers to data that needs to be stored because it continues to exist after the program that creates and uses it has stopped executing.

Polymorphism the ability to hide different implementations behind a common interface.

Presentation layer	a term that relates to a layered architecture, describes the packages and classes that are used in the system's interface.
Primary key	attribute that uniquely identifies a single occurrence of a data item in a relational database table.
Private	a private feature is usually interpreted to be one that can only be used by an instance of the owning class.
Problem definition	a brief initial summary of what has been discovered during the requirements elicitation process.
Problem domain	the area of knowledge or activity relating to the problem that the system is to solve.
Problems and requirements list	a structured and detailed list of problems and requirements uncovered during requirements elicitation.
Protected	a protected feature is usually interpreted to be one that can only be used by instances of the owning class or a subclass (or other descendent) of the owning class.
Prototyping	an iterative method of developing a system, instead of using traditional structured methods. A working model of the system may be constructed at an early stage in development for the purpose of establishing user requirements and later discarded. Alternatively, a working model is sometimes used as the basis for design and implementation of the final system (as in iterative development).
Public	a public feature is usually interpreted to be one that can be used by instances of any class.

Public interface	the operations and attributes of an object or class that can be seen by others in the system.
Rational Unified Process (RUP)	a widely used version of the Unified Software Development Process, marketed by the Rational Corporation.
Real use case	real use cases show detail of design and implementation decisions insofar as they affect the user. See also *Essential use case*.
Reflexive message	the call by an object to itself to invoke one of its own methods while it is executing another method. Also known as a self-referencing message.
Relational database	a well-established and widely used type of database that is based on tables.
Relationship	a link between classes. During analysis a relationship represents something that occurs in the real world that is significant for the system. During design it represents a navigable path.
Requirement	a feature or behaviour of the system that is desired by any person or organization affected by the system, such as users, clients, developers, management.
Requirements elicitation	the stage of requirements engineering which aims to gather as much information as possible about the problem domain, the clients' and users' current difficulties and what they would like the intended system to do for them
Requirements engineering	the process of establishing what is wanted and needed from a software system. Requirements engineering covers the three stages of elicitation, specification and validation.

Requirements specification	the stage of requirements engineering during which the information from the elicitation process is analysed and recorded using textual and diagrammatic modelling techniques to represent the problem and the proposed solution.
Requirements validation	the stage of requirements engineering which checks that the recorded requirements correspond to the intentions of the clients and users about the system.
Responsibility	an obligation that one class has to provide a service for another.
Return	describes the transfer of control back to the calling object. Sometimes data is associated with a return.
Reuse	programming with existing software modules rather than coding them from scratch each time.
Reverse engineering	the process of reconstructing a design model, such as a class or sequence diagram, by examining the code.
Scenario	a scenario represents one instance of a use case, describing a particular sequence of events that may occur in trying to reach the use case goal.
Self-referencing	see *Reflexive message*.
Self-transition	occurs when an object remains in the same state in response to an event.
Sequence diagram	illustrates the behaviour specified in a scenario, with the interactions shown in a time sequence.

Service	the set of publicly available operations belonging to a class.
Set method	a method that initializes or changes the value of an attribute.
Signature	the signature of an attribute or an operation is its public interface.
Simulation	a computer program that models a complex real-world situation.
Single-threaded	a single-threaded system is one where only one process at a time executes.
Software platform	the software used to implement and run a system.
Specification	a definition or description of what is wanted and needed from a software system. See also *Requirements specification*.
Specification by contract	describes operations in terms of the services they deliver.
State	represents a period of time during which an object of a class satisfies some condition or waits for an event.
State diagram	diagram illustrating the behaviour of a single class in response to events in the system.
State transition	the response of an object to an event; usually involving movement of the object from one state to another.

Static method   a static method is one that can be invoked without having to create an instance of the class to which it belongs.

Stereotype   specialized use of a modelling element, which allows us to extend the basic set of UML modelling elements. A stereotype is usually identified by a label inside a pair of guillemets « » such as «include» and «extend».

Structured English   a subset of English that may be used to specify operations.

Subclass   a specialized version of another class (the superclass).

Subsystem   a system which is itself part of a larger system.

Superclass   a generalized version of another class (the subclass).

Superstate   a state drawn round all or some of the states in a state diagram in order to simplify the diagram and avoid clutter.

Swimlane   found in activity diagrams. A swimlane indicates which agent, person or object is responsible for a set of activities.

Synchronization bar   used in activity diagrams. A synchronization bar indicates the start or end of parallel processing.

Synchronous message   a message sent from one object to another, where the sending object waits for a response from the receiving object.

System   a set of interrelated objects or elements that are viewed as a whole and designed by human beings to achieve a purpose; it has a boundary within which it lies and outside of which is the environment.

System life cycle   see *Life cycle*.

Table   repository of data in a relational database. Tables store data in a row-column format; each column stores a field, or attribute of the data, and each row stores a record, typically the complete set of values for a single data object.

Traceability   the ability to track a requirement through the development process and identify where it is implemented in the final system code.

Transient object   an object that is created and deleted during an interaction.

Transition   see *State transition*.

Unified Modelling Language (UML)   a set of diagrammatic techniques, specifically tailored for object-oriented development, which have become an industry standard for modelling object-oriented systems.

Use case   specifies the functionality that the system will offer from the users' perspective. A use case specifies a set of interactions between a user and the system to achieve a particular goal.

Use case beneficiary   the most important actor associated with a use case. The purpose of the use case is to achieve the goal for the beneficiary.

Use case description   documents what the use case does; see also *Expanded use case description*.

Use case realization   the development of a use case from its initial identification during requirements elicitation to its implementation.

User   any organization or person that uses the system to input or process data, or who receives the results of such processing.

User interface   interaction between the user and the system.

Validation   see *Requirements validation*.

Visibility   describes the accessibility of an attribute or operation. Visibility can be public, private or protected.

Workflow   in object-oriented development activities, such as analysis, design and implementation are referred to as workflows.

«extend»   stereotyped relationship between two use cases. A use case linked by an «extend» relationship specifies significant alternative behaviour.

«include»   stereotyped relationship between two use cases, such that behaviour common to several use cases can be shared between them.

E Answers

The answers given in this section are one possible set of solutions. If your answers are different, it does not necessarily mean they are wrong – there are almost always many possible solutions that are equally satisfactory. If your answer is very different from ours you should discuss it with your tutor.

Chapter 2

Exercise 2.1

Interview Plan			
System: **Wheels**		Project reference: **Wheels/04**	
Participants:	**Naresh Patel (Chief mechanic for Wheels)** **Simon Davis (Developer)**		
Date **24 February 2004**	Time **9.30 am**	Duration **30 minutes**	Place **Storeroom office**
Purpose of interview **Preliminary meeting to discuss procedures and problems with the current system, relating to handling the bikes**			
Agenda • **current procedures for recording details of bikes** • **current procedures for hiring bikes** • **current procedures for checking bikes** • **problems with the current system** • **initial ideas on how these could be addressed** • **follow-up actions.**			
Documents to be brought to interview • **list of bike details from the computer** • **any records of checks on bikes** • **any other documents relating to current procedures.**			

Figure E.1   The interview plan

Exercise 2.2

a   How many bikes are purchased from suppliers at one time?

b   What happens usually when a bike is checked and how is the outcome recorded?

c   Is the process different for specialist bikes?

d   How do you cope when it's Annie's day off and you have to deal with hiring bikes for customers?

e   Do you find the current procedures easy to use?

f   How could the current procedures be improved?

Exercise 2.3

Other useful requirements might include:

• Produce a report on the damage done to different bikes

• Use customer details for marketing purposes, special offers, etc.

• Produce a report on the relative popularity of different types of bike.

Exercise 2.4

See Figure E.2

Exercise 2.5

• A customer, Sheena Patel, arrives at the shop to return a bike

• Annie contacts the mechanics to ask for someone to come and check the bike

• Annie looks out the relevant bike card and checks Sheena's name and address

• Annie makes sure that the bike being returned is the one on the card

• She confirms that the bike is being returned on time by checking the return date against the current date

• One of the mechanics checks the bike and finds some damage to the front wheel

• He shows the damage to the customer, Sheena, and informs her that there is a charge of £10 to cover the repair

• Annie returns Sheena's deposit, minus £10 to cover the cost of repair to the damage

• Annie writes out a receipt for Sheena.

Wheels customer survey

We are planning to expand our business to enable you to hire a range of sports items as well as bikes, and we would very much value your views on the best way to do this.

Please spare a few minutes to answer the questions below and return the form to Annie in reception.

Please answer questions 1 and 2 by ticking one of the boxes:

1. Roughly how many times have you hired a bike from us in the past year?

   no hire ☐   once only ☐   2–5 times ☐   6–10 times ☐   more than 10 times ☐

2. In the boxes below please tick the items you would be interested in hiring from us

   skateboard ☐
   surfboard ☐
   golf clubs ☐
   tennis racket ☐
   squash racket ☐
   badminton racket ☐

3. For each of the statements (a)–(c) below, circle the number that is closest to your own view. 1 means that you strongly agree with the statement, and 5 means that you strongly disagree.

		strongly agree			strongly disagree	
a	I would like to be able to hire a wider range of items	1	2	3	4	5
b	I would like to hire sports items	1	2	3	4	5
c	I would like to hire sports items for my family	1	2	3	4	5

4.

Are there any other items that you would like to hire from Wheels? YES/NO	If yes, please give details:
Any other comments:	

If you would like more information about our bikes please give your details:

Your name: _____

Your address: _____

_____

Thank you for completing this questionnaire.

Figure E.2   The Wheels customer survey

Exercise 2.6

Table E.1:   Answer to Exercise 2.6

No.	Source	Date	Description	Priority	Related reqs.	Related docs.	Change details
2.1	Interview with Annie Price	10/02/04	Keep record of essential customer details (name, address, contact details, etc.)	Essential	2.2	Current bike cards	

Chapter 3

Exercise 3.1 Library system

a   Use case: Issue book; Actor: Librarian

b   Use case: Issue book; Actor: Librarian

c   Use case: Issue book; Actor: Librarian

d   Use case: Handle book return; Actor: Librarian

e   Use case: Search catalogue; Actor: Member

f   Use case: Reserve book; Actor: Member

g   Use case: Add new book; Actor: Librarian.

Notice that scenarios a, b and c, although they document quite different sequences of events, are for the same use case: 'Issue book'. All three scenarios have the goal of lending a book to a customer but take different routes to achieve it; in the case of scenario c the goal is not achieved at all. See Figure E.3 for use case.

Exercise 3.2 Library system

The «include» relationship indicates that the 'Reserve book' use case always uses the functionality specified in 'Search catalogue'. The use case description for 'Reserve book' will not have to duplicate functionality already described in the 'Search catalogue' use case description. See Figure E.4 for use case.

Exercise 3.3 Cool Cuts

a   Use case: Make appointment; Actor: Junior

b   Use case: Make appointment; Actor: Junior

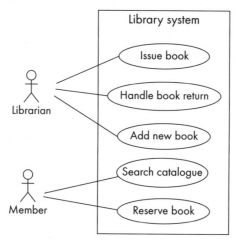

Figure E.3   Library use case diagram

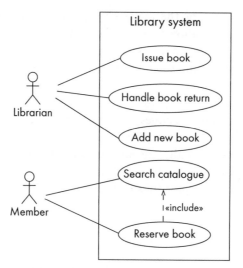

Figure E.4   Library use case diagram with «include»

c Use case: Make appointment; Actor: Junior

d Use case: Maintain staff list; Actor: Manager

e Use case: Handle customer payments; Actor: Junior

f Use case: Maintain product list; Actor: Junior.

Junior is not the job title of any employee at Cool Cuts: it describes the way certain employees are permitted to use the computer system; a role. Juniors can make appointments, maintain the product list and take customer payments. Trainees, the part-time

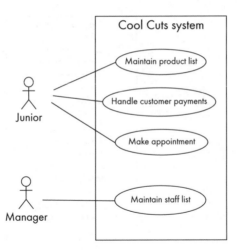

Figure E.5   Cool Cuts use case diagram

receptionist or the manager use the system in this way. Only the manager is allowed to update the staff list. We have used this device, rather that modelling each job title as an actor, to stop the diagram getting too cluttered.

Exercise 3.4 Cool Cuts

This version assumes that the use case 'Maintain product list' always uses 'Find product'. Conversely, 'Handle customer payment' only occasionally needs to use 'Find product'. This covers situations where customers want to buy products like shampoo as well as paying for their haircut.

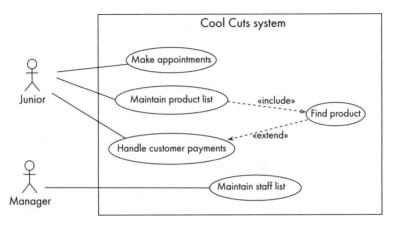

Figure E.6   Cool Cuts use case diagram with «include» and «extend»

Exercise 3.5 Cool Cuts

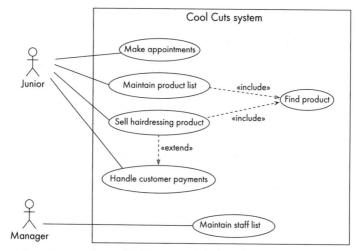

Figure E.7   *Cool Cuts use case diagram with 'Sell hairdressing product' as a separate use case*

'Sell hairdressing product' is now modelled as a separate use case. The «extend» link to 'Handle customer payments' indicates that the functionality in 'Sell hairdressing product' will sometimes form part of the 'Handle customer payments' use case, i.e. customers may sometimes buy a hairdressing product when they pay for their cut and blow dry. The association link to the actor Junior indicates that 'Sell hairdressing product' is a use case that can take place independently, not necessarily as part of 'Handle customer payments'. The «include» link to 'Find product' indicates that 'Sell hairdressing product' always uses 'Find product'.

Exercise 3.6 Dentist's system

Part a

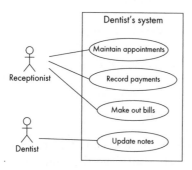

Figure E.8   *Dentist use case diagram*

Part b   i Use case 'Maintain appointments'

- Katherine phones the dentist to make an appointment

- Joanne, the receptionist, asks when she would like to come

- Katherine says Monday 8th November

- Joanne says there are free appointments at 10.00am and 2.00pm

- Katherine says she will come at 2.00pm

- Joanne records the appointment.

ii Use case 'Maintain appointments'

- Ann phones the dentist to make an appointment as soon as possible

- Joanne says there are free appointments on Monday 11th October at 9.00am, 11.15am or 11.45am or on Wednesday 13th October at 2.00pm

- Ann says she will come Monday 11th October at 9.00am

- Joanne records the appointment.

iii Use case 'Maintain appointments'

- Alan comes into the waiting room after seeing the dentist. The dentist has told him to make another appointment in 10 days

- Joanne says that will be Thursday 16th September

- Joanne looks up the system and finds there are no free appointments on that day

- She says there are free appointments on Friday 17th September at 8.45am, 11.00am and 12.15pm or on Monday 20th September at 9.00am and at 10.30am

- Alan says he has forgotten his diary and will phone later to make an appointment.

Notice that, although these scenarios record very different sequences of events, they all have the same goal, i.e. to make an appointment – although in the last case this goal is not achieved.

Exercise 3.7 Dentist's system

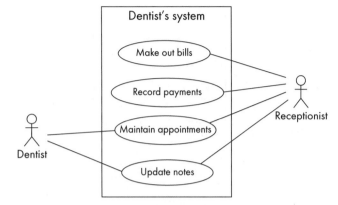

Figure E.9   Dentist s system use case diagram with added information

Exercise 3.8 Automatic ticket system

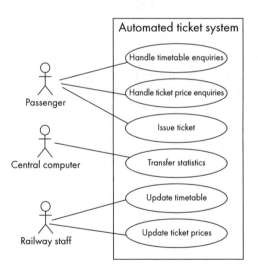

Figure E.10   *Automatic ticket machine use case diagram*

The central computer is modelled as an actor because it receives output from the system, it is a beneficiary. Although they are modelled as stick figures, actors do not have to be human.

Exercise 3.9 Quick Bites system

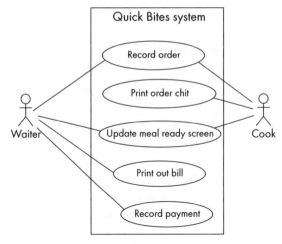

Figure E.11   *Quick Bites use case diagram*

Both the Waiter and the Cook are associated with the use case 'Record order': the Waiter inputs the order to the system and the Cook receives it – he reads it from his screen. The same two actors are associated with the use case 'Update meal ready screen': the Cook inputs the information and the Waiter receives it and updates the screen when he has served a customer.

Exercise 3.10

If you notice that two or more of the use cases have a chunk of functionality in common, it may be worth extracting the common functionality and putting it in a new use case. The new use case must then be linked to the ones from which you originally extracted the functionality by an «include» relationship. The new use case then provides functionality that is integral to any use case linked to it by an «include» relationship. This is conceptually very similar to using a function or procedure in a computer program. It is an economical way of reusing functionality.

Exercise 3.11

If we want to specify a chunk of behaviour that is additional or exceptional to the normal sequence of events in a use case, we can create a new use case for that behaviour and specify an «extend» relationship between the new and the original use cases.

Exercise 3.12 View Us video system

Part a

Scenario 1. Use case: Loan a video

- Lucy comes into the shop
- She finds two videos she wants to borrow
- She takes the empty video covers to the counter and says she wants to borrow them tonight
- She presents her membership card
- Phil, the assistant, finds the videos
- He scans the barcode on the membership card
- Lucy's details come up on the screen
- Phil checks that Lucy still lives at 6 Privet Drive
- He sees that she has no videos outstanding and does not owe View Us any money
- He scans the barcodes on the videos and hands them to Lucy
- Phil takes the money for the rental and says Lucy must return the videos by 8pm the next evening
- The system prints a receipt
- Lucy leaves the shop with the videos.

Scenario 2. Use case: Loan a video

- Ian comes into the shop
- He finds a video he wants to borrow for one night
- He takes the video case to the counter
- Phil asks for his membership card
- Ian says he isn't a member but he'd like to become one
- Phil takes details of his name, address, telephone number, and bank account number and sort code
- He prints out a membership card for Ian
- He scans the video barcode
- Phil takes the money for the rental and says Ian must return the video by 8pm the next evening
- The system prints a receipt
- Ian leaves with the video and his new membership card.

Scenario 3. Use case: Return a video

- Rachel comes into the video shop with three videos she borrowed the previous day

- She hands them to Phil

- Phil scans the video barcodes

- He checks that the videos are back in time and that Rachel doesn't owe them any money

- Rachel leaves the shop.

Scenario 4. Use case: Manage members

- Hannah comes into the shop and says she wants to become a member

- Phil takes details of her name, address, telephone number, and bank account number and sort code

- He prints out a membership card for Hannah

- He asks Hannah if she wants to borrow a video now

- She says 'No'

- She leaves with her new membership card.

Scenario 5. Use case: Return a video

- Andy comes into the shop with two videos to return

- The videos are a day late

- Phil is busy with another customer

- Andy puts the videos into the returned video box and leaves

- When Phil has finished with his customer he retrieves the videos and scans the barcodes

- He notices that they are a day late and checks that the system has registered this against Andy's name.

Scenario 6. Use case: Manage videos

- Kim, the View Us manager, arrives with a box of new videos

- Phil and Kim sort through the videos allocating barcodes and prices: newly released videos are more expensive to rent than older ones

- Kim enters the details of the new videos on to the system.

Scenario 7. Use case: Loan a video

- Tony comes into the shop

- He chooses three videos

- Phil scans his membership card

- He notices that Tony still has two videos out; they are three days overdue

- He says he cannot let Tony borrow any more videos until he returns those still out.

What dictates the splitting of a sequence of events into separate use cases is primarily what the clients see as distinct jobs. This is often influenced by where the time intervals come. Normally there is a gap between the time a customer borrows a video and the time they take it back; so borrowing a video and returning it are perceived as separate jobs and modelled as separate use cases.

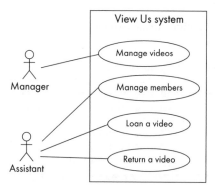

Figure E.12   *Original use case diagram for the View Us video system*

Part b   Diagram incorporating new information about reservations

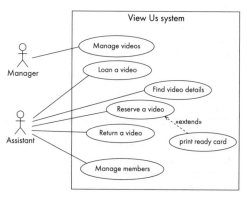

Figure E.13   *View Us use case diagram with reservation and find video details added*

Part c

Use case: Find video details
Actors: Assistant
Goal: To find recorded details of a specific video

Description:
The system searches for a specific video using information supplied from the input screen (e.g. barcode, title, actor name). The system locates the best match and displays the details on the screen.

Use case: Loan a video
Actors: Assistant
Goal: To lend a video to a customer

Description:
A customer chooses a video and gives their membership card and the video to the assistant. The assistant scans the customer's membership card and checks if they owe any money or have outstanding loans. The system searches for a specific video using the barcode scanned from the video they wish to borrow. The system locates the required video and displays the details on the screen. The assistant checks that this is the video the customer wants to borrow and looks to see what the rental cost is for this video. The system then registers the loan transaction.

Use case: reserve a video
Actors: Assistant
Goal: To find a specific video and reserve it for a member

Description:
The system searches for a specific video using information supplied from the input screen (e.g. barcode, title, actor name). The system locates the best match and displays the details on the screen. If this is the video the customer wants to reserve, and there are no copies in stock, it is marked as reserved. The assistant scans the member's barcode so that the system can record who made the reservation.

Figure E.14   High-level use case descriptions of the View Us system

Part d

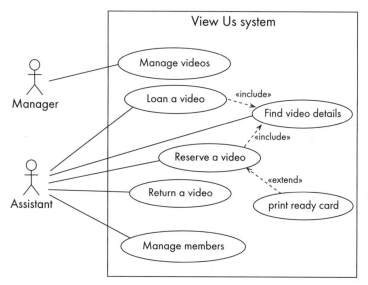

Figure E.15   View Us use case diagram avoiding duplicated functionality

Part e   i

> **Use case:** Print ready card
> **Actors:**   Assistant
> **Goal:**   To print out a postcard stating that a reserved video is available
>
> **Overview:**
> The assistant uses the system to find details of the member who reserved
> the video. A postcard is printed with the member's name and address and
> the title of the video.
>
> **Typical course of events:**
>
> | Actor action | System response |
> |---|---|
> | 1   The Assistant asks for details of the reserving member | 2   Displays details of the reserving member |
> | 3   The Assistant requests a printed postcard | 4   Prints a postcard with the name and address of reserving member and title of the video |

Figure E.16   Expanded description of the 'Print ready card' use case

Part e   ii

Use case: Return a video
Actors: Assistant
Goal: To register the return of a video by a customer

Overview:
A customer returns a video. The assistant scans the video barcode and finds
the record of the loan transaction. If the video is late back the system will
indicate this and a fine will be registered on the customer's record. The
system then checks whether the returned title has been reserved by another
member. If so the video is placed on the reserved shelf under the counter
and a postcard is printed and sent to the reserving customer.

Typical course of events:

Actor action	System response
1 A customer returns a video	
2 The Assistant scans in the barcode	3 Displays the load transaction
4 The Assistant indicates that the video has been returned	5 Indicates if overdue
	6 Checks for reservation
7 Assistant returns video to shelves	

Alternative courses:

At step 5   if a video is overdue, the system calculates the overdue fee
                   and adds it to the customer's record.

At step 6   if the video has been reserved, the assistant asks the system
                   to initiate the use case 'Print ready card'. The Assistant then
                   places the video on the reserved shelf under the counter
                   instead of returning it to the normal shelves.

Figure E.17   *Expanded description of the 'Return a video' use case*

Part f

Use case: Loan a video
Actors: Assistant
Goal: To lend a video to a customer

Overview:
A customer chooses a video and gives their membership card and the video
to the assistant. The assistant scans the customer's membership card and
checks if they owe any money or have outstanding loans. The system searches
for a specific video using the barcode scanned from the video they wish to
borrow. The system locates the required video and displays the details on
the screen. The assistant checks that this is the video the customer wants
to borrow and looks to see what the rental cost is for this video. The system
then registers the loan transaction.

Typical course of events:

Actor action	System response
1 A customer chooses a video	
2 The Assistant scans in the membership card barcode	3 Displays customer details
4 The Assistant agrees the details	
5 The Assistant scans in the video barcode	6 Displays video details including hire
7 The Assistant agrees the cost and registers the loan	8 Stores the loan transaction
9 The Customer pays for the loan	
10 The Assistant records the payment	11 Prints a receipt

Alternative courses:

Steps 2, 3 & 4   For a new customer, details must be entered into the system
at this stage and a membership card printed.*

Steps 3 and 4   If the customer has too many videos already out on loan,
he may not borrow any more until he returns some.

Steps 3 and 4   If the customer owes money for late returns, he may not
borrow any videos until his debt is paid.

* Ideally this should be modelled by adding an «extend» relationship linking 'Loan a video'
to 'Manage members'. At this point the use case description should read: For a new
customer initiate the use case 'Manage members'

Figure E.18   Expanded description of the 'Loan a video' use case

Chapter 4

Exercise 4.1

Emptying your pockets, etc. produces a heap of objects. By categorizing them and naming the category, you are defining the class to which they belong. By dividing them into subcategories you are defining specialized classes. By pulling items apart, you are defining an aggregation (or composition) relationship between a whole class and its parts.

Exercise 4.2

Part a

StudentModuleResults
studentName
studentNumber
moduleName
moduleCode
result

Part b

Clothes
itemNumber
garmentDescription
colour
sizeRange
price

Part c

Book
ISBN
title
author
publisher
yearOfPublication

Exercise 4.3

a   Banking system: Customer, Account, CurrentAccount, DepositAccount, OnlineAccount, PersonalAccount, BusinessAccount

b   Drawing package: Shape, Triangle, Circle, Rectangle, Square, Line

c   Library system: Book, Member, Loan, Reservation

d University human resources system: Employee,
   AdministrativeStaff, AcademicStaff, TechnicalStaff, Grade

e Mail order system: Product, Customer, Order, Payment.

Exercise 4.4

Object/Class	Category
Customer	People
Account, CurrentAccount, etc.	Conceptual
Shape, Triangle, etc.	Conceptual
Book	Physical
Member	People
Loan	Conceptual
Reservation	Conceptual
Employee	People
AdminStaff, AcademicStaff, etc.	People
Grade	Conceptual
Customer	People
Product	Physical
Order, Payment	Conceptual

Exercise 4.5

Concept	Definition
a	14
b	11
c	7
d	13
e	5
f	10
g	3
h	1
i	6
j	12
k	4
l	8
m	9
n	2

Exercise 4.6

blueSide.try()
blueSide.conversion()
blueSide.dropGoal()
blueSide.penalty()
blueSide.displayScore()

Exercise 4.7

Part a

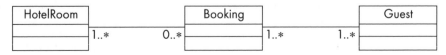

Figure E.19   Answer to Exercise 4.7a

Part b

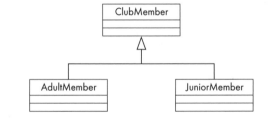

Figure E.20   Answer to Exercise 4.7b

Part c

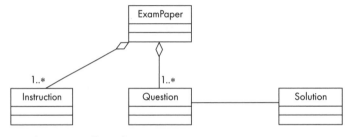

Figure E.21   Answer to Exercise 4.7c

Part d

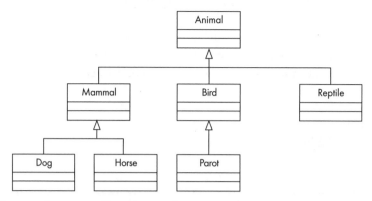

Figure E.22   Answer to Exercise 4.7d

Part e

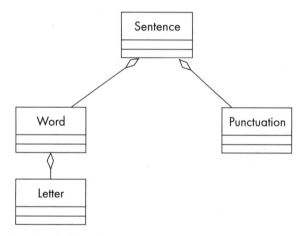

Figure E.23   Answer to Exercise 4.7e

Part f

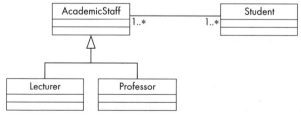

Figure E.24   Answer to Exercise 4.7f

Exercise 4.8

Part a The attributes of a Staff card object are:
cardNumber, name, dept., expiryDate

Part b The attributes of a Wholesale customer object are:
name, address, phone#, email, account#, creditLimit, contactName

Exercise 4.9

Additions to Table 4.3 are:

Table E.2: *Answer to Exercise 4.9*

Object name	Class	Attributes	Response to greet() message
george	Briton	language: English	Good morning
antonio	Italian	language: Italian	Buongiorno

Exercise 4.10

The message would be: jojo.perform()

Exercise 4.11

See Table E.3.

Notice that we have not completed an entry for AnimalRobot as it would make no sense to define behaviour and values for an unspecified type of animal. Although a method has been defined for its perform() operation, common sense tells us that this call can never be instantiated and should be declared abstract. We can do this by annotating the class with the word {abstract}, see Figure E.25.

Figure E.25 *Abstract class*

Exercise 4.12

The abstract classes in the Robot hierarchy are Robot, HumanoidRobot, DomesticRobot and AlienRobot because they have no method defined for the perform() operation; also AnimalRobot (see answer to Exercise 4.11).

Table E.3: Set of objects with classes, attribute values and responses from the Robot hierarchy

Object name	Class	Attributes	Response to perform() message
jamie	CookRobot	meansOfMobility: two legs language: English	prepare meal
sophia	MaidRobot	meansOfMobility: two legs language: Italian	clean stairs
jeeves	ButlerRobot	meansOfMobility: two legs language: English	answer door
mart	MartianRobot	meansOfMobility: wheels language: Martian numOfWheels: 8	transmits reports to earth in Martian
john	WierdoRobot	meansOfMobility: wheels language: ⲧⲁⲩⲕⲧⲻⲕ numOfWheels: 6	converses with other heads in ⲧⲁⲩⲕⲧⲻⲕ
pat	DogRobot	meansOfMobility: four legs noise: Woof bestTrick: fetch stick noisy: True	fetch stick and say 'Woof, Woof, Woof, Woof'
felix	CatRobot	meansOfMobility: four legs noise: miaow bestTrick: catch mice extraTrick: climb up curtain	catch mice and say 'Miaow' and climb up curtain

Exercise 4.13

The output would be:

- prepare meal

- clean stairs

- answer door

- transmit to earth in Martian

- converse with other heads in ⲧⲁⲩⲕⲧⲻⲕ

- fetch stick and say 'Woof, Woof, Woof, Woof'

- catch mice and say 'Miaow' and climb up curtain.

Exercise 4.14

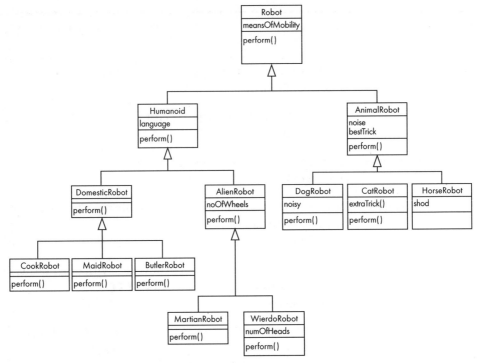

Figure E.26   Robot hierarchy with new class HorseRobot

i   HorseRobot inherits the attributes: meansofMobility, noise, best trick.

Notice that the HorseRobot class also has a new attribute, shod. For a class to be a specialization of its parent class, it must have some distinguishing feature. Different values for its attributes only qualify it to be a different object of that class. HorseRobot does not redefine the perform() method, so it must have some new feature.

ii   HorseRobot inherits unchanged AnimalRobot's method for perform().

Exercise 4.15

Part a

```
Robot automaton[];
    int i;
    automaton = new Robot[8];

    automaton[0] = new CookRobot();
    automaton[1] = new MaidRobot();
    automaton[2] = new ButlerRobot();
    automaton[3] = new MartianRobot();
    automaton[4] = new WierdoRobot();
    automaton[5] = new DogRobot();
    automaton[6] = new CatRobot();
    automaton[7] = new HorseRobot();
```

Figure E.27   *Answer to Exercise 4.15a*

Part b

```
for (i=0;i<8;i++)
{
automaton[i].perform();
}
```

Figure E.28   *Answer to Exercise 4.15b*

Chapter 5

Exercise 5.1

a   A system for a medical centre: doctor, nurse, patient, appointment, prescription, medication

b   A system for a video hire shop: video, video copy, customer, hire

c   A system for a car park which allows entry with an ID card: car, barrier, car sensor, ID card

d   A system allocating equipment to local schools: school, equipment item, supplier.

Exercise 5.2

Object	Category
doctor, nurse, patient	People
appointment	Conceptual
prescription	Conceptual
medication	Physical
video	Physical
video copy	Physical
customer	People
hire	Conceptual
car, barrier, car sensor, ID card	Physical
school	Organization
equipment item	Physical
supplier	People or Organization

Exercise 5.3

Part a

Mr Major, the town's only dentist, has a computer system to help him keep track of patients' appointments and dental treatment. Mr Major's receptionist makes appointments with patients either when they phone up or when they are back in the waiting room after treatment. Sometimes patients phone to cancel appointments or to change them. Mr Major keeps notes on the system about his patients' treatments – these are updated each time he sees a patient. The receptionist also makes out bills for patients and records payments on the system.

See Table E.4 for a list of rejected candidate objects in the dentist's system and the reasons for rejection

Objects retained as possible classes: patient, appointment, dental treatment, payment.

Part b

Your local railway station is going to install automatic ticket dispensing machines. Each machine will be able to give passengers up-to-date train timetable and ticket price information. The machines must also issue tickets and transfer statistics about ticket sales to a central computer system. Railway staff must be able to update ticket prices and timetable information.

See table Table E.5 for a list of rejected candidate objects in automatic ticket system and reasons for rejection.

Objects retained as possible classes: timetable, ticket information, ticket sales.

Table E.4:   *Candidate objects in dentist's system and reasons for rejection*

Objects	Reasons for rejection
Mr Major	outside the scope of the system, Mr Major is a user of the system
town	outside the scope of the system
dentist	duplicate of Mr Major (and therefore also outside the scope of the system)
computer system	whole system
receptionist	outside the scope of the system, the receptionist is a user of the system
waiting room	outside the scope of the system
notes	attribute of dental treatment
bill	output of the system

Table E.5:   *Candidate objects in automatic ticket system and reasons for rejection*

Objects	Reasons for rejection
railway station	outside the scope of the system
ticket dispensing machines	whole system
passengers	outside the scope of the system – system users
ticket price	attribute of ticket information
ticket	output of the system
statistics	duplicates ticket sales
computer system	outside the scope of the system
railway staff	outside the scope of the system – system users

Exercise 5.4

a A Customer in a banking system: accountNo., name, address, phoneNumber

b A library Member: memberNo., name, address, readerCategory (adult/junior/pensioner)

c A university Lecturer: employeeNo., name, address, phoneNumber, dateOfBirth, speciality, roomNo., extensionNo.

d A Student: studentId, name, homeAddress, universityAddress, dateOfBirth, degreeCourse

e A Patient in a dentist's system: patientNo., name, address, phoneNumber, dateOfBirth, category (private/health service).

Exercise 5.5

Concept	Definition
a	2
b	5
c	4
d	3
e	6
f	1

Exercise 5.6

The object diagram shows the object name and which specific bike was hired by which customer. This information is not on the class diagram.

Exercise 5.7

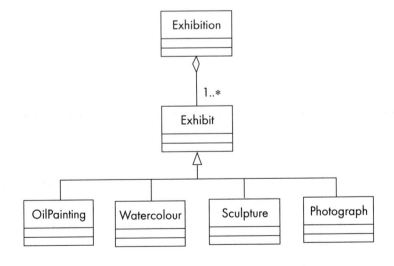

Exercise 5.8

a Yes, the multiplicity at the Order end of the Customer/Order relationship is one or more.

b An order consists of at least one order line.

c No, the multiplicity at the Order end of the Payment/Order relationship is one only.

d There is one product in each order line.

e It is an inheritance relationship, a CD is a kind of product.

f Yes, the multiplicity at the OrderLine end of the Product/OrderLine relationship is zero or more.

Exercise 5.9

Part a[1]

Part b

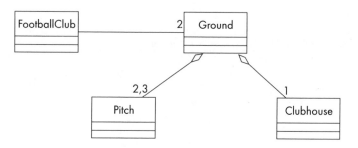

Part c

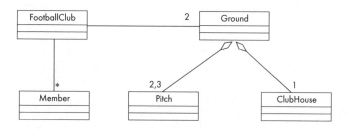

---

1. *Remember that where the multiplicity is one only, the '1' symbol may be omitted (see Chapter 4)*

Part d

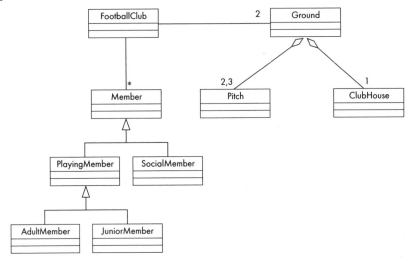

Part e

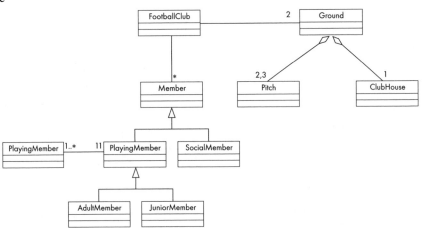

Part f

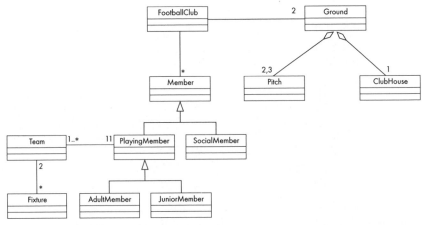

Exercise 5.10

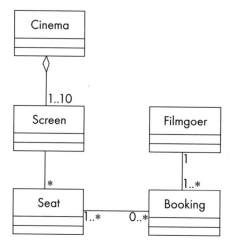

Exercise 5.11

Part a

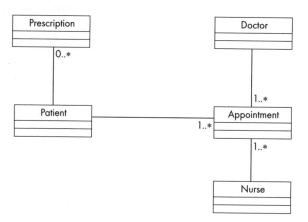

Note that there is no separate class for medical records. This is because the information that would be held in this class is already part of Patient.

Part b

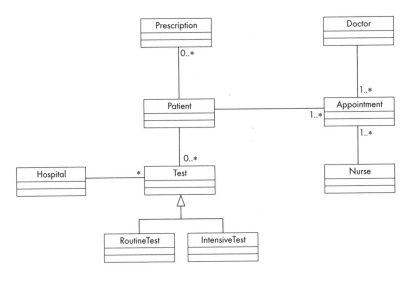

Exercise 5.12

a Yes, the multiplicity at the Account end of the Customer/ Account relationship is one or more.

b Yes, both these are types of account and a customer can have more than one.

c A deposit is a kind of transaction.

d According to the diagram, there is no direct link. A cash machine is related to a branch through a customer and a transaction. However, this does not mean that the cash machine is at that branch, just that the customer has used that cash machine and banks at that branch.

Exercise 5.13

Part a

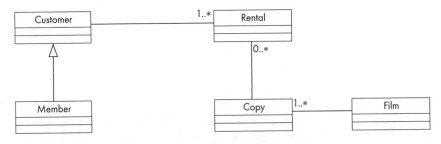

Member = membershipNumber + name + address + phoneNumber + {type of film}

Exercise 5.14

a   No, delivery address is optional.

b   Yes, date required is mandatory.

c   Between 1 and 2 first names or initials for each customer.

d   Yes, an order can have any number of order lines.

e   You would add a comment, e.g.

   (delivery charge) * if customer lives > 10 miles away*.

f   orderLine = product# + productDescription + productCategory + quantity + productCost + costOfLine

   productCategory = ["men's" | "women's" | "children's" | "outdoor" | "sport"].

Exercise 5.15

TextBook = preface + $_6${chapter}$_{10}$ + (glossary) + bibliography
chapter = introduction + {section} + summary
glossary = {term + definition}

Exercise 5.16

OfferCard = vendorDetails + propertyDetails + {offerDetails}

vendorDetails = vendorName + vendorAddress + vendorPhone

propertyDetails = propertyAddress *if different from vendorAddress* + propertyType + propertyPrice

propertyType = ["Detached" | "Semi" | "Terraced" | "Bungalow" | "Flat"]

offerDetails = name + contactPhone + offerPrice + outcome

Chapter 6

Exercise 6.1

Mother	
Responsibility	*Collaborator*
Invite friends	Form teacher
Book magician	
By food and drink	
Prepare birthday cake	Baker

Exercise 6.2

Mail order company	
Responsibility	*Collaborator*
Update product details	Supplier
Get list of existing customers	Company database
Get new brochure design	Marketing department
Get list of other potential outlets	Marketing department

Exercise 6.3

Class	*Operation*
Reservation	findMember(videoCode)
	printPostcard(memberDetails)

Exercise 6.4

Class	*Operation*
Member	findMember(membershipCode)
Video	findVideo(videoCode)
Loan	Loan()
Payment	printReceipt()

Exercise 6.5

Class	*Operation*
Loan	findLoan(videoCode)
	calcDaysOverdue()
Reservation	checkReservation(videoCode)

Exercise 6.6

- calcDaysOverdue( ) : no.Days, latenessFine

- This operation works out whether a video has been returned late and if so by how many days. If it is late, the lateness fine is calculated

- The video must have been returned by the customer, the loan details must have been found

- The number of days' loan is added to the start date and then compared with today's date to calculate if the video is late and by how many days. The daily loan rate is multiplied by the number of days late to give the lateness fine

- This operation calls Video.calcCharge(no.Days)

- This operation sets the Loan attributes dateReturned and latenessFine.

Exercise 6.7

Part a

Conditions		1	2	3	4
			Rules		
Customer uses store credit card		N	Y	N	Y
Customer shops in store		N	N	Y	Y
Actions					
No points		X			
1 point per £ spent				X	
2 points per £ spent			X		
4 points per £ spent					X

Part b

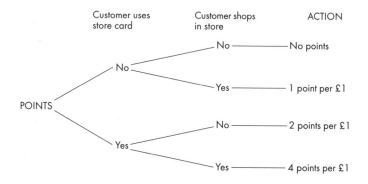

Customer uses store card	Customer shops in store	ACTION
No → No → No points
No → Yes → 1 point per £1
Yes → No → 2 points per £1
Yes → Yes → 4 points per £1

POINTS

Exercise 6.8

Part a

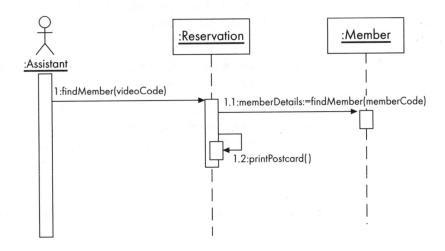

Part b

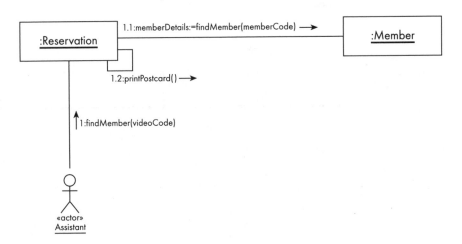

Exercise 6.9

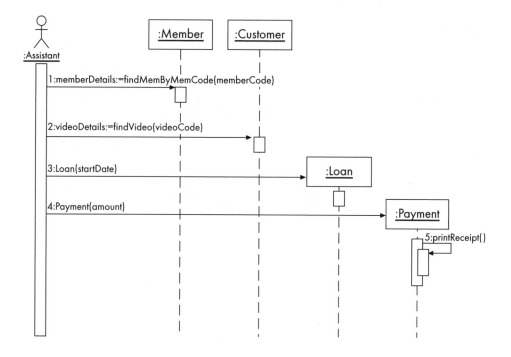

Exercise 6.10

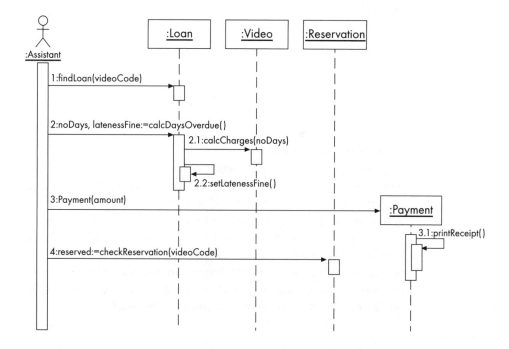

Chapter 7

Exercise 7.1

Part a

Part b

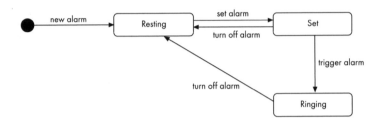

Part c

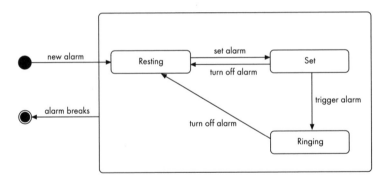

Exercise 7.2 Estate agent's property.

A property is registered as available for sale with an estate agent when the vendor contacts the agent with instructions. The agent markets the property until an offer to buy it has been made and accepted; the property is then under offer and a contract for sale is drawn up. Once contracts have been exchanged, neither side can back out of the deal. The sale of the property is completed when the money is handed over. The buyer can pull out of the deal while the property is under offer, and the vendor can take the property off the market at any time before contracts are exchanged.

Exercise 7.3

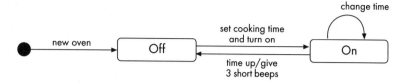

Exercise 7.4

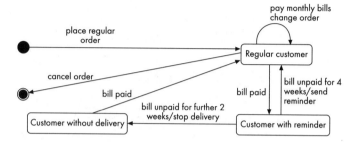

Exercise 7.5

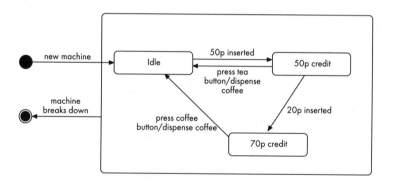

Exercise 7.6

a This event does not affect the state of the object.

b An existing user has to enter his or her password.

c The message is displayed when the new user enters their details into the system.

d The user can change the delivery address while the order is in the Checkout state.

e No.

f The life of an object ends once the order is dispatched or if the user cancels the order.

Chapter 8

Exercise 8.1

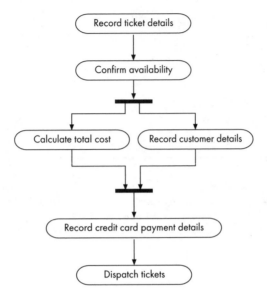

Exercise 8.2

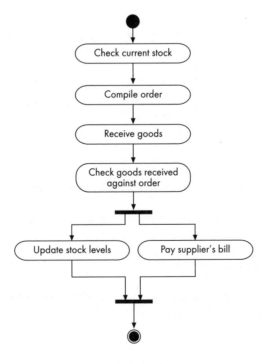

Exercise 8.3

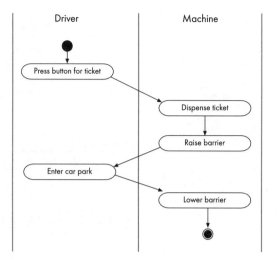

Exercise 8.4

Part a

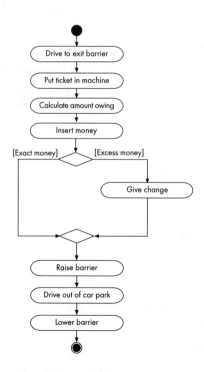

Part b

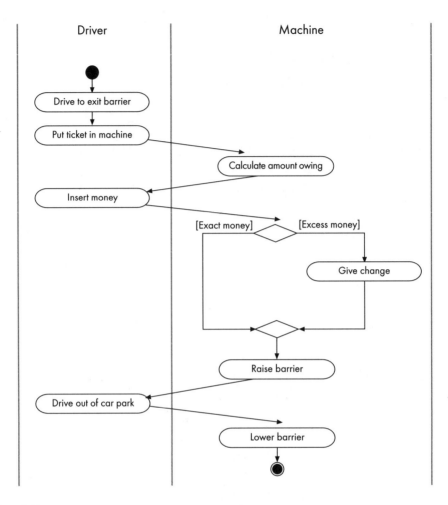

Exercise 8.5

See Figure E.29

Exercise 8.6

Answer is b.

Exercise 8.7

a   Customer details must be recorded before the amount owing is calculated.

FALSE

b   If the title is not available, a new title is input.

FALSE

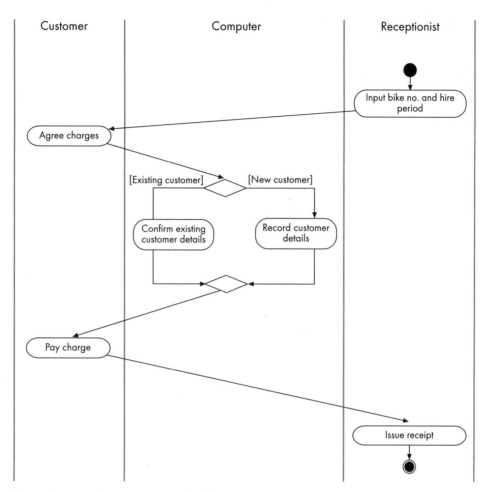

Figure E.29   Answer to Exercise 8.5

    c The transaction must always be confirmed immediately after the credit card details are recorded.

    FALSE

    d The credit card details must be recorded before the transaction is confirmed.

    TRUE

    e Customer details are only recorded if the title chosen is available.

    TRUE

Exercise 8.8

Answer is d.

Exercise 8.9

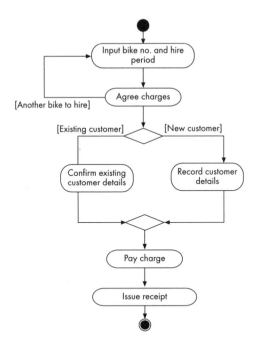

Exercise 8.10

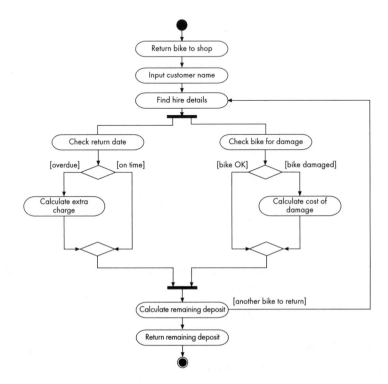

Chapter 9

Exercise 9.1

The Ordering package depends on the Stock package because there is a client–server relationship between OrderLine (in the Ordering package) and Product (in the Stock package).

Exercise 9.2

```
                    ┌─────────────────────┐
                    │ Wheels Bike Hire    │
                    └─────────────────────┘

                      Hire details screen

  Customer name       Sheena James

  Bike details        1591               Scott

                      Atlantic Trail     woman's


  Start date          12/02/04

  No. of days         7

  Deposit paid        £50.00

  Hire fee paid       £8.00              Return to main menu


  record: |◄ ◄ |    1  ► ►| ►*| of 1
```

Exercise 9.3 Hire

HireID	Start date	No. of days	Date returned	Lateness deduction	Damage deduction
04/141	3/04/04	2	5/04/04	£0.00	£0.00
04/142	3/04/04	7	10/04/04	£0.00	£5.00
04/143	6/04/04	5	11/04/04	£0.00	£0.00
04/144	6/04/04	10	16/04/04	£0.00	£0.00
04/145	7/04/04	2	9/04/04	£4.00	£0.00

Exercise 9.4

This relationship could be implemented:

a   As three separate tables, one for each class and one for the association

b   As two tables with a foreign key (CustID) in the Hire table.

Chapter 10

Exercise 10.1

At analysis, an association reflects a real-life relationship between two classes which might be of significance in the system. At design, an association means that there must be a navigable path between two classes, so that objects of those classes can communicate. On the design diagram, the direction of the navigability will be specified.

Exercise 10.2

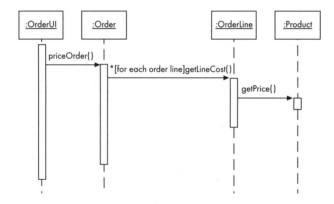

Exercise 10.3

Part a   See Figure E.30.

Part b   The class diagram would need a new class Supplier, associated with the Product class. The sequence diagram is shown in Figure E.31.

Exercise 10.4 Object identifiers:

Step 1   The higher-level menu will have the object identifier of the Issue Bike interface/control object.

Step 2   The :IssueBikeUI calls a static method on the Bike class. A static method is one that can be invoked without having to create an instance of the class to which it belongs. It is

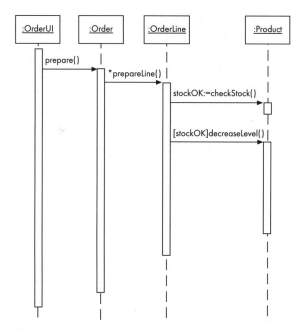

Figure E.30   Answer to Exercise 10.3a

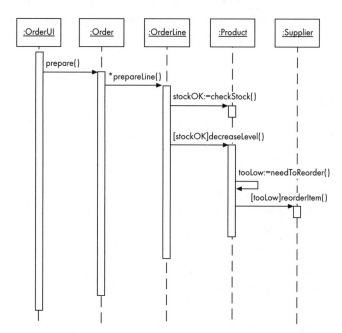

Figure E.31   Answer to Exercise 10.3b

also globally visible so no identifier is needed. Bike has an array of identifiers for all the :Bikes. When it finds the :Bike with a matching bike#, it returns its object identifier to :IssueBikeUI which stores the identifier. The :IssueBikeUI then calls the matching :Bike to get the details.

Step 3   :IssueBikeUI uses the :Bike identifier stored in step 2 to send it a calculateCost(no.Days) message. The number of days, used as a parameter to this message, is input by the actor and stored by :IssueBikeUI for use in step 6.

Step 4   :IssueBikeUI creates a new Customer object, passing in the name, postcode and telephone details. It then stores the new :Customer identifier.

Step 5   :IssueBikeUI creates a new Payment object, passing the stored :Customer identifier from step 4. :IssueBikeUI stores the object identifier of the new Payment object.

Step 6   :IssueBikeUI creates a new Hire object. The attribute startDate is set to today's date, the attribute, numberOfDays, is set to the number of days stored by :IssueBikeUI in step 3.

Step 7   :IssueBikeUI sends a calcTotalPayment() message to :Payment, using the identifier it stored in step 5.

Step 8   :Payment issues a receipt. To do this it needs to get information from Customer object (name and postcode); the relevant :Customer's identifier was passed as an argument to its constructor.

Chapter 11

Exercise 11.1

Part a   The constructors are on lines:

    04   public European()
    14   public Briton()
    25   public Frenchman()
    36   public German()
    47   public Italian().

Part b   The keyword is: extends, on line 11.

Part c   The output would be:
Good morning
Bonjour
Guten Tag
Buongiorno

Exercise 11.2

Part a

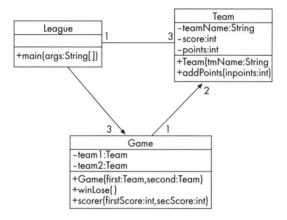

Part b

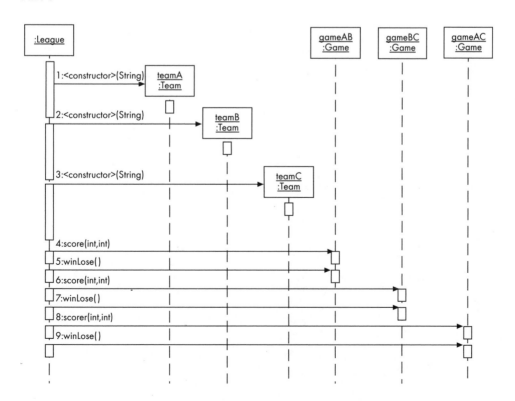

Part c   The output from main() would be:

Team	Points
Alan	2
Ian	1
Martin	3

Index